1993-96 EDITION

THE RULES BOOK

ERIC TWINAME
REVISED BY BRYAN WILLIS

The 1993–96 International Yacht Racing Rules explained

SHERIDAN HOUSE

Published 1993 by
Sheridan House Inc.
145 Palisade Street
Dobbs Ferry, NY 10522

Reprinted 1994 (twice)

Library of Congress Cataloging-in-Publication Data

Printed in England by Clays Ltd, St Ives plc

ISBN 0-924486-49-X

Dedication: To my mother and father who taught me the first rule I knew

ACKNOWLEDGEMENTS

Some of the interpretations and the idea of using an almost comic-strip presentation first appeared in my articles for *Yachts and Yachting* whose readers very usefully pounced on my interpretative mistakes. The International Yacht Racing Union kindly allowed us to reprint sections of the racing rules, and the Royal Yachting Association gave me a unique opportunity to sharpen up my wits and rule knowledge by asking me to join their racing rules committee three years ago.

The manuscript came in for a hard time under the perceptive eyes of Bryan Willis, Andrew Pool, Graham Donald, Nick Martin and the National Sailing coach, Bob Bond, who checked the book for its use in teaching and for ease of understanding. The chairman of the IYRU and RYA racing rules committees, Gerald Sambrooke-Sturgess, was kind enough to read and correct the manuscript as carefully as if he had written it himself. Almost all their suggestions and corrections have been worked into the book.

Clive Gordon and the Parkway Design Group produced the quite superb design and layout with more than just professional competence and imagination. They were also amazingly patient.

Everyone I have dealt with in Adlard Coles and Granada, especially Jeremy Howard-Williams, Bruce Thomas and Rab MacWilliam, have responded with exceptional warmth and enthusiasm to the project. But my biggest debt is to Oliver Freeman. It was Oliver, when managing editor, who persuaded me to write the book and shaped it with me at every step of the way, even when he no longer worked for the company. Did I say my biggest debt? I was forgetting Jill.

To all of you who have helped, thank you.

Eric Twiname
March 1977

Eric's tragic death in 1980 meant a great loss both to his friends and to yachtsmen everywhere. His *Rules Book* has helped countless helmsmen to grasp the principles of the racing rules, and in making the changes necessary for the book to comply with the current rules, I have been careful not to change Eric's unique method of presentation.

Bryan Willis
January 1989

CONTENTS

THE RULE CHANGES

The major differences between the 1989–92 and the 1993–96 racing rules

Every year at the Conference of the International Yacht Racing Union, improvements and amendments are made to the racing rules, but only every four years (after the Olympic Games) are the 'new rules' published. This fifth edition of *The Rules Book* has been revised to include the changes that come into force on 1 April 1993. Most of the changes are for clarification, but some change the way the game is played. To readers new to racing, the changes are irrelevant as they have been built into the book, but those who have been racing a while will need to know what these changes are; this new section is for them.

The Answering Pennant (red and white striped flag) continues to mean that there is a postponement of unlimited time. The 'AP over a numeral pennant' meaning a postponement for a particular number of hours, and the 'AP over A' meaning postponed to another day, both remain. But there is a new signal of 'AP over H' ('H' for home) meaning that there is a postponement, and new signals will be made ashore (rule 4.1).

The race committee will continue to signal an individual recall (code flag 'X') when one or more identifiable yachts are over the start line itself, but will now ignore those yachts over the line extensions. The reason is that those who are on the course side of an extension will know that they are over, and to give a recall signal may confuse those who are just behind the actual line at the start (old rule 8.1 new rule 7.1).

Code flag 'N' displayed on its own used to mean 'race abandoned'; now it means not only that the race is abandoned, but also that further signals will be made in the starting area. That's not much of a change, but there is a new signal 'N over H' (H for home) which means that the race is abandoned and new signals will be made ashore. The 'N over X' (abandon and re-sail) and the 'N over first substitute' (race cancelled) have been removed as the idea is that the race committee will decide on the water to abandon the race, and decide later whether the race should be re-sailed or cancelled. It can abandon a race at any time, even before the starting sequence has begun, but now, as before, the race cannot be abandoned after the start except for a specific reason: an error in the starting procedure, foul weather, a mark shifted or missing, insufficient wind to complete the course in the time limit, or some reason directly affecting the fairness of the competition (rules 4.1 and 5.4).

There is some new wording in fundamental rule B which says that by participating, competitors agree to be governed by the rules, to accept any penalties imposed (subject to appeal) and not to sue the organisers! (Fundamental rule B.)

There are now hundreds of drugs which a sailor cannot take, many of which are available without a prescription from the local drug store. To be more exact, a competitor's urine sample tested for drug abuse must not prove positive. Since the vast majority of sailing events have no testing facilities, the rule is usually ineffective because competitors are not permitted to lodge protests. The list of banned substances and banned methods is so big and new drugs are added so frequently that the IYRU Medical List is not included in the rule book. The rule will be of interest only to the few with high aspirations, but those few will need to take advice from coaches and team doctors if they have any doubts at all, as the penalties are severe and automatic. Drinking too much coffee could lead to a one year ban by the IYRU which is unlikely to address 'intent'; those needing medication can seek dispensation when considering entering an event where there is testing (new rule 17 and Appendix A2).

A new three-letter sail number system has been introduced so that all sails measured after 1 April 1993 must carry the new three letter national letters, except that they need not be carried in home waters unless the race or series is an international championship. A 'grandfather rule' allows sails measured before April 1993 to carry the old letters, but all sails will need to comply after March 1997. Of course, the requirement will continue to apply only at international events. Britain changes from K to GBR, United States of America must add an A to their US to make USA, and Australia will become AUS (old rule 25, new rule 25 and Appendix B3).

Weight jackets (which are permitted only when class rules prescribe) must now be worn outside everything else – including the buoyancy aid (new rule 61.2(b)).

Under the old rules, when a race continued unexpectedly after sunset (sunset is always at a specific time each day), a yacht could be disqualified after protest for not displaying lights in accordance with the requirements of the International Regulations for Preventing Collisions at Sea. Now lights (and fog signals) are required only 'when safe pilotage requires', a phrase to be interpreted by a protest committee if there is a protest (old rule 66, new rule 65).

There is now a clear rule requiring a yacht that is not yet racing or that has completed her race not to seriously hinder a yacht that is racing. If a yacht infringes this rule and there is a hearing, a protest committee now has no option but to penalise (old rule 31.2, new rule 30.1).

There is a new rule prohibiting a yacht from deviating from her proper course to interfere with a yacht that is exonerating herself (doing a 720 degree turn for an infringement of part IV B or C, or a 360 degree turn after hitting a mark). Under the old rules, in the last race of a fleet race series where yacht A's sole objective was to drive yacht B down the fleet, yacht A could prevent yacht B from ever taking a penalty. And yes, it happened! (new rule 30.2).

'When serious damage results from a collision, a yacht that had the opportunity but failed to make a reasonable attempt to avoid the collision shall be penalised.' Previously only the right-of-way yacht was subject to this rule. There were several examples over the past few years of a give-way yacht completely disabling a right-of-way yacht, and while the right-of-way yacht limped home, the give-way yacht did a 720 degree penalty and sailed on; now she can be disqualified. (The right-of-way yacht could, and still can, claim redress (rule 69)) (rule 32).

When, before the start, a leeward yacht is luffing above close-hauled, and the windward yacht attains, 'mast abeam', the old rules required the leeward yacht to simply stop luffing; now she is required to bear away to close hauled. An overtaking yacht gaining an overlap to leeward, while sailing higher than close-hauled when the windward yacht will have to alter course to keep clear, will infringe the rule as she establishes the overlap. A leeward yacht without luffing rights may not 'close the gap' by sailing higher than close-hauled unless she tacks or unless the windward yacht would not 'have to alter course to keep clear' (old rule 40, new rule 38.1).

Under the old rules, if a starting limit mark was placed on the pre-course side of the line the mark could not be said to 'begin, bound or end a leg' and therefore never had a required side, and yachts could ignore it. With the new wording, a starting mark has a required side from the time a yacht is 'approaching the line from the pre-course side to start', so if it's reasonably close, it must be left on the correct side as a boat comes to the line to start. However, the obligations to leave it on one side or the other must be stated in the sailing instructions; just to say there will be an IDM (inner distance mark) would be meaningless (rule 51.3).

Rule 42 (Rounding or passing marks and obstructions) has been reordered and the argument as to whether a leeward yacht could claim room at a starting mark has been resolved: no yacht has the right to room at a starting mark when approaching the line to start even if it is an obstruction (unless it's not surrounded by navigable water) (old rules 42(b) and 42.4 new rule 42(a)).

It is clearer that a luffing yacht with luffing rights which is 'luffing as she pleases' must nevertheless not cause serious damage (new words in new rule 39.2 which was 38.1).

Under the old rules, a leeward yacht without luffing rights sailing below her proper course could luff as quickly as she pleased up to her proper course. Now if she doesn't have luffing rights she must give the windward yacht an opportunity to keep clear (that is, she is subject to rule 35) (new words in new rule 39.2 which was 38.1).

Under the old rules a yacht with a small overlap to leeward (and therefore without luffing rights) was not permitted to tack, though only match racers ever protested about it. Now this is permitted; and so too can a yacht, sailing downwind with a small overlap to windward, gybe without infringing (new rules 39.1 and 39.3).

The definition of 'mast abeam' was described rather badly in the old rule 38.2(a) and repeated (although not quite the same) in the old rule 40. There were two interpretations in common use, and the difference between them concerned a windward yacht that was sailing higher than the leeward yacht, but whose helmsman was abreast of the leeward yacht's mast. Some thought she was mast abeam, others thought she could never attain mast abeam when she was sailing higher than the leeward yacht. The term has now been removed from the rules of part IV and added to the definitions, and is worded such that a windward yacht attains the 'mast abeam' position when sailing higher than the leeward yacht when her helmsman is abreast the mast of the leeward yacht (old rule 38.2(a) – new definition).

When a windward yacht hails to a leeward yacht that there is something to windward, the leeward yacht must give room to the windward yacht to pass the something. The old rule required the leeward yacht merely to stop luffing (old rule 38.2, new rule 40.2).

The title of the 'simultaneous tacking rule' is changed to help clarify that the rule applies at any moment the yachts are both tacking (or gybing) at the same time, not just when the commencement is at the same moment (rule 41.4).

The rule that said 'a yacht that hails when claiming the establishment or termination of an overlap or insufficiency of room at a mark or obstruction thereby helps to support her claim' has been deleted. It really didn't mean much, because the 'rule' didn't require anything. A hail of 'water' at a mark never did give you any rights to room (it's the overlap that counts), but I continue to recommend that, well before the critical 'two lengths', if you are the skipper of an inside yacht with other than an obvious overlap it can do no harm to talk to the skipper of the outside yacht (eg 'Overlap – do you agree?'). If you're the skipper of a yacht clear ahead with less than a length between your stern and the bow of the following yacht you should talk to the skipper of the boat astern (eg 'Clear ahead – do you agree?'). If you're not being given sufficient room, there's no harm in calling 'water'. Even when you get no response, and in spite of the deletion of the rule, such a procedure will help you when there is a protest (old rule 42.1(f)).

If you hit a mark you may take a 'turn penalty'. The old rule used to require a 720 degree turn, the new rule requires only a turn of 360 degrees. The sailing instructions could, of course, and still can, change this, and might require a yacht to retire or do a 720 degree turn or re-round, or take some other penalty. The new rule also clarifies that not only must a yacht get clear as soon as possible after touching, but that when she is clear, she must do the turn immediately (rule 52.2.(a)).

Establishing an overlap between a continuous obstruction (such as a river bank) and a yacht clear ahead, when there is not room to pass in safety at the time the overlap is established, was and still is an infringement. I mention this only because the new wording of rule 42.3(b) may not be as clear on this point as the old rule, and some might think the yacht gaining the overlap when there is insufficient room to pass in safety is merely not entitled to room (rule 42.3(b)).

Rule 43.1 used to start: 'When two close-hauled yachts are on the same tack and safe pilotage requires the yacht clear ahead or the leeward yacht to make a substantial alteration of course to clear an obstruction . . . she shall hail the other yacht . . .' There was a flaw here in that the outside/astern yacht had only to bear off a little so that she wasn't close-hauled and she would escape the obligation of having to respond to the hail. The loophole has been closed; only match racers would have thought of such a mean trick anyway (rule 43.1 and 43.2).

This covers the rare situation of a windward mark that is also an obstruction, and a yacht inside or ahead which needs to tack and cannot do so without colliding with another yacht; when the hailed yacht can fetch the obstruction/mark she can hail a 'refusal'. Under the old rules a second hail from the hailing (inside/ahead) yacht would oblige the hailed yacht to tack and the hailing yacht to retire or take a penalty. This confusing 'second hail' provision has been removed. A second hail now can be used to reinforce the first when it is thought the first wasn't heard, without the danger of it resulting in a penalty. However, the inside yacht needs to be aware that she might be trapped with no way to escape (rule 43.3).

Now to the rules about propulsion; rocking to facilitate steering is now permitted (rule 54.2(b)). The crew may now 'exaggerate the rolling that facilitates steering the yacht through a tack or gybe'. The reference to movement of the mast away from the vertical has been deleted. Under the old rule if the crew moved to leeward to release the jib sheet causing the mast to move to leeward, then as the yacht went through the tack and the mast moved to leeward on the new tack, the rule was infringed. So now you can roll tack or gybe, with the restriction of 'speed at the end of the tack or gybe not greater than it would have been in the absence of the tack or gybe' still applying (rule 54.3(a)). Pumping the spinnaker guy used to be prohibited; now you can pump the guy. Pumping the main used to be restricted to the full purchase; now you can grab all the sheets and pump with a 1:1 purchase if you want to (rule 54.3(b)).

The old rule about the spinnaker pole required that when a pole was used with a spinnaker, it had to be carried only on the side opposite to the boom; now it can be used either side with a spinnaker or a foresail. Furthermore, a spinnaker may now be set without a spinnaker pole, and if a pole is set, then there is no longer a requirement for the tack to be in close proximity to the end of the pole. The term 'whisker pole' has been included for those classes that don't have spinnakers (and therefore no spinnaker poles). The change should eliminate a lot of 'technical' protests, especially in match racing (rule 64.2).

The new rules make it clear that a yacht, having decided to take a turn penalty for touching a mark, or a 720 degree turn for infringing a rule of part IV, must not only get clear as soon as possible after the incident but, that once she is clear, she must immediately make her turn(s) (old Appendix 3, now Appendix B1 1.1 and rule 52.2(a)).

A yellow flag may now be used in place of an 'I' flag for signalling what used to be called a 'percentage penalty' and is now called a 'scoring penalty'. Sailing instructions may need to insist on an 'I' flag if customs officers get excited about all the requests for customs clearance! (Appendix B1).

When the 'scoring penalty' system (which used to be called 'percentage penalty' system) is in force, unless a yacht accepts the penalty (by displaying 'I' or a yellow flag) at 'the first reasonable opportunity which is usually immediately' then she loses the chance for a 20% penalty. Under the old rules this was increased to 50% at a hearing; under the new rules the protest committee must disqualify her (old Appendix 3, new Appendix B1 2).

Where there is contact that is neither minor nor unavoidable, a third yacht may retire or take a penalty in relation to the incident, whereas the old rule required one of the yachts involved in the contact to retire or take a penalty. It is still true to say that if neither yacht involved in the collision protests, and no yacht retires, or takes a penalty, then both yachts will be penalised at a hearing (rule 33).

Under the new rules, when a yacht infringes a rule of part IV and hits a mark in the same incident, she need do just a 720 degree turn rather than a 720+360. There was nothing in the old rules to cover this (Appendix B1 1.1).

Under the old rules when no alternative penalty (such as the 720 degree turns) was prescribed in the sailing instructions, a protesting yacht could inform the protested yacht at any time that she was going to protest – even after the race (although the flag had to be displayed at the first reasonable opportunity). Now there is an obligation on a yacht involved in an incident that wishes to protest to hail 'protest (or words to that effect)' immediately; and if not involved (for example in the case of a third yacht protesting two others for colliding and not protesting, retiring, or taking a penalty) then at the first reasonable opportunity (rule 68.2).

Under the old rules, a code flag 'B' was always acceptable, no matter what was said in the sailing instructions; under the new rules a red rectangular flag is also acceptable no matter what the sailing instructions say. (Under the old rules protests were being ruled as invalid when the sailing instructions prescribed a 'B' flag and the yacht displayed a red flag without swallow tails.) The words 'which is normally immediately' have been added to emphasise the importance of displaying the flag promptly (rules 68.3(a) and (b)).

The old rules required that a protest be lodged within two hours of the protestor finishing; now it is within two hours of the last yacht. The sailing instructions may, and often do, vary this time limit (rule 68.6).

There is no longer any reference to a protest fee, and hopefully any organising authority or race committee that in the past has required a protest to be accompanied by a fee, will in future drop the requirement (old rule 68.7).

Sometimes a sailing instruction can be infringed whilst not racing and it was difficult to know to which race the penalty should apply. There is a new rule to say that the penalty applies to 'the race sailed nearest to the time of the infringement' (rule 74.4(b)).

Under the old rules, the protest committee could penalise a yacht that infringed rule 54 (Propulsion) without a hearing. Now the sailing instructions will need to specifically give the protest committee that power. Without such a prescription, infringements of rule 54 are like any other, and a penalty can be applied only after a valid hearing. Even when there is a prescription allowing the protest committee to disqualify without a hearing, the disqualified yacht continues to be entitled to a hearing upon request (rule 70.1(b)).

Under the old rule it was not clear whether the protest committee had the right to ban an excessive number of witnesses. It is now clear that a yacht can bring any number of witnesses (though experienced skippers will know how detrimental it can be to call too many). The protest committee could and still can itself call anyone as a witness (rule 73.3).

When a yacht that was required to keep clear, damages a right-of-way yacht, the right-of-way yacht can claim redress. The word 'physically' has been added to the rule, to clarify that the right-of-way yacht needs to be physically damaged (this includes the crew being injured to a degree needing more than minor medical treatment) before she can successfully claim redress; 'damage' to the position in the race or series is not a legitimate reason. (The yacht will also need to satisfy the protest committee that her finishing position was materially prejudiced through no fault of her own, of course (rule 69).)

It is now clear that a yacht may obtain redress when her finishing position in a series (rather than just a race) has been materially prejudiced. Many sailors feel it is already too easy to get redress (for example, average points). However, there is no change in the limited number of legitimate reasons for giving redress (rule 69).

What is currently called the 'Olympic Scoring system' is renamed 'The Bonus Point Scoring System'. This is because some, if not all, classes in the next Olympics will not use this scoring system (Appendix B2).

LEARNING THE RULES

The rules of sailing are complex. There's no getting away from that. But there are ways of making rule knowledge much more accessible and the rules themselves easier to understand. This book is written very much with those two aims in mind.

Anyone who races sailing boats needs to know something about the rules. To begin with you only need know enough to get a boat round the course without fouling the others. Later the rules become tactically important because they define what moves you are allowed to make when trying to overtake other boats and, just as important, what tricks other people might legitimately use in trying to overtake you.

So the crucial point about learning the sailing rules is that your knowledge needs to be a working knowledge. There is little point in learning the rules merely to be able to quote chapter and verse. That won't help you on the water, whereas a good working knowledge certainly will, since rule knowledge is a vital department of your racing skills – as important as knowledge of wind and weather.

The International Yacht Racing Union's (IYRU) racing rule book is something most people approach at best reluctantly. For one thing it's usually only approached at all when you've got a problem. Which puts it immediately into the category of garages, police stations and dentists. But with the difference that most times you turn to the rule book you will find something that either you can't quite understand or that contradicts something you thought you did know.

This book therefore approaches the whole problem the other way round, starting from the real live situations that you're liable to come across while racing. So rather than looking for a rule which might apply to the situation in question, you can turn straight to that situation and read which rule applies, how it applies and why it applies. To make this possible, the situations are arranged here, not to the basic logic of the IYRU rule book, but to a logic based on your perception of situations as you meet them on the water.

There are several things that anyone who knows anything at all about sailing will be able to tell you about a collision or near miss, whether they have ever seen a rule book or not. The first thing they'll be able to say is whereabouts on the course the incident happened. They shouldn't find it too difficult either, to say which tacks the boats were on or whether they were tacking or gybing. And already, by answering these questions correctly, over 90 per cent of racing incidents can be eliminated and we are left with, at most, 10 per cent. The sections of the book have therefore been arranged to correspond to parts of the course, with subdivisions into incidents where boats are on opposite tacks, on the same tack, tacking or gybing.

In this way, when you are trying to unravel the rights and wrongs of a particular incident, you can quickly home in on the relevant 5 or 10 per cent of possible incidents. Among these, the one you want will be easy to find. Having found it, you can read why one boat is in the right and the other in the wrong, why a particular rule applies, which rule that is and, on difficult points, which appeals cases support the interpretation. The rule referred to can then be looked up in the IYRU rule book (reproduced in the back of this book, starting on page 93).

So far I have only mentioned the book's use in providing a post-mortem analysis after a rule infringement. But if you're a racing helmsman you constantly need to know just what you can do during a race without infringing any rules. You can certainly build up this knowledge by tearing around the course hitting other boats and being protested against afterwards, but by far the best way to learn is to keep your rule knowledge running in advance of your sailing skills.

Some right-of-way problems are much more common than others, so the situations dealt with here are graded so that you can, if you like, sit down and work up your rule knowledge to a level that fits in with your other racing abilities.

The incidents and situations interpreted in the book are graded on three levels. These levels are:

1. rules everyone who races should know (dealt with on pages 5 to 9)
2. racing at the top end of a club fleet
3. top-level national and international competition and team racing

For the purpose of learning the rules, the book should not be read from cover to cover in the usual way. That would be too big a bite at once and probably pretty confusing, unless you already know the rules quite well. Instead, the best approach is to decide what level of rule knowledge you want from the book beforehand, then to ignore everything listed as being beyond the level you've set yourself.

Take the example of a helmsman who has raced for a couple of seasons, and who wants to improve his rule knowledge so that he is at least on a par with the people who are winning his club races. His approach to learning would be to read all items marked by one boat (but not those marked by two boats), checking back to any rules referred to, but ignoring the appeal case references.

If you work in this way you needn't read from the front of the book to the back, but will learn faster by picking a particular section – mark-rounding from an offwind leg, for example, – and first studying only that section, rather than trying to take in too much at once. Re-reading, dipping into the book at random – but not yet reading beyond the level you've set yourself – are all useful parts of the learning process. For really keen groups of people, and particularly for children, quizzes are an obvious way of livening up the process.

Learning is also speeded up considerably by using the book as a reference after racing to check the rights and wrongs of any incidents or near misses you experienced during the race. When using the book in this way, of course, you would not restrict yourself to the grading levels, since an incident you want to know about might be one of those rare ones in group 3.

One important word of warning, though. What may look like two identical situations in different sections of the book will sometimes have opposite interpretations. This is because the position on the course is crucial. For example, when two boats collide within two lengths of a mark, the boat in the wrong is liable to be the one that is in the right if you take the mark away and have them in open water on a leg of the course. It is vital to make sure you read and bear in mind the leg of course the boats are on–which is why that information is printed at the top of every page.

The interpretations are, as far as possible, not my own but those of the IYRU, the RYA (Royal Yachting Association) and the USSA (United States Sailing Association). Throughout I have included references to their most useful published appeals, so anyone can look these up if they want to. At protest meetings – whether you are on the committee or one of the warring parties – the relevant appeal case placed on the table is usually decisive – and gratifying. You are instantly a rule expert. No longer is it a question of 'my opinion is this . . .' but 'this is what the definitive IYRU, RYA or USSA appeal says', which is difficult for a protest committee to refute, or for a competitor who has just been disqualified to argue about.

The IYRU appeal cases are accepted as definitive anywhere (except in the very rare case of a more recent published national appeal conflicting; then the national appeal might apply in that country). The RYA appeals apply in British clubs and classes and any others under the RYA's jurisdiction; the USSA appeals apply only in the USA. Elsewhere national appeals of the country concerned govern, but in the absence of a national or IYRU appeal on a point of interpretation for races held outside Britain or the

USA, an RYA or USSA appeal which clarified the point would usually be accepted by a protest committee in that country. The national authority would always have the chance of reversing the decision on appeal – if the dispute went that far.

The rules themselves are revised once every four years and those used in this edition are valid until early 1997. These rules together with the RYA prescriptions can be bought in a booklet from the Royal Yachting Association, Romsey Road, Eastleigh, Hampshire SO5 4YA, England. So can the RYA appeals cases. The IYRU racing rules alone and its appeals can be bought from the IYRU at 60 Knightsbridge, London SW1X 7JX, and USSA appeals from the USSA, P.O. Box 229, Newport, Rhode Island, 0284, USA.

THE RULES EVERYONE WHO RACES SHOULD KNOW

An understanding of these first few pages of introduction to the rules enables a racing helmsman to keep out of trouble and provides the logical framework which underlies all the right of way rules, however complex. These are the most important four pages in the book.

The sailing rules are designed to prevent collisions and to promote fair sailing. So when boats collide, or when a right-of-way boat is forced to steer clear, the boat in the wrong should be penalised. The voluntary penalty is retirement from the race or, when 720 degree penalties are in force, two full penalty turns. If a helmsman in the wrong does not take the voluntary penalty soon after the incident, another competitor or the race organisers may lodge a protest. In the protest meeting the boat in the wrong is disqualified. The basic right-of-way code is quite simple, but it is important to know that the right-of-way in open water is fundamentally different from that at marks of the course or other obstructions.

Basic right-of-way in open water

When neither boat is about to sail round a mark but are both in open water:

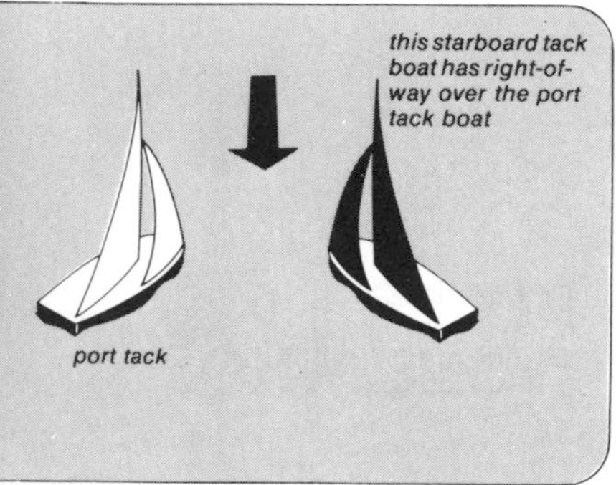

1. A boat on port tack keeps clear of a boat on starboard tack (rule 36).

2. A windward boat keeps clear of a leeward boat (rule 37.1).

3. A boat which is tacking or gybing keeps clear of one that isn't (rule 41).

4. A boat clear astern of another keeps clear of the one ahead when they are both on the same tack (rule 37.2).

Basic right-of-way at a windward mark

At a windward mark – that is a mark of the course which you have been tacking to reach – the basics are:

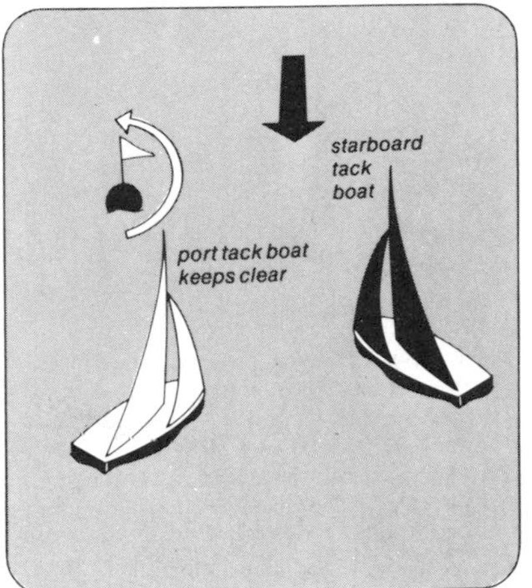

1. When on opposite tacks, take the mark away and apply the principles as in open water (rule 42(b) and 36).

2. When on the same tack, the boat next to the mark must be given room to round by the boat outside (rule 42.1 (a)).

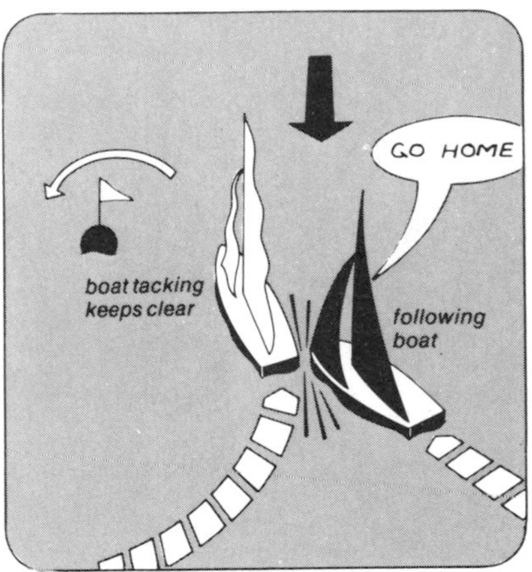

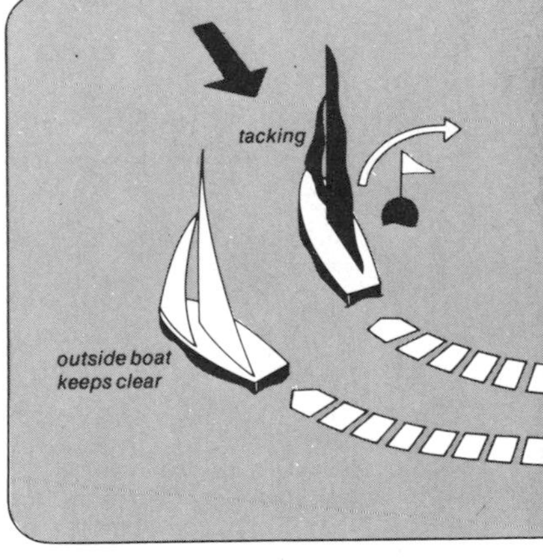

3. When a boat is tacking round the mark, she must keep clear of any following boat (rule 42.2(b)) but any boat outside her must give her room (rule 42.1(a)).

Basic right-of-way at an offwind mark

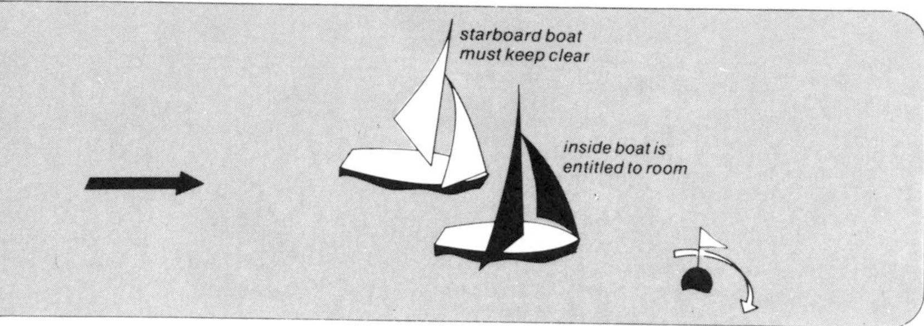
starboard boat
must keep clear
inside boat is
entitled to room

At an offwind mark – that is one you have sailed to on a close reach, broad reach or run – the basics are:

1. The boat on the inside at the mark must be given room to round (rule 42.1(a)). The port and starboard rule (36) does not apply here.
2. A boat which approaches the mark clear ahead of another has the right to gybe round the mark; the other boat must keep clear (rule 42.2(a)).
3. The boat on the inside must not round so wide that she sails into a boat that is giving her room (rules 36, 37, 41.1).

Basic rights before and at the start

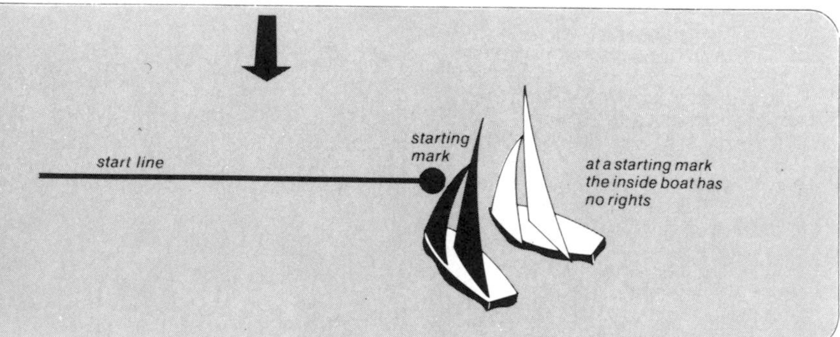
starting
mark
start line
at a starting mark
the inside boat has
no rights

The rules before the start are slightly different in some details from those after the start. Collisions are common before the start, and it is important to realise that if you are either out of control or are pre-occupied in adjusting a halyard, you can be penalised in a collision with a boat which has right-of-way. So if you're going to mess about with your boat just before the start, make sure you're on starboard tack. If you infringe a rule in the 'preparatory period' (usually five minutes before the start), you will have to retire or take a penalty.

No yacht has the right to room at a starting mark when approaching the line to start (unless the mark is not surrounded by navigable water).

The luffing rules

windward boat
must keep clear
the leeward boat
has the right to luff

There are some rules (rules 39 and 40) about the right for a leeward boat to luff after starting that are important to understand. After the start, when you are overtaking a boat to windward, the leeward helmsman has the right to throw his boat head to wind as sharply as he likes. If he hits you, you are the one who will be penalised for not keeping clear. Before starting and clearing the line, he may only slowly luff (rule 38).

Boats, cruising, in other races and motor boats

The IYRU yacht racing rules apply only between boats which are racing, either in the same or different races. Sailing boats have right-of-way over motor boats, but in confined waters ships have right-of-way over yachts. It should always be remembered that the rules are primarily intended to enable people to avoid collisions.

When a boat which is racing meets one which is cruising, a different set of right-of-way rules apply: they are the International Regulations for Preventing Collisions at Sea (IRPCS). Although essentially the same as the basic IYRU rules explained above, there are two important differences! The IRPCS code does not allow luffing, and a boat which is overtaking must keep clear, regardless of which tacks the boats concerned are on. As a matter of courtesy, though, boats not racing should always do their best to keep clear of those racing.

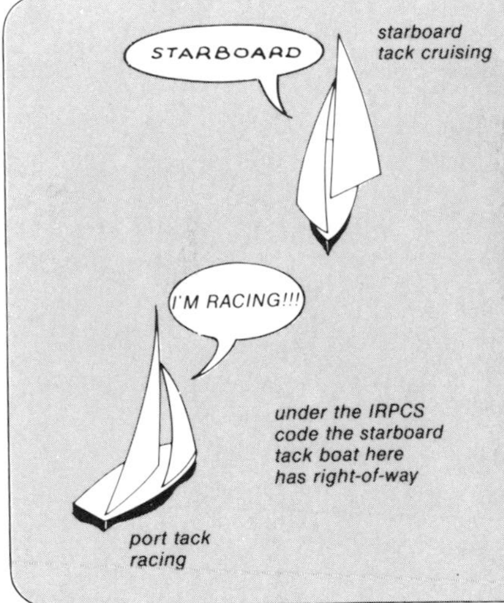
STARBOARD
starboard
tack cruising
I'M RACING!!!
under the IRPCS
code the starboard
tack boat here
has right-of-way
port tack
racing

DEFINITIONS

The rules are built on simple and precise ideas; these are the building blocks and they must be understood if the full meaning of the rules is to become clear.

Racing

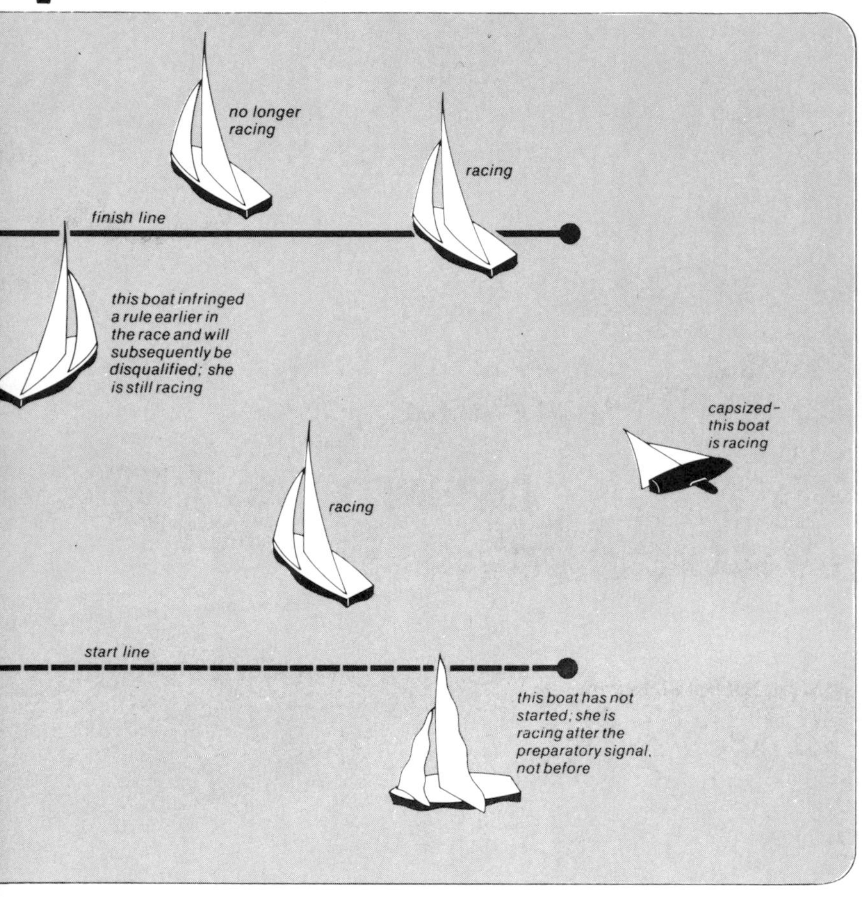
no longer
racing
racing
finish line
this boat infringed
a rule earlier in
the race and will
subsequently be
disqualified; she
is still racing
capsized -
this boat
is racing
racing
start line
this boat has not
started; she is
racing after the
preparatory signal,
not before

The international racing rules apply to boats which are racing or about to race. Penalties for infringing the rules come into force after the preparatory signal (usually 5 minutes before the starting signal) and apply to a boat until she has finished and cleared the finish line. A boat not racing (before the preparatory signal or after finishing) will be penalised if she seriously hindered a boat that is racing (rule 30).

A boat which infringes a rule without realising it and which therefore continues racing and is later disqualified after a protest does not lose her right-of-way status during the race. She is racing throughout and carries exactly the same rights under the rules as other boats racing (IYRU appeal case 2). To continue to race knowing that a rule has been infringed is a violation of fundamental rule D (Accepting Penalties).

Port tack and starboard tack

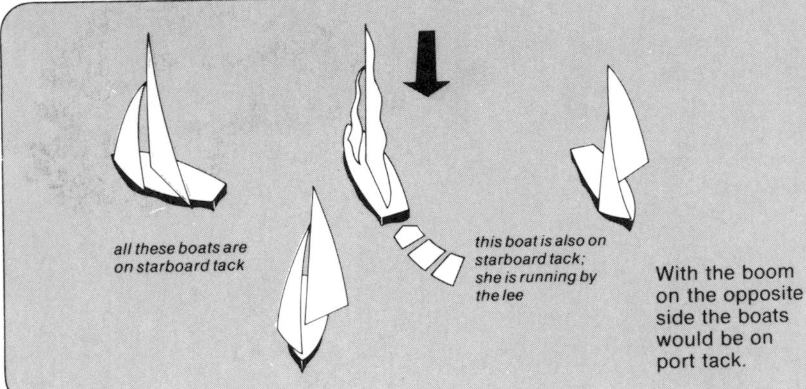
all these boats are
on starboard tack
this boat is also on
starboard tack;
she is running by
the lee
With the boom
on the opposite
side the boats
would be on
port tack.

A boat is on starboard tack when her mainsail is on her port side. Conversely, a boat is on port tack when her mainsail is on her starboard side. Helmsmen who have problems knowing which tack they are on can usefully paint 'starboard tack' on the starboard side of the boom and 'port tack' on the port side. It saves having to think.

Close-hauled and free

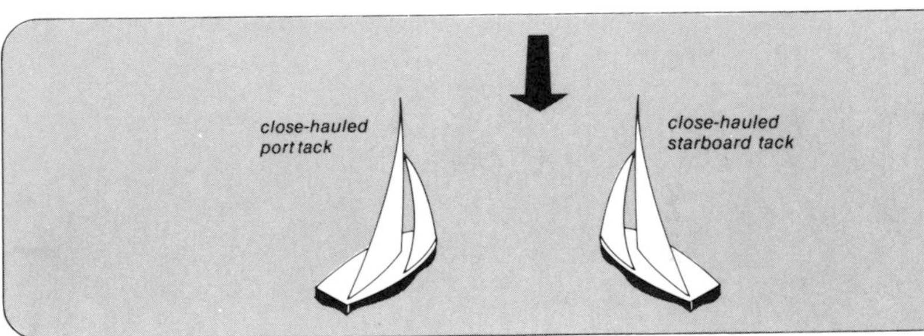
close-hauled
port tack
close-hauled
starboard tack

The term 'close-hauled' defines a direction of sailing in relation to the wind; this is different for different classes of boat and to a lesser degree among boats of the same class. The official rule book definition reads: 'A yacht is close-hauled when sailing by the wind as close as she can lie with advantage in working to windward'.

The terms 'beating', 'beating to windward' and 'on the wind' are all sometimes used to mean close-hauled.

Windward and leeward

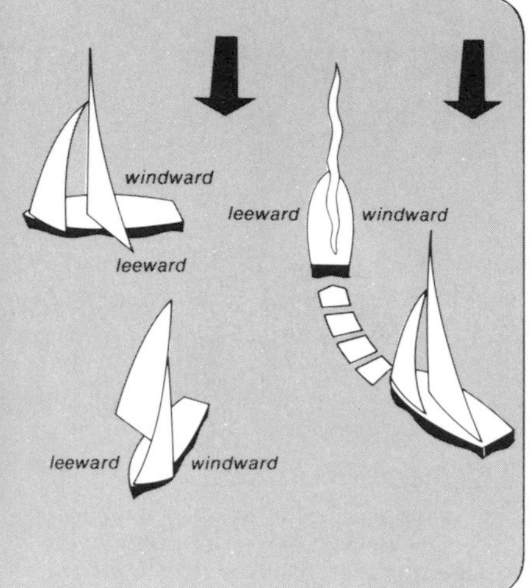

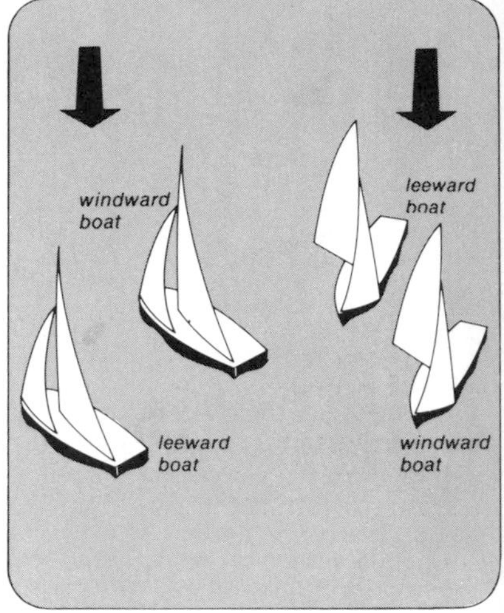

The leeward side of a boat is the side that the mainsail is being carried; or if head to wind, on the side the mainsail was before she became head to wind. The opposite side is the windward side.

When two boats are overlapped on the same tack the leeward one is the one on the other's leeward side. The other boat is the windward one.

Luffing

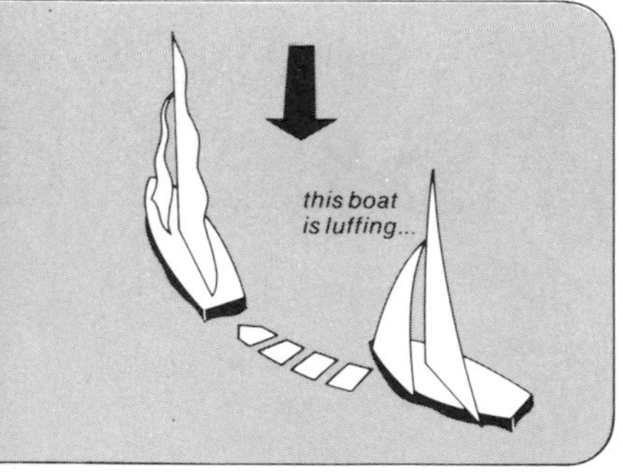

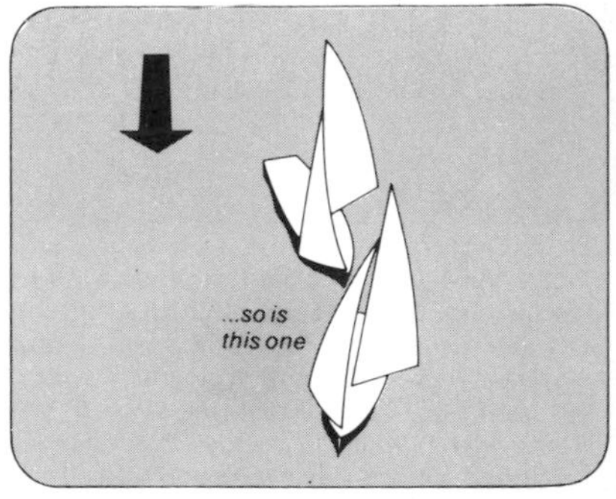

A boat which is luffing is altering course towards the wind. Other phrases commonly used (though not in the rules) to mean the same as luffing are: 'hardening up', 'pointing up' and 'putting the helm down'.

Bearing away

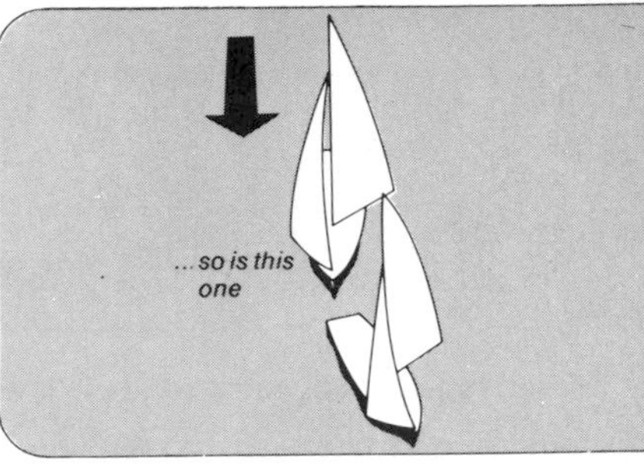

A boat which is bearing away is altering course away from the wind. Bearing away stops when the boat begins to gybe. Other phrases commonly used (though not in the rules) to mean the same as bearing away are: 'bearing off', 'bearing down', 'freeing off' and 'putting the helm up'.

Tacking

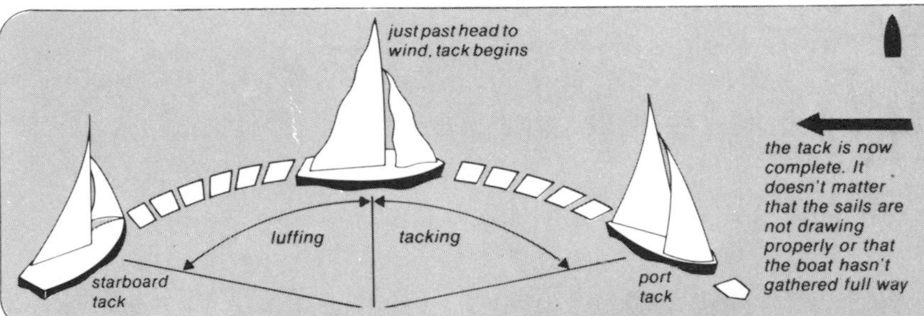

When people talk about tacking they usually mean the whole manoeuvre from first putting the helm down to getting under way on the new tack. The rule book definition is much narrower than this. The boat first luffs, and her tack is not defined as beginning until after she has passed through the eye of the wind. Tacking continues until the boat has reached a close-hauled course on the new tack.

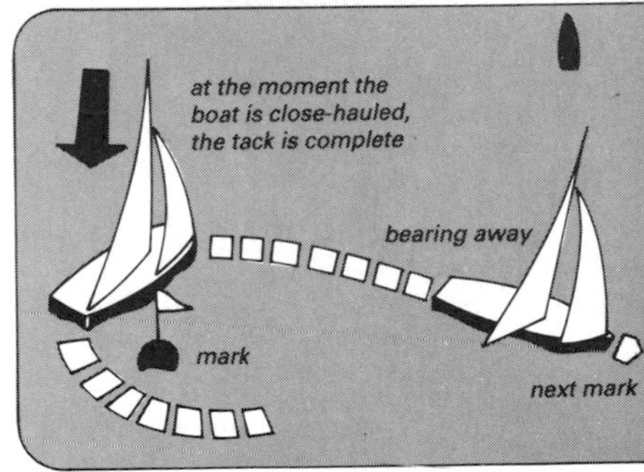

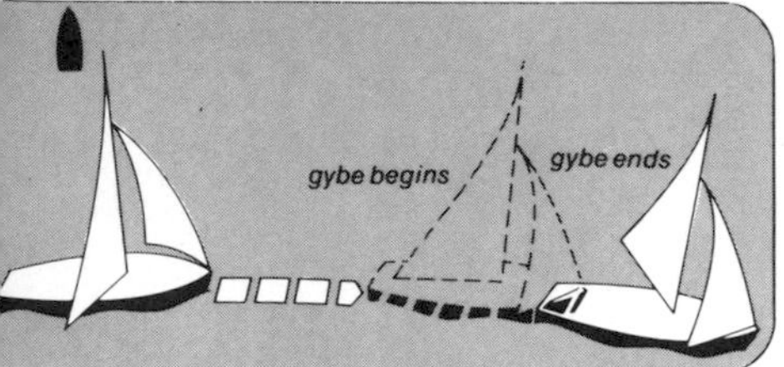

Gybing

Gybing happens much more quickly than tacking. The gybe begins when, with the wind aft, the boom crosses the centreline; it ends when the mainsail has filled on the other tack.

Overlapped, clear astern and clear ahead

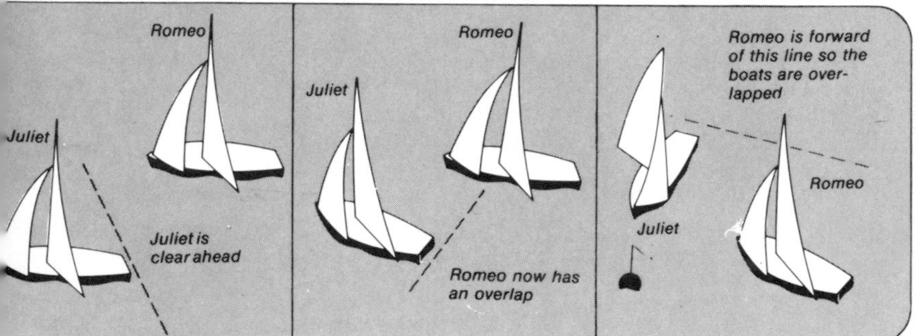

'A yacht is clear astern of another when her hull and equipment in normal position are abaft an imaginary line projected abeam from the aftermost point of the other's hull and equipment in normal position. The other yacht is clear ahead...' (Definition in Part I of the rule book.)

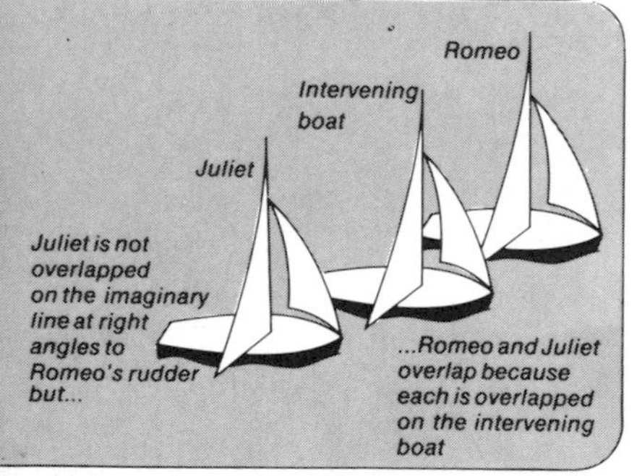

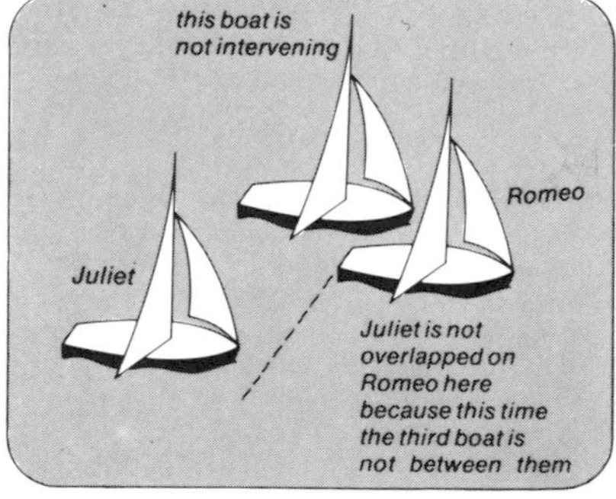

'The yachts overlap if neither is clear astern; or if, although one is clear astern, an intervening yacht overlaps both of them...' (Definition.)

Obstruction

'An obstruction is any object, including a vessel under way, large enough to require a yacht, if more than one overall length away from it, to make a substantial alteration of course to pass on one side or the other, or any object which can be passed on one side only, including a buoy when the yacht in question cannot safely pass between it and the shoal or object which it marks.' (Definition).

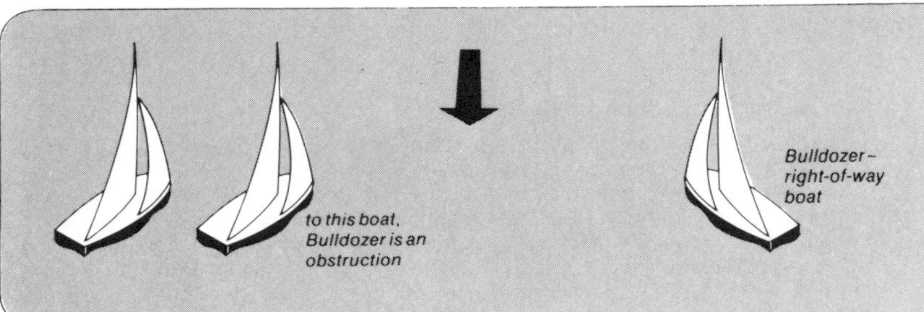
to this boat,
Bulldozer is an
obstruction
Bulldozer –
right-of-way
boat

Obstructions include shorelines, heavy patches of weed, fishing nets, shallows, moored boats, motor boats, crusing boats and, in some situations, other boats racing. Right-of-way boats and boats which refuse to give way, are out of control or capsized all rate as obstructions.

Mark

'A mark is any object specified in the sailing instructions which a yacht must round or pass on a required side. Every ordinary part of a mark ranks as part of it, including a flag, flagpole, boom or hoisted boat, but excluding ground tackle and any object either accidentally or temporarily attached to the mark'. (Definition.)

A dinghy tied to a mark does not count as part of the mark, unless specified in the sailing instructions (RYA appeal case 7 1971); nor does anything that has accidentally become attached to it or is only temporarily attached.

A mark's ground tackle is not counted as part of the mark (USSA appeal No. 3), but when a boat runs into the mooring line and is drawn onto any part of the mark, above or below water, she is counted as having hit the mark (USSA appeal No. 59).

Windward leg

A windward leg or, as it's often called, a beat, is a leg of the course which is sailed close-hauled, and on which the mark that ends the leg can not be reached without putting in at least one tack.

these are both
windward legs

Offwind leg

Any leg which is not a windward leg is an offwind leg. A free leg (the rule book's term) or a downwind leg mean exactly the same.

Starting and finishing

Starting is dealt with at the beginning of the special section on starting (page 21) and finishing is dealt with at the beginning of the special section on finishing (page 79).

Postponement and abandonment

A postponed race is one which is not started at its scheduled time and which can be sailed at any time the race committee may decide.

The race committee may abandon a race at any time, even before it has started or after some boats have finished. It may re-schedule a replacement race or declare it void (ie cancel it). Before the starting signal, the committee may abandon for any reason; after the starting signal the race can be abandoned only for one of the reasons listed in rule 5.4(c). After abandonment, the race committee has to consider carefully what is the right action to take, or lay itself open to requests for redress.

Collision

A collision happens when there is contact between any part of one boat (including all rigging, sails and sheets) or her crew and part of another boat or her crew.

Proper course

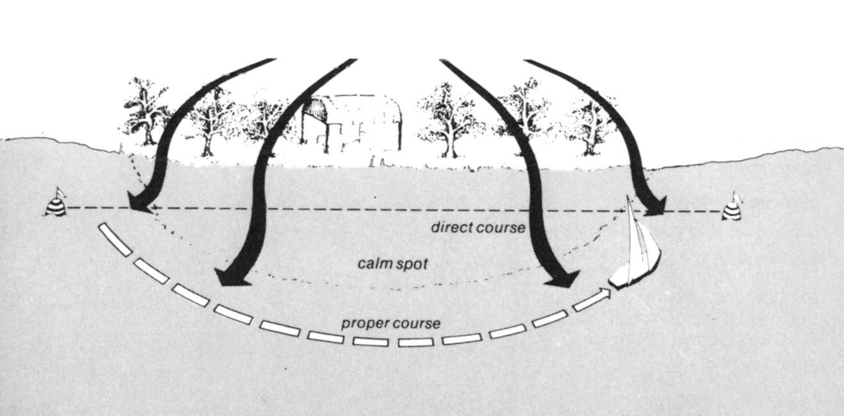

direction
of next mark
proper course for this boat
as she surfs down a wave may
well be 15 or 20 degrees
low of the straight line
course tothe next mark

'A proper course is any course which a yacht might sail after the starting signal, in the absence of other yacht or yachts affected, to finish as quickly as possible . . .' (Definition.) The reference to other yacht or yachts affected means that a helmsman is not sailing his proper course if, for example, he bears away solely to gain a tactical advantage over a boat or boats just behind or overlapping him.

Proper course refers to the course the boat makes good and not the direction she is pointing (RYA case 9 1969 and USSA Appeal No. 79).

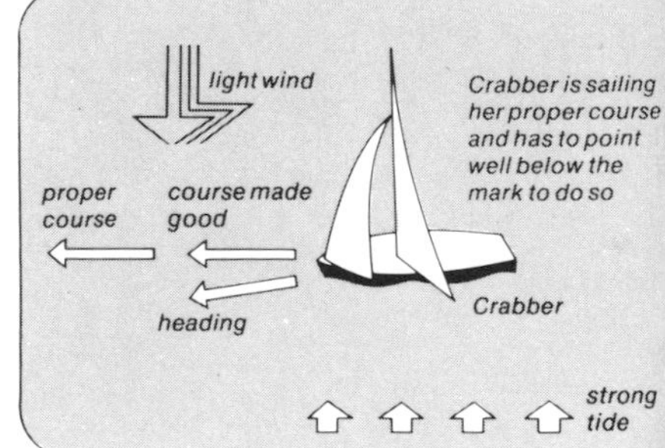
light wind
Crabber is sailing
her proper course
and has to point
well below the
mark to do so
proper
course
course made
good
heading
Crabber
strong
tide

There is no proper course before the starting signal.

Helmsman

Someone of either sex who is steering a sailing boat. Referred to as he.

Yacht

The IYRU rule book uses the word 'yacht' to mean any sailing boat. In the official language of the rule book, sailboards, Optimists, Lasers and 505s, for example, are all yachts, though no-one who sails them would normally refer to them as yachts – except in jest.

THE START

The starting period covered in this section runs from the moment a boat receives her preparatory signal to the moment after the starting signal when she starts.

Timing of starts

A race is usually started by a 10 minute warning signal, a 5 minute preparatory signal and the start signal. If there is an error of timing between the 10 minute and 5 minute signals, the starting signal must follow exactly 5 minutes after the preparatory signal – unless the race is then postponed. A national authority or a race committee through its sailing instructions may specify different timings. This often happens in team races where a 6 minute, 3 minute, start sequence may be used (rule 4.3).

The timing is taken from the visual signals, not from the sound signals (rule 4.5).

The racing rules come into force with the back-up of penalties at the 5 minute preparatory signal (Definition of racing Part 1 of the rules).

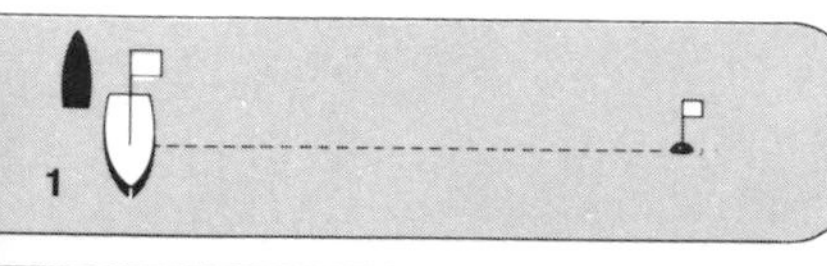

Start lines

A start line will usually be one of the following:

(a) A line between a mark and a mast on the committee boat or place clearly identified in the sailing instructions (1).

(b) A line between two marks (2).

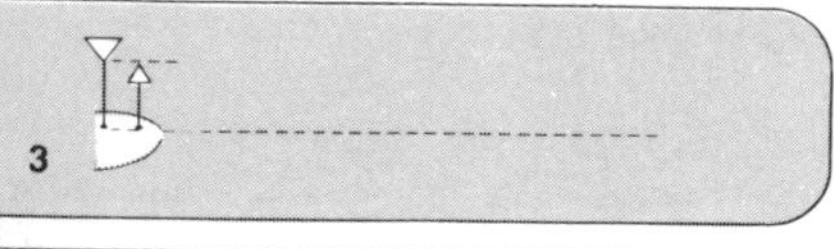

(c) The extension of a line through two stationary posts (3), which may have a mark at or near its outer limit, that boats must pass inside (4).

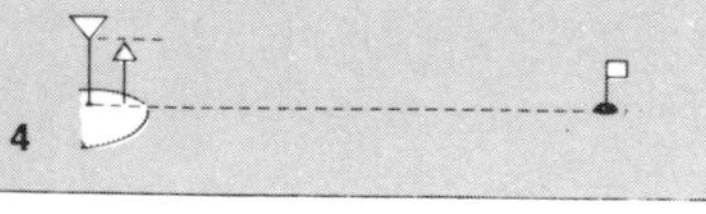

Inner distance mark (IDM)

On starting lines of types (1), (3) and (4) an inner distance mark may be laid, but will have an effect only if the 'sailing instructions state what the obligations of yachts are (for example 'yachts shall pass between the mark and the outer starting mark' or 'yachts shall not pass between the mark and committee boat'). Unless otherwise stated in the sailing instructions, this mark (like all other starting marks) 'begins to have a required side when [a yacht] is approaching the starting line from the pre-course side to start'. Unless the sailing instructions state otherwise, before you are 'approaching the line to start, you can pass either side of it'.

Over the line at the start

When any part of a boat, her sails, rigging, equipment or crew is on the course side of the start line at the starting signal the boat is a premature starter (rule 7).

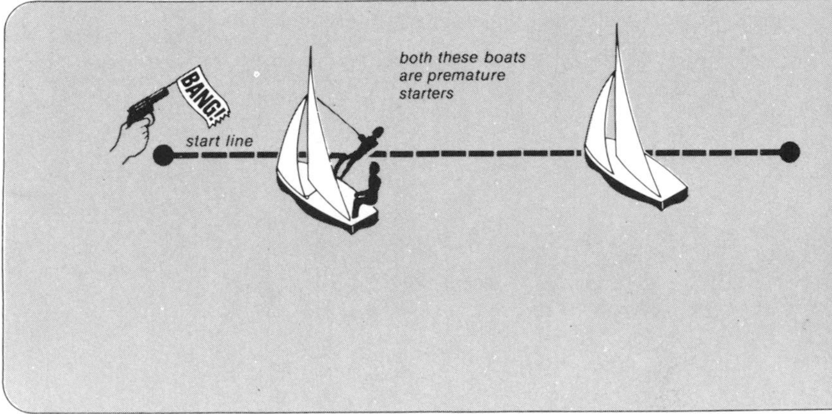
BANG!
start line
both these boats
are premature
starters

When one or more boats are premature starters, the race officer must make a sound signal and display code flag 'X'.

A boat which has started prematurely must now re-start or be disqualified. But a premature starter who does not realise her error is not required to go back and re-start when the visual signal is not accompanied by the prescribed sound signal (rule 7.1 and IYRU case 70).

When a recalled boat has returned completely to the pre-start side of the start line, she can start correctly. The 'X' flag is lowered once the last of the premature starters has returned to the pre-start side of the line, or four minutes after the starting signal, whichever is the earlier (rule 7.1).

Any boat anchored before the start with part of her ground tackle on the course side of the start line at the start signal becomes a premature starter because the anchor and warp are part of the boat's equipment (rule 7.1).

When code flag 'I' has been displayed, any boat whose hull, equipment or crew is on the course side of the start line during the minute before the start must sail round one end of the line before starting. She may not just dip back over the line (rule 51.1(c)).

Hitting a starting mark

A boat which collides with a starting mark after the preparatory signal can stay in the race provided she immediately sails clear of other boats and makes a 360 degree turn.

720 degree penalty for an infringement before the start signal

When the sailing instructions specify that the 720 degree penalty is in force the turns must be done at the first reasonable opportunity after the infringement. This means sailing clear of other boats to find a space. (720 degree turns are dealt with in detail on pages 86–7.)

An infringement just before the starting signal will therefore result in a much more severe penalty than an infringement soon after the preparatory signal.

If the infringement occurs before the wrong-doer has started (or if he is a premature starter not yet returned) then the 720 must be done at the first reasonable opportunity, whichever side of the line that happens to be. If at the end of doing the 720 he is on, or on the course side of, the line he must go back behind the line and re-start.

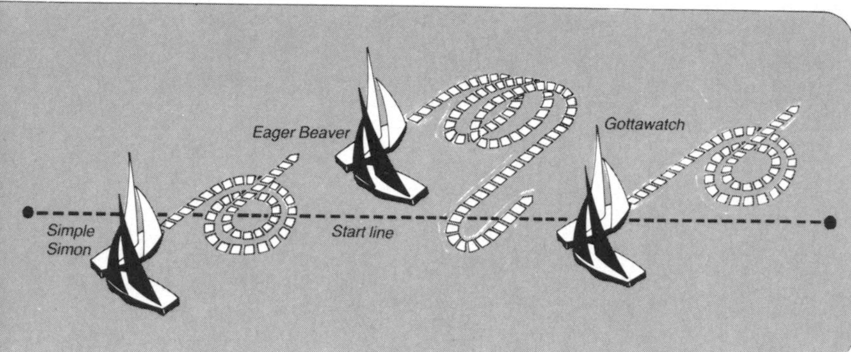

It is two seconds after the starting signal and all these port tackers have infringed Rule 36. They must do a 720 as soon as they can. Eager Beaver was a premature starter and will then have to go back behind the line and start; Gottawatch started before he infringed; Simple Simon starts as he commences his 720.

Anchored, moored, tied up or still ashore

A boat may be disqualified for being ashore, moored or tied up after the preparatory (5 minute) signal (rule 53). If she doesn't sail about the vicinity of the start line between the preparatory and starting signals or does not start, she is counted as a non-starter (rule 74.5).

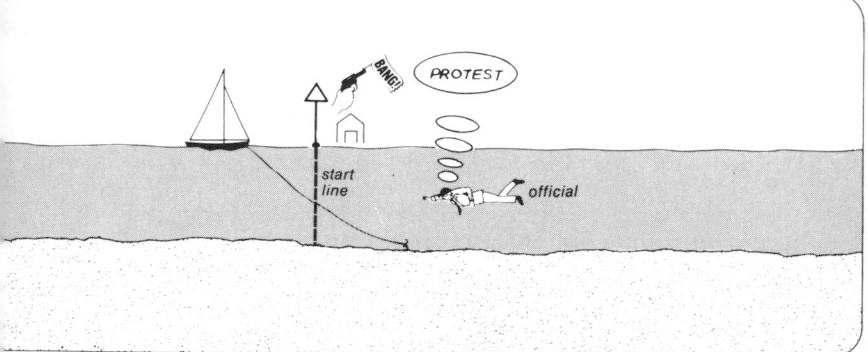

If she does get to the vicinity of the line before the starting signal, she must be ranked as a starter (rule 74.5) and can only be disqualified under rule 53 after a proper protest hearing. A helmsman cannot exonerate himself under this rule by taking any alternative penalties since they only apply to the right-of-way rules in Part IV of the rule book. Rule 53 is in Part V.

A boat may be anchored after the preparatory signal or held by a member of the crew standing in the water, and no rule is broken (rule 53). However, if an anchor is over the line at the start, the boat is reckoned to be a premature starter.

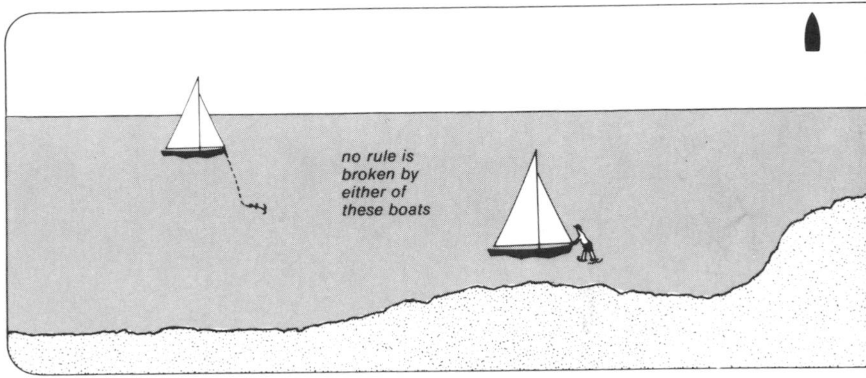
no rule is
broken by
either of
these boats

General recall

When the race officer can't pick out all the premature starters, or when the start is unsatisfactory in some other way, he can abandon the start by flying the First Substitute and making two or more sound signals after the starting signal.

The procedure for the re-start is then:

1. First Substitute is lowered to the accompaniment of a sound signal.
2. After one minute a new preparatory signal is made (including the class signal when system 1 of rule 4.3(a) is in use).

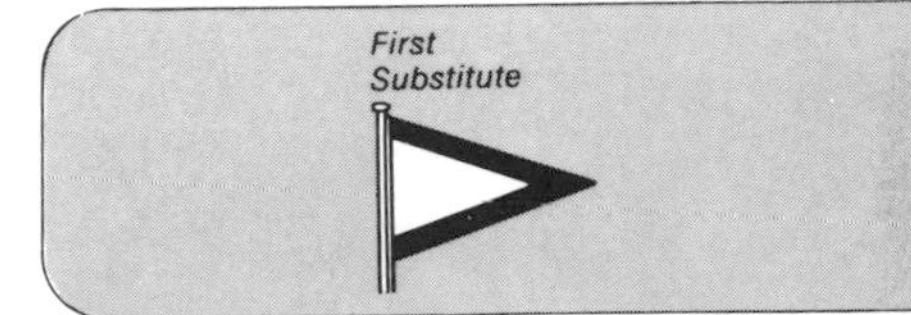
First
Substitute

Once again, though, the sailing instructions may give a different procedure. This would have precedence over the IYRU standard procedure.

Any boat which commits a foul on the abandoned start is not barred from competing in any subsequent starts unless the sailing instructions specifically say so (and that is very rare except in very populous starts) (rule 7.2(b)).

Postponement

A race may be postponed by flying the Answering Pennant. The race will then be started after the scheduled time at the discretion of the race committee. The warning signal is made one minute after the Answering Pennant is lowered, accompanied by a sound signal.

Answering
Pennant

RIGHT-OF-WAY

Starting

A boat starts when any part of her hull, crew or equipment first crosses the start line after the start signal in the direction of the first mark (except that if she is subject to the 'round the ends rule' she must first sail round an end). (Definition of Starting and rule 51.1(c).)

two seconds after the start gun:
this boat touched a starting mark just before the starting signal, so she will need to do a 720 and then go back and start
this boat was over the line at the gun so has not started, but is racing
direction of first mark
this boat has started
start line
this boat has not yet started, even though the gun has gone, but she is racing
this boat infringed a rule just before the starting signal so she has to do a 720 before she can start

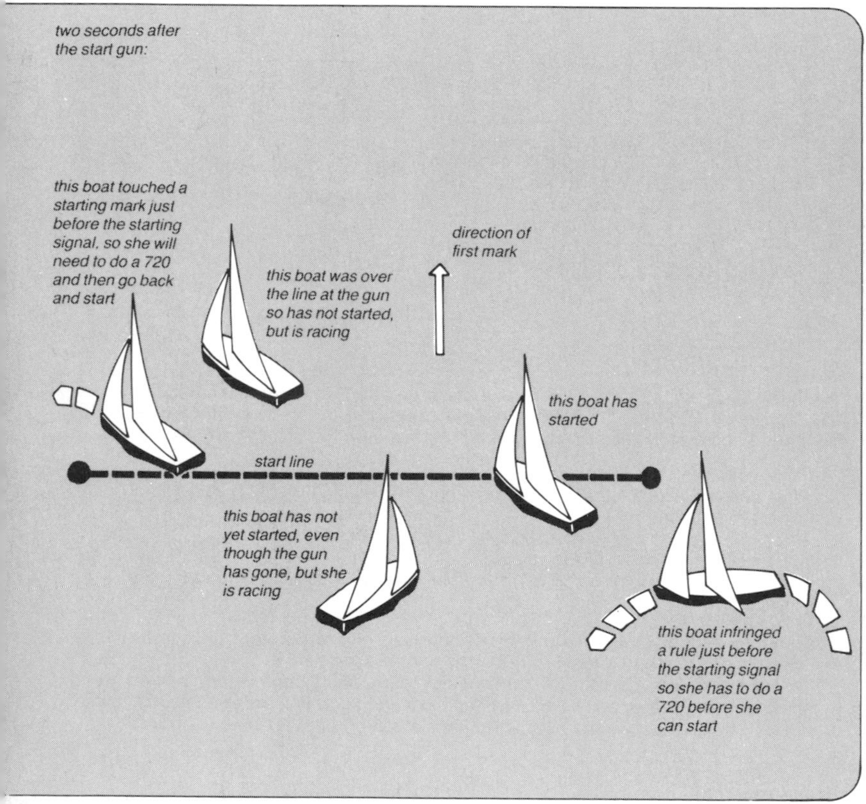

No room at a starting mark

When approaching the line to start a windward boat (white) is not entitled to demand room from any leeward boat (black) at a starting mark (rule 42(a)).

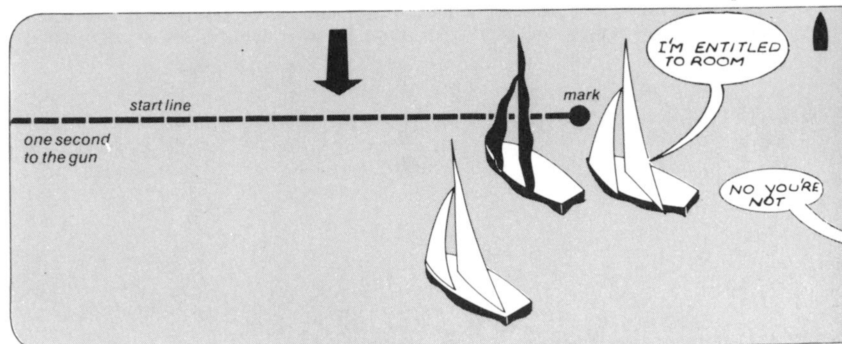

But after the starting signal the leeward boat is not entitled to squeeze the windward boat out at the mark by sailing either:

1. above (that is, upwind of) the course to the first mark *or*
2. above close-hauled (rule 42(a)).

The mark must be a starting mark and surrounded by navigable water for this ruling to apply.

In the to-ing and fro-ing before the start, though, a windward boat is entitled to room at a starting mark, but only if it's an obstruction. The 'no water' rule applies only 'when approaching the line to start'.

At the other end of the start line, if there is just a small buoy, the leeward boat is not entitled to room (rule 42(a)). The black boat here may only luff, slowly, above close hauled, if the white boat is not 'mast abeam' and is able to respond.

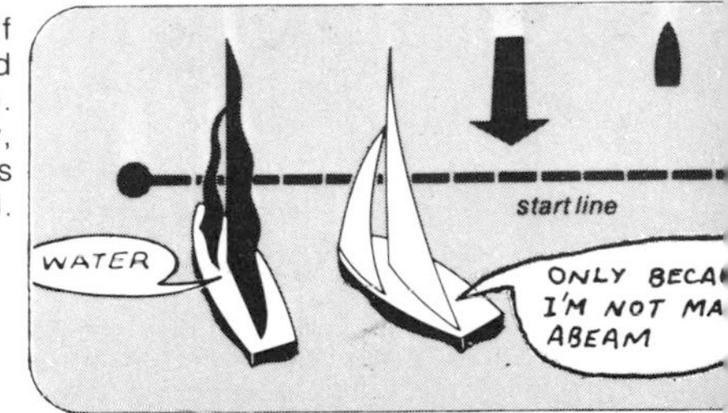

The position is quite different if the starting mark cannot be sailed round or the line's length is limited by, say, a pier. A windward boat is then entitled to room at that mark or pier (rule 42(a)).

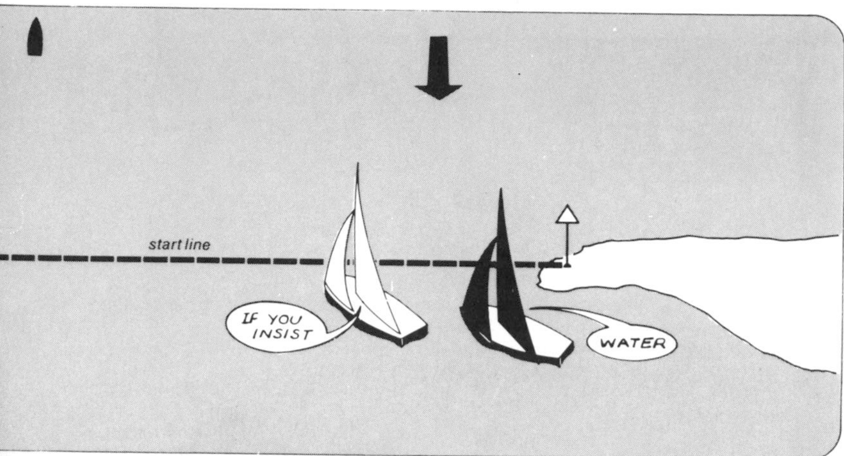

Altering course to start

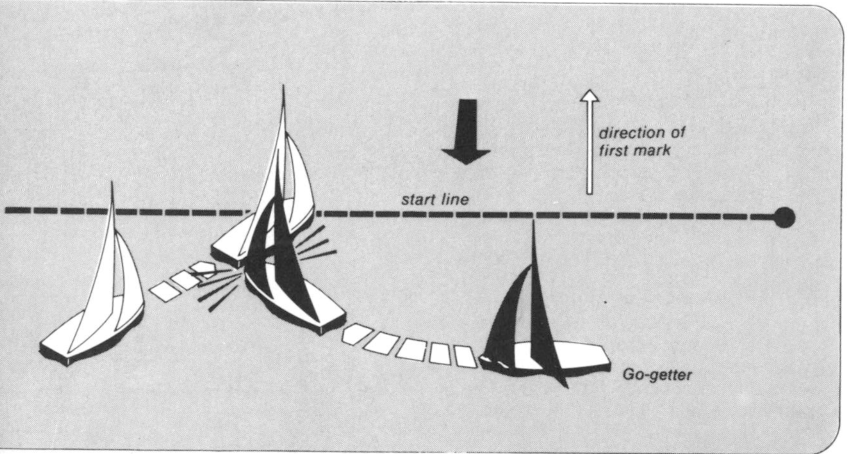

A boat which is assuming a proper course after the starting signal does not have to worry about any non-right-of-way boats which are on the opposite tack, whereas at any other time in the race (except at marks) she would (rule 35(b)(i)).

Go-getter is altering course to start and white is in the wrong. If she were not starting, **Go-getter,** as right-of-way boat, would be in the wrong for altering course in a way that obstructs a boat which was keeping clear.

Luffing before the start

The luffing rules that apply before a boat starts are fundamentally different from those that apply later. A luff may not be fast before she starts and the acquisition of luffing rights is quite different.

After the preparatory signal (5 minute) but before she has started and cleared the start line:

1. A leeward yacht may luff a windward boat slowly and in such a way that the windward boat has 'room and opportunity to keep clear' (rule 38).
2. The leeward boat has the right to luff as high as head to wind (again slowly) when the windward boat is aft of the mast abeam position – regardless of how the two boats came together (rule 38).

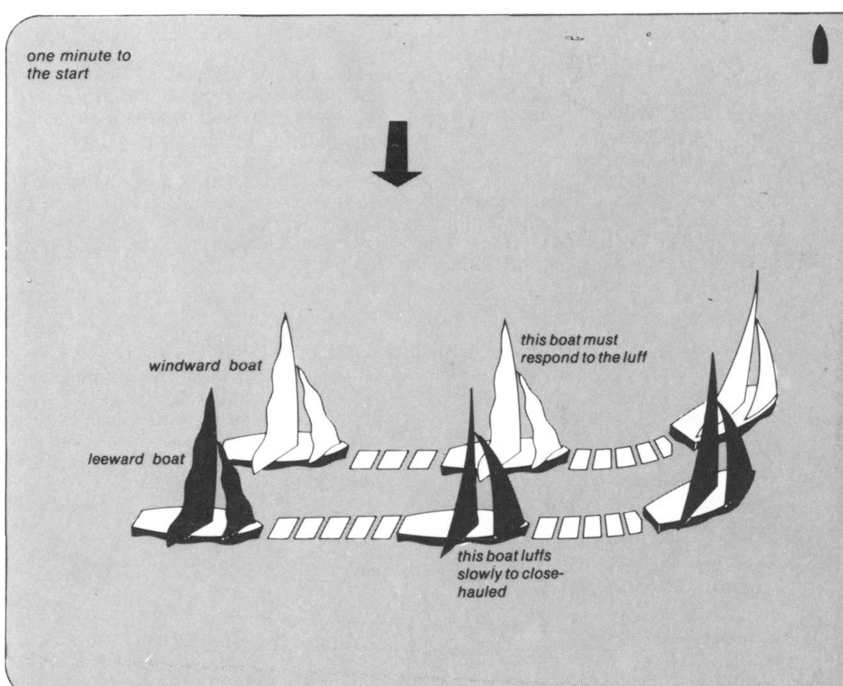
one minute to
the start
windward boat
leeward boat
this boat must
respond to the luff
this boat luffs
slowly to close-
hauled

The windward boat has not dropped behind the 'mast abeam' position (explained on page 72), so the leeward boat may not luff above close-hauled.

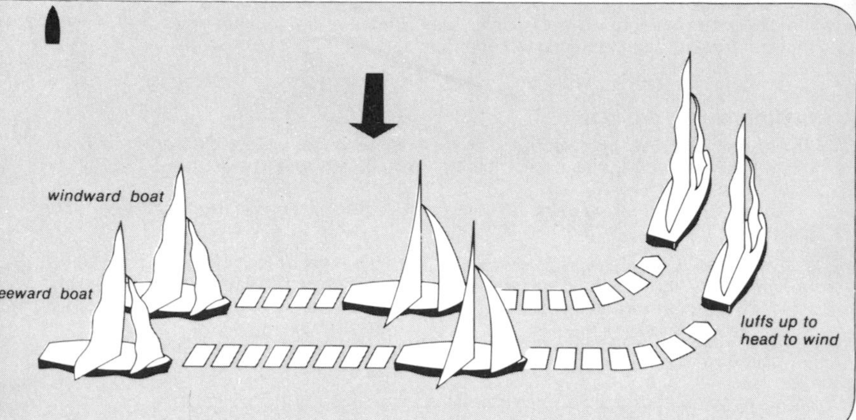

The leeward boat here is entitled to carry on luffing slowly until she is head to wind – provided the windward boat doesn't gain the 'mast abeam' position or move forward of it and provided the windward boat does not hail 'that an obstruction, a third yacht or other object limits her ability to keep clear' (rules 39.2 and 40.2).

If, for example, the windward boat was idling when the luff began, she would require time to gather way and respond to the luff. The leeward boat has to give her this opportunity. It is important to remember that the first movement of the windward boat's stern is responding to a luff is inevitably *towards* the leeward boat. The windward boat would not be disqualified in a pre-start luffing incident if she made every reasonable effort to avoid the leeward boat's luff from the moment the luff began.

3. A luff which is higher than close-hauled can be stopped by the windward helmsman if he reaches the 'mast abeam' position. He simply hails 'mast abeam' and the leeward boat must bear away to close-hauled (rule 40.1).
4. When more than one boat is overlapped upwind the leeward boat may not luff higher than close-hauled unless she has the right to luff *all* the overlapped boats (rule 40.3).
5. A windward helmsman can hail to stop the leeward boat luffing when he can't respond because of an obstruction (rule 40.2). A starting mark surrounded by navigable water does not rate as a legitimate obstruction when starting to leeward of it.

Over the line at the start

While a premature starter is sailing the course, she carries full rights. But at the moment she begins her manoeuvre to return, she loses the protection of the main right-of-way rules (rule 44).

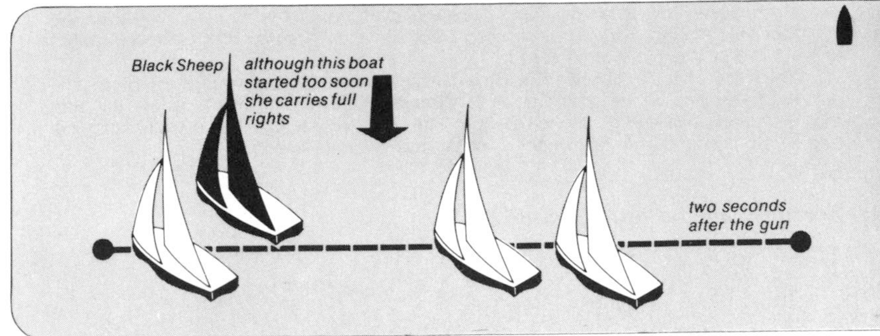

Now **Black Sheep** lets her sails flap to slow down. Her manoeuvre to return has begun and she must keep clear of all other boats (rule 44).

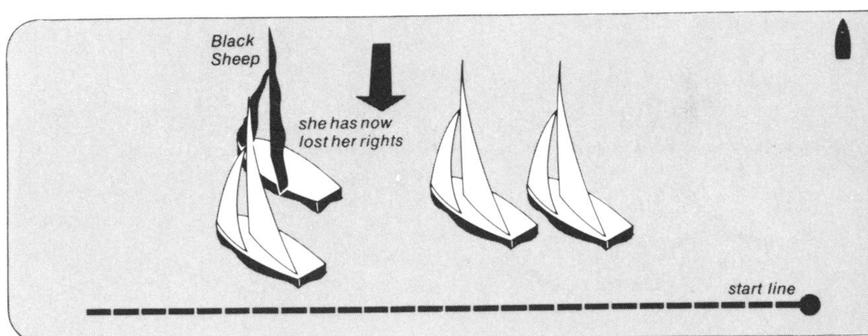

Once back on the pre-start side of the line **Black Sheep** gets back her rights, but she cannot make use of them immediately. She must allow boats over which she has right-of-way 'ample room and opportunity to keep clear' (rule 44.1(b)).

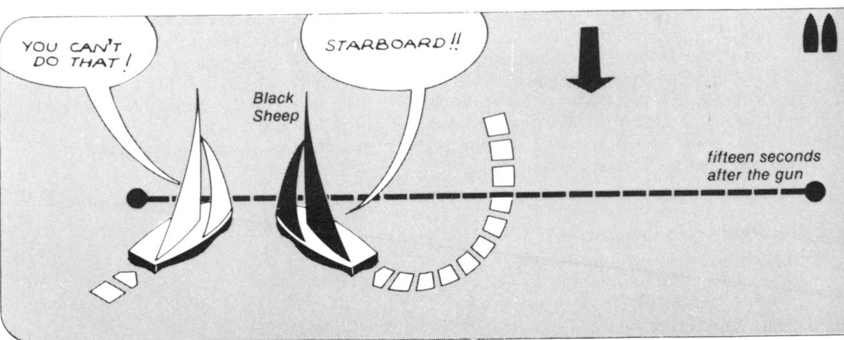

Black Sheep has acted too fast in claiming starboard rights. She has not given the port tack boat enough opportunity to keep clear. On this showing, **Black Sheep's** return to the fold would only be temporary.

When code flag 'I' has been displayed, any boat whose hull, equipment or crew is on the course side of the start line or its extensions during the minute before the start must sail round one end of the line to start. She may not just dip back over the start line (rule 51.1(c)). The sailing instructions, though, may override this rule.

Starting from the wrong side of the line

STARBOARD YOU LOT

Cowboy

two seconds to go

YOU'LL BE LUCKY

start line

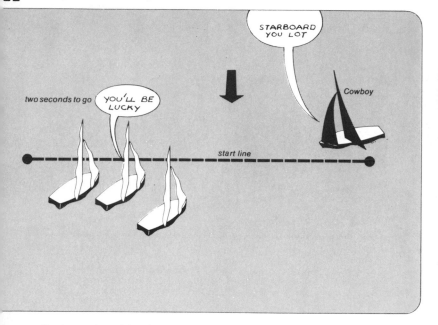

Cowboy enjoys right-of-way for 2 seconds more, then loses it as soon as the gun goes if she is caught with any part of the boat or crew on the wrong side of the line at the gun (rule 51.1(b) and 44.1(a)). If she gets behind the line in 2 seconds she has the right to head up and start as explained in 'Altering course to start', page 28.

But look out for any special starting provisions in the sailing instructions; they may override the IYRU rules that apply here.

Overtaking to leeward

This is very common before and at the start, though the rules that apply are much the same as would apply at any other time in the race.

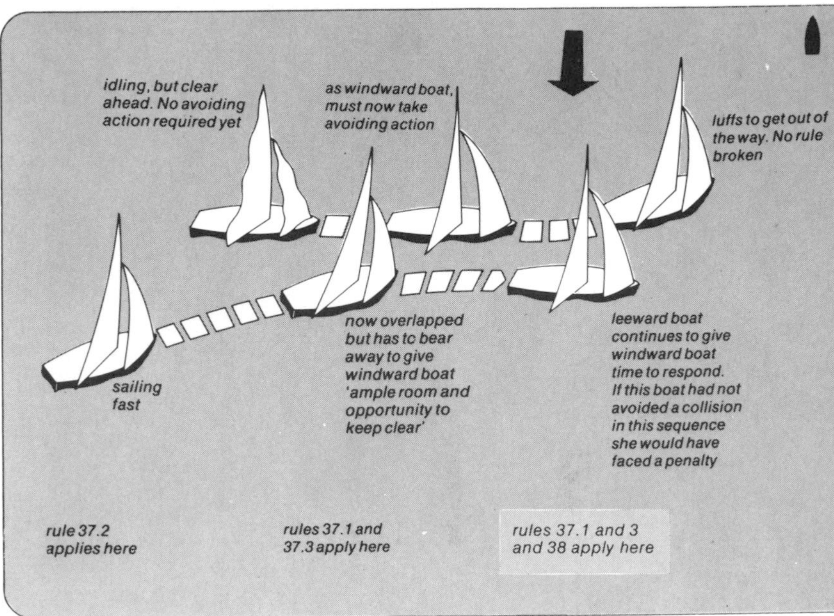
idling, but clear ahead. No avoiding action required yet
as windward boat, must now take avoiding action
luffs to get out of the way. No rule broken
now overlapped but has tc bear away to give windward boat 'ample room and opportunity to keep clear'
leeward boat continues to give windward boat time to respond. If this boat had not avoided a collision in this sequence she would have faced a penalty
sailing fast
rule 37.2 applies here
rules 37.1 and 37.3 apply here
rules 37.1 and 3 and 38 apply here

Ample room and opportunity (rule 37.3) means more than just 'sufficient', and the benefit of any doubt must go to the windward boat.

The one big difference in the overtaking rights-of-way before and after starting is in the rights of the leeward boat to luff (pages 30 and 72).

WINDWARD LEG

A windward leg is one that a boat can complete only by putting in at least one tack.

OPPOSITE TACKS

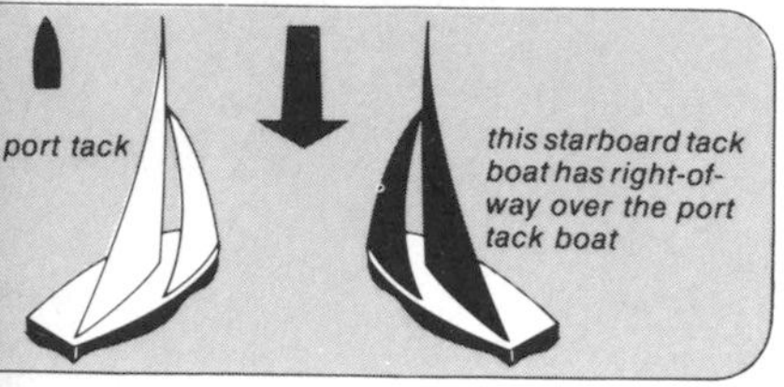

Port and starboard

A port tack boat gives way to a starboard tack boat (rule 36).

When there is no collision and a close-hauled starboard tack boat bears away to miss the port boat's stern, the onus of proof is on the port tack helmsman to show that the starboard boat would have missed had she held her course (RYA case 1 1973, USSA case 32 and IYRU case 113).

The port tack helmsman may hail 'hold your course' but this hail is not binding on the starboard boat, which can still bear away to miss and protest (USSA case 137). In dinghies, though, it is no bad thing for the starboard helmsman to hold his course in these circumstances. A rudder or transom clipped saves any argument.

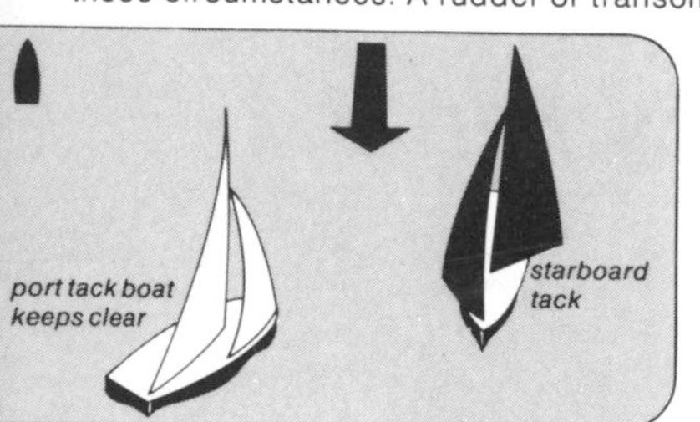

A starboard tack boat sailing free has right-of-way over a close-hauled port tack boat, so long as the starboard tacker does not alter course in a way that prevents the port tack boat keeping clear (rules 35 and 36).

Port and starboard when the starboard tack boat alters course

A port and starboard incident where the starboard tack boat alters course and hits – or claims she could have hit – a port tacker is quite different from the straightforward port and starboard case above. This situation is controlled by rule 35, which is designed to deny *carte blanche* to alter course and hit give way boats.

The white boat on starboard is in the wrong because she altered course when the port boat was properly keeping clear. Nor can an offwind starboard tack boat legitimately alter course to hit a port tack boat that is sailing a course to keep clear.

Even when there is a windshift, rule 35 can override the basic port and starboard rule (IYRU case 52, RYA case 5 1974 and USSA case 157). To use the windshift as a defence at a protest hearing, black would have to establish to the committee's satisfaction that she was clearly going to cross white before the windshift complicated matters.

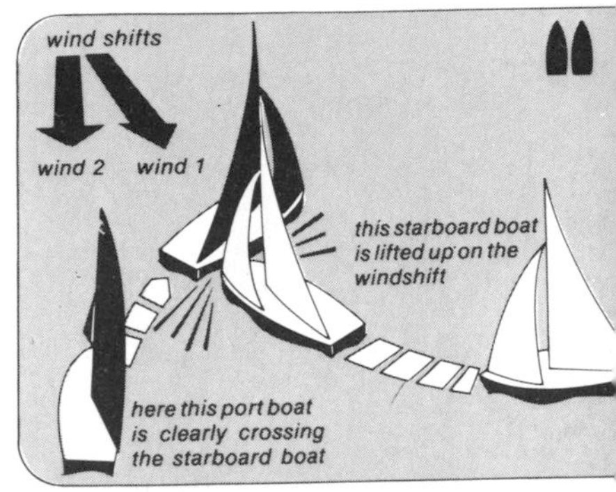

here this port boat is clearly crossing the starboard boat

Port and starboard when starboard tack boat has just tacked

'A yacht shall neither tack nor gybe into a position which will give her right of way unless she does so far enough from a yacht on a tack to enable this yacht to keep clear without having to begin to alter her course until after the tack or gybe has been completed' (rule 41.2).

The boat which has just tacked (**Jack-in-the-box**) has the onus of satisfying the race committee that the tack was completed far enough from the other boat (rule 41.3). Protest committees are too often apt to place the onus on the port tack boat, merely because the port and starboard rule is basic. In cases like this one they would be wrong to do that.

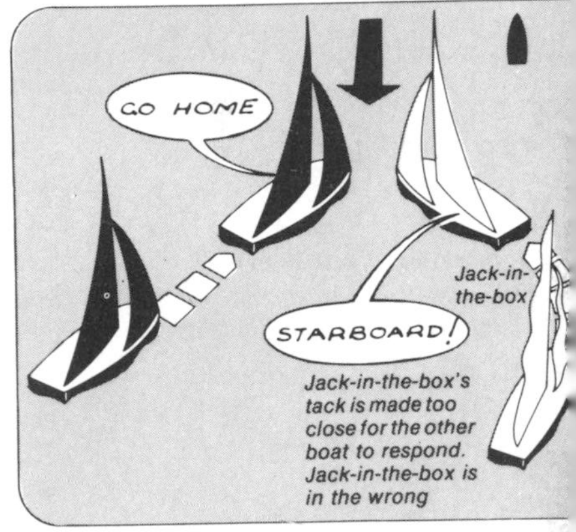

GO HOME
Jack-in-the-box
STARBOARD!
Jack-in-the-box's tack is made too close for the other boat to respond. Jack-in-the-box is in the wrong

Calling 'starboard'

There is no obligation to call 'starboard', but anybody who makes a habit of not hailing would soon become pretty unpopular – particularly when tacking onto starboard a few lengths away from a port tack boat.

The starboard tack boat on the right breaks no rule by hailing 'starboard', putting the port tack boat about, then tacking.

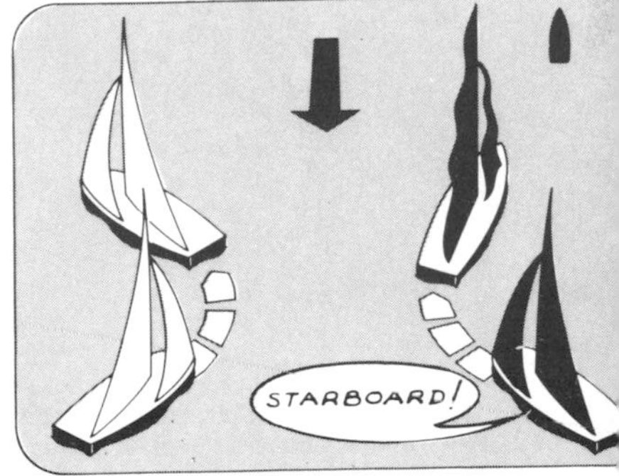

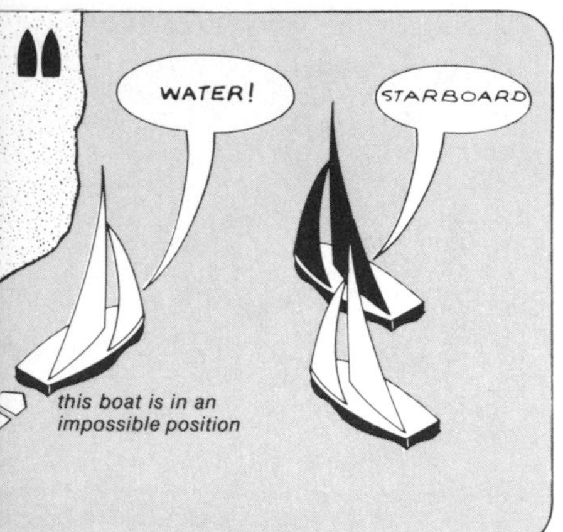

Opposite tack boat requiring room for an obstruction

There is, curiously, no way that a port tack boat which is prevented from tacking by an obstruction can legitimately force starboard tack boats to tack and give her room. Only when she calls for room before tacking onto port can she put the starboard tackers about without infringing the rules (rule 43, explained opposite). Otherwise the port and starboard rule (36) applies, in spite of the fact that the port tack boat's only escape may be to bear away hard or go aground.

SAME TACK

Windward and leeward

When two boats are beating on the same tack and the one to windward is not sailing as close to the wind as the leeward one, the windward boat must keep clear (rule 37.1).

The leeward boat may not sail above her proper course (close-hauled here) unless she has luffing rights (rule 39.1 and 39.2).

If the leeward boat has come up from clear astern, she must allow the windward boat 'ample room and opportunity to keep clear' from the moment the overlap is established (rule 37.3). This may mean that the leeward boat has to bear off initially, but the windward boat is required to respond by luffing above her close-hauled course if necessary. Again, the initial onus to keep clear is on the boat which has newly acquired right-of-way (the leeward one).

The crew or helmsman of the leeward boat may not deliberately reach out, sit out or trapeze with the prime intention of hitting the windward boat (RYA case 6 1971). This is penalised under the fair sailing rule.

Luffing

The rule is exactly the same as for an off-wind leg (page 72). I should mention one situation, though, which only crops up on the beat; it represents a particularly sharp, but legitimate, use of the luffing rule.

From the moment the leeward boat completes a tack there is a new situation and if the leeward boat has luffing rights when she completes her tack, then once she's given the windward boat an opportunity to keep clear, she may luff as sharply as she likes, up to head to wind (Definition of Clear Astern, rules 39.2 and 41.2). Though she is not entitled to cause serious damage (rule 32).

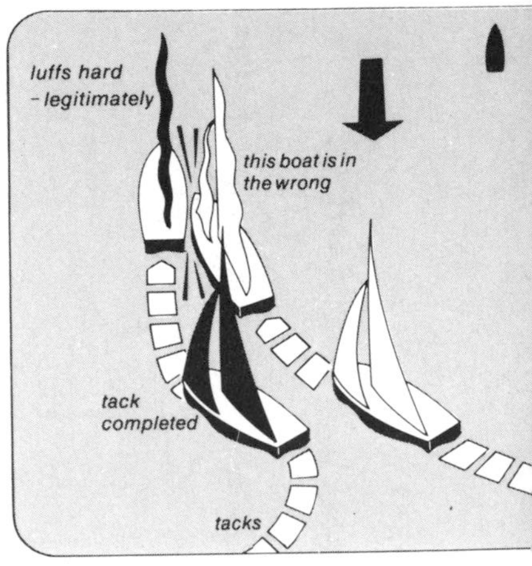

Bearing down

Provided the leeward boat isn't made to alter course to avoid hitting the windward boat, the windward boat may bear away below close-hauled as white does here.

This would not be allowed on an off-wind leg because rule 39.3 (sailing below a proper course) forbids it, but that rule applies only to free legs, not beats. It is also worth remembering that it is the leg itself that counts, not the actual point of sailing, so if two boats have overstood a weather mark the windward one may bear down on the other since, although sailing free, they are still on the windward leg. (A windward leg is defined on page 17.)

Calling for room at a continuous obstruction

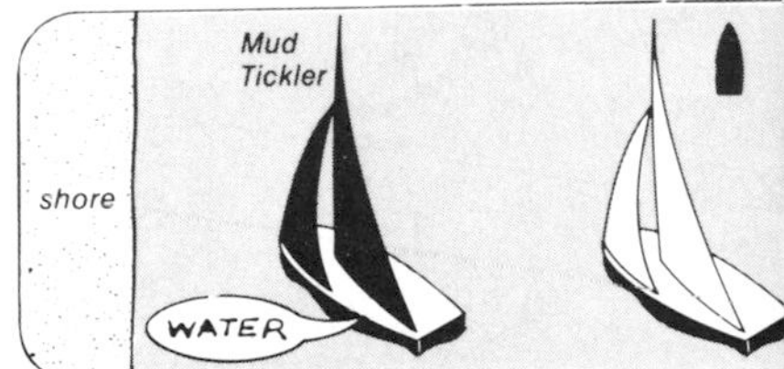

If **Mud Tickler** carries on she'll hit the shore; if she tacks she'll hit white. The rules provide a way out of this one provided both boats are on the same tack as they are here: **Mud Tickler** can hail 'water',

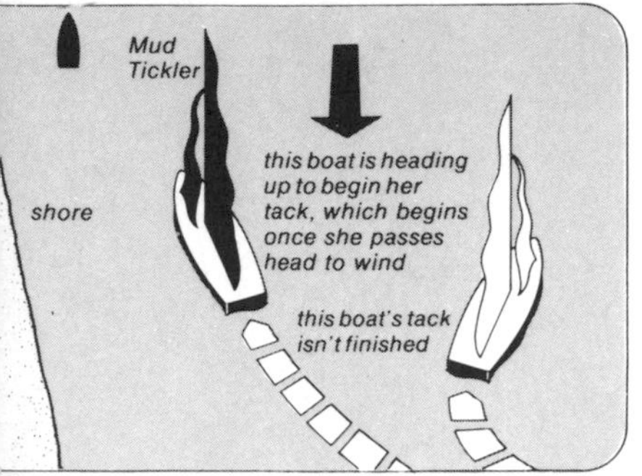

'shore room' or something similar at white before tacking. (But if she makes the call after tacking she'll be in trouble, as explained on page 38).

The white boat here must now respond either by immediately:

1. tacking *or*
2. hailing 'you tack' (rule 43.2(b)).

If white chooses to tack, **Mud Tickler** must begin to tack immediately she is able to tack and clear the white boat (rule 43.2(a) and USSA case 108). But **Mud Tickler** is not entitled to hail and tack simultaneously into white (rule 43.1).

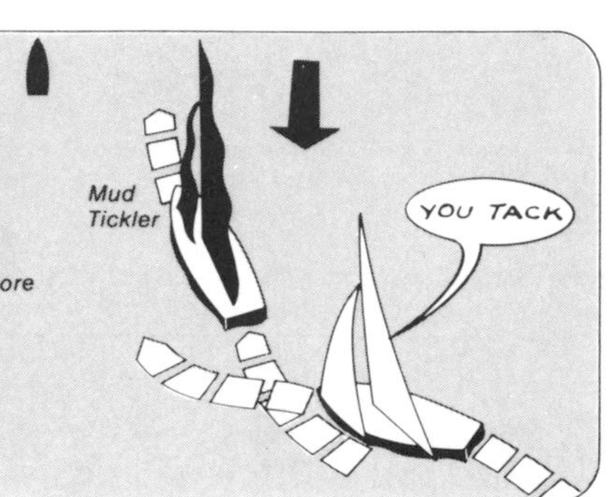

White may prefer to let **Mud Tickler** tack, keep out of her way and really squeeze into the shore herself. Then white must call 'you tack' and avoid **Mud Tickler.** The onus is now entirely on white to keep out of the way (rule 43.2(b)(ii) and (iii)).

Once white has made her 'you tack' call, **Mud Tickler** must tack immediately. If she doesn't she can be protested against – even if there is no collision (rule 43.2 (b)(i)).

The commonest problems in these situations come up when short tacking against a tide, and hinge on how far apart the boats need to be before the inshore boat's call for water is invalid. There is no set number of boat lengths - the distance will vary according to the conditions and the type of boat – but the criteria for deciding are quite clear. The inshore boat is not entitled to hail for water when:

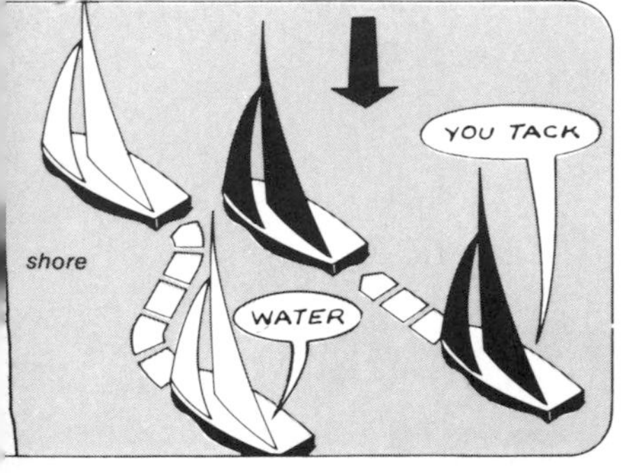

1. she can tack out from the shore and back again onto her original tack without tacking in the other boat's water *or*
2. she can tack and bear off behind the other boat without difficulty.

The white boat here is able to tack out from the shore and back onto her original tack without tacking in black's water. White's hail was therefore illegal. Black must still respond to the hail (for example by hailing 'you tack') and may then protest. However, if the protest committee is satisfied that it was reasonable for white to believe she could not tack with the possibility of not being able to keep clear of black, then white's hail will be ruled as valid, even though, as it turned out here, white was in fact able to keep clear of black after completing her tack onto port.

In this sequence, white's call was dubious, but since she believed she was going to find it difficult to tack and clear black, she had the right to hail.

Black took a chance by hailing 'you tack' but, as it turned out, white was able to tack and bear off behind black without difficulty, so there was no infringement (rule 43.1 and USSA case 108).

Calling for room at a non-continuous obstruction

A non-continuous obstruction is one which can be passed on either side and requires a boat not less than a length away to make a substantial alteration of course to miss it. Moored boats, miniscule islands, capsized boats, other boats sailing and motor boats may all be non-continuous obstructions (the definition is on page 17).

Once the 'water' call has been made here by black, white must respond exactly as in the section above (rule 43). The fact that white would have missed the obstruction anyway doesn't matter. Nor does it matter that black chose to tack rather than bear off and go to leeward of the obstruction. There is no rule which dictates that a boat should take the shortest route around an obstruction. Although if black would only need to make a small alteration of course when one length away, the rules don't allow her to call for water to tack; she must then make the course change, staying on the same tack (USSA case 81).

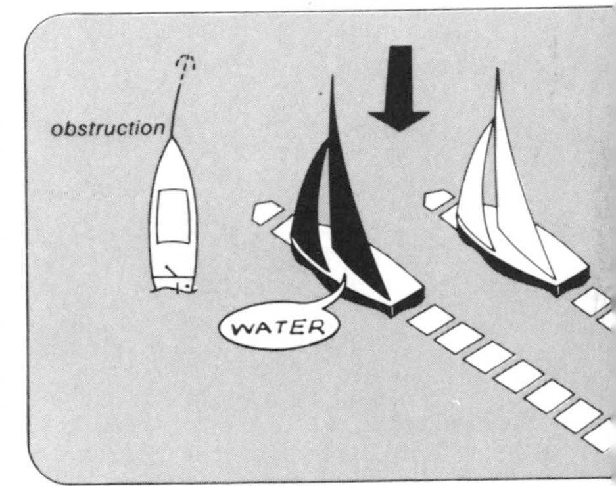

A starboard tack boat as an obstruction

One of the commonest obstructions to sea room is a starboard tack boat. Usually it will be close-hauled but it can be running free.

Stool-pigeon is entitled to hail for water to tack, and the white boat must either tack immediately or call 'you tack'. **Stool-pigeon** has to see this situation coming in good time or she'll be too late to call and won't be able to get out of the starboard tacker's way (rule 43 and definition of an obstruction).

When **Stool-pigeon** calls clearly for room to tack in good time, and white fails to respond, the responsibility is entirely white's and no blame falls on **Stool-pigeon** for white's failure to tack. (As USSA case 142 conflicts with IYRU case 6 here, I have taken the IYRU interpretation since, though earlier, it will apply everywhere outside the United States.)

Instead of tacking, **Stool-pigeon** can choose to bear away astern of the starboard boat, since an obstruction can be taken on either side, but she must then give any room white might need if she needs to take action to avoid the starboard boat and wishes to go underneath (rule 42.1(a) and definition of obstruction).

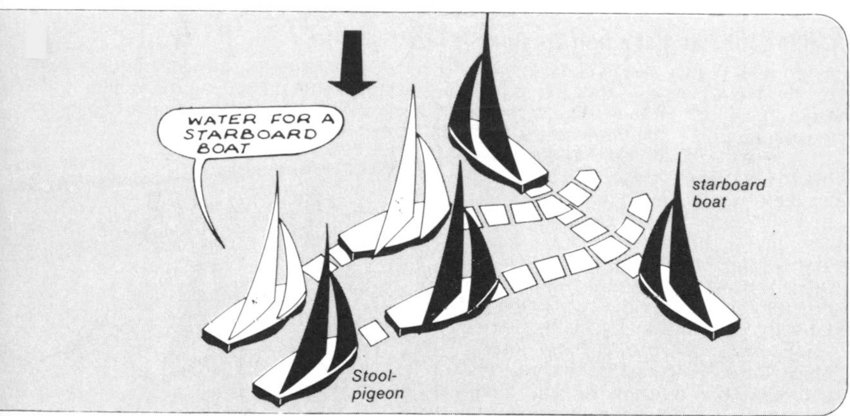

If white asks for water to bear off behind the starboard boat at the same moment as **Stool-pigeon** asks for room to tack, **Stool-pigeon**'s call governs. White only gets room if **Stool-pigeon** chooses not to hail for room to tack, in which case **Stool-pigeon** must give room whether or not white hails (USSA case 131).

Forcing another boat to overstand a weather mark

The team racing ploy of holding an opponent on the same tack to sail beyond the lay line and overstand the weather mark is explained on page 64.

TACKING

Tacking in the water of a starboard tack boat

A boat which is tacking is required to keep clear of a boat which is not tacking (rule 41). Tacking is explained on page 15.

Even when the tacking boat has completed her tack she is not necessarily in the clear. Any nearby boat on a tack has no need to alter course to avoid her until her tack is complete – that is, until her boom is across and she is heading on a close-hauled course (though her sails needn't be filling).

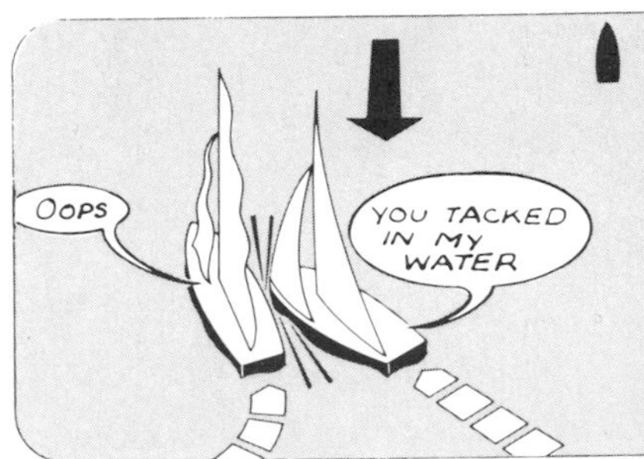

In a protest, the onus is on the boat that tacks to satisfy the protest committee that she did so far enough ahead to allow the boat already on the tack to keep clear (rule 41.3 and RYA case 3 1970). In a close tacking incident the boat which is tacking can often help to establish the facts to the satisfaction of a protest committee by calling at the time, 'I'm round now', then counting steadily 1,2,3,4...and stopping when either there's a collision or the other boat overlaps. In spite of the onus of proof, it is possible to tack quite close from port to starboard without breaking any rules.

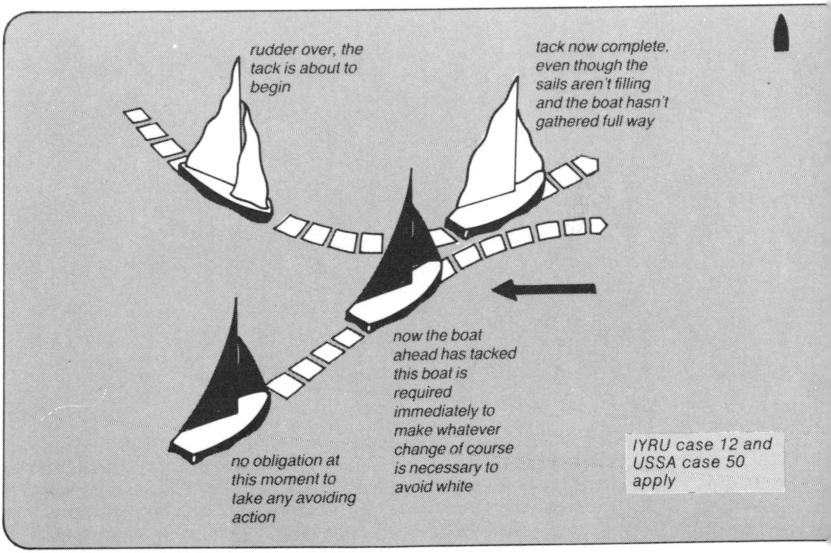

rudder over, the tack is about to begin

tack now complete, even though the sails aren't filling and the boat hasn't gathered full way

now the boat ahead has tacked this boat is required immediately to make whatever change of course is necessary to avoid white

no obligation at this moment to take any avoiding action

IYRU case 12 and USSA case 50 apply

Tacking in the water of a port tack boat

It is not possible to tack as close to another boat when going from starboard tack to port as it is in going from port to starboard.

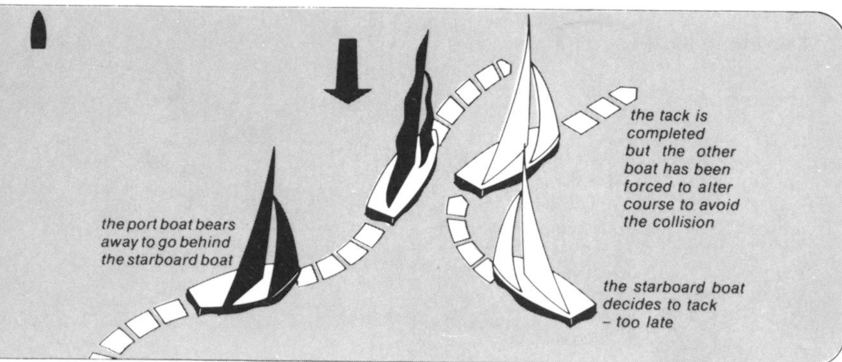
the tack is completed but the other boat has been forced to alter course to avoid the collision
the port boat bears away to go behind the starboard boat
the starboard boat decides to tack – too late

White is in the wrong under rule 35 – which is the one that bars a right-of-way boat from altering course when a give way boat is sailing a course to keep clear. For white to be in the wrong here under rule 35 a protest committee must establish that the port tack boat (black) began to bear off to go behind white before white had altered course to tack.

Once black has borne off, the situation is treated as a close-hauled boat (white) tacking in front of a close reaching boat (black) and the tacking in water rule (41) applies.

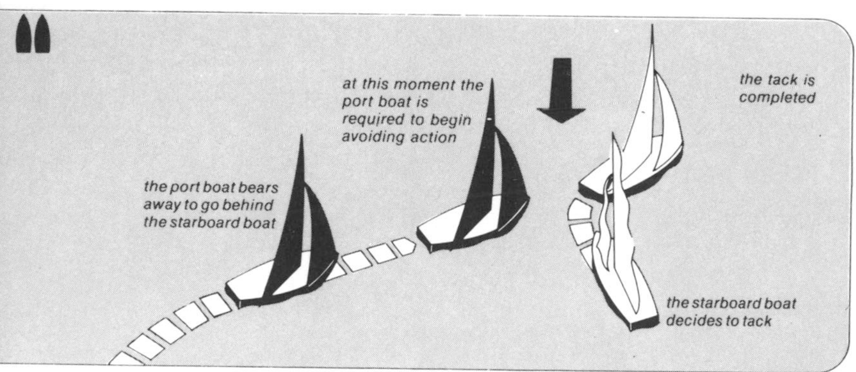
at this moment the port boat is required to begin avoiding action
the tack is completed
the port boat bears away to go behind the starboard boat
the starboard boat decides to tack

At the moment white's tack is completed, black must take whatever avoiding action, including going head to wind, necessary to avoid white. In practice, the port tack boat would head up back to close-hauled as soon as the other boat was seen to be tacking; but for the purposes of deciding a case like this in protest, premature avoiding action by black would not automatically exonerate the tacking boat (rule 41.3).

Simultaneous tacking

When two boats are tacking at the same time, the one on the other's port side keeps clear (rule 41.4).

The easy way to remember simultaneous tacking or gybing onus is quoted in *Elvström Explains* – 'If you're on the right, you're in the right'.

The rule does allow Black's helmsman to wait for the other boat's helm to go down and then put his own down, since tacking only happens from the moment a boat goes past head to wind until she is pointing on the new close-hauled course. This takes a little time. As long as the tacking of each boat coincides, they are defined as tacking simultaneously (USSA case 129). In dinghies and small keel-boats it can be risky to tack immediately after crossing close ahead of a port tack boat – especially if the port tack boat has borne away to miss the starboard tacker's stern, since she'll be moving extra fast into any tack she might make.

MARK ROUNDING

The mark-rounding rules come into effect when a boat is 'about to round the mark', and continue until the mark is left astern.

Where the mark-rounding rules come into force

The special rules which apply to rounding marks and obstructions are in Part IV Section C of the IYRU rules. Rules of that section override rules of Section B with which they conflict. For simplicity's sake here I have dealt separately with mark-rounding. Obstructions are dealt with in the sections on windward legs and offwind legs.

The mark-rounding rules come into force when the leading boat of the pair (or bunch) is 'about to round' the mark. This is usually at two boat-lengths but in heavy seas or with a tidal stream increasing the boat's speed over the ground, or when the boats are fast catamarans, or

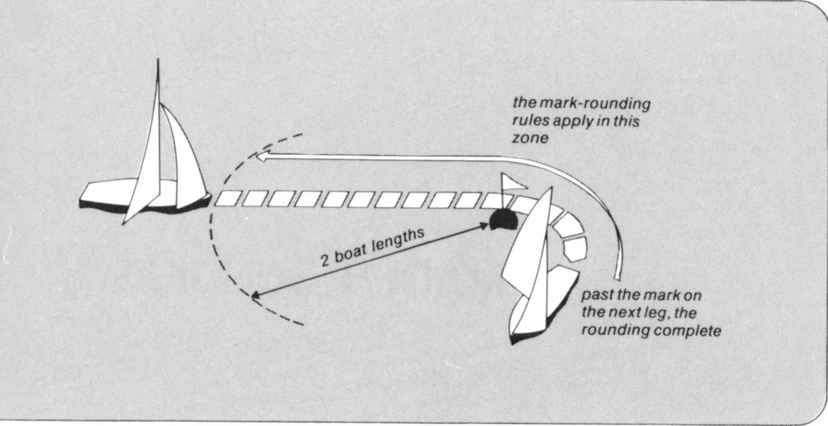
the mark-rounding
rules apply in this
zone
2 boat lengths
past the mark on
the next leg, the
rounding complete

A boat overlapped on another which is already in the two lengths circle is also governed by the mark-rounding rules (42.1).

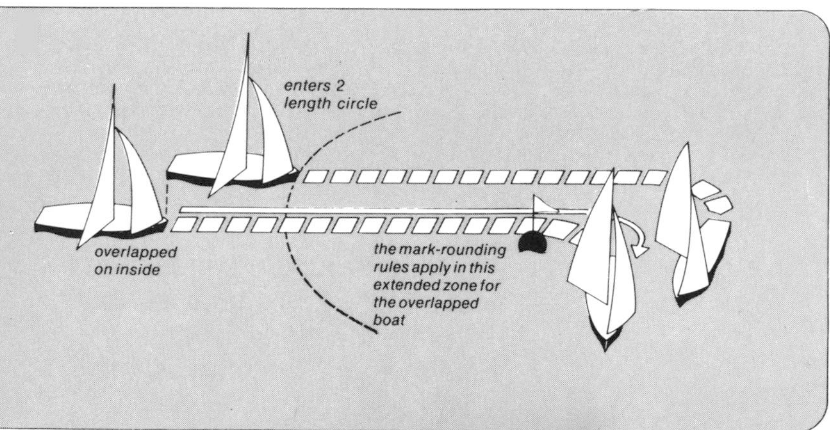
enters 2
length circle
overlapped
on inside
the mark-rounding
rules apply in this
extended zone for
the overlapped
boat

when a big bunch of boats is coming together at the mark, this distance could be much more. The mark-rounding rules apply until the mark has been rounded or passed (rule 42).

The most usual cases where the zone in which the mark-rounding rules apply can extend further back than two lengths are when:

1. Several boats are overlapped
   The outside boats are required to give room as the boats are 'about to round the mark' (rule 42) which may mean giving room well before the two lengths circle.
   or
2. A leading boat is physically incapable of giving room. For example, a multi-hull travelling fast (in boats other than multi-hulls this special provision, rule 42.3(a)(i), is rarely used).

The penalty for hitting a mark

A boat is exonerated for hitting a mark if she does a '360'; that is, sails well clear of all other yachts as soon as possible and remains clear while making a complete turn, including a tack and a gybe (or a gybe and a tack).

A boat is counted as hitting a mark when any part of her hull, crew or equipment touches it. So a neat hand-off or a spinnaker sheet touching a flag on the mark is a touch (rule 52 and definition of a mark). The mark's mooring line or chain is not counted as part of the mark (definition again).

When a boat hits the 'wrong' side of a mark (sails the wrong side of it and hits it) she must first go off and do her 360, and then come back and round it on the right side though if she can do her 360 round the mark, then she need not round it again.

Forced onto a mark by another boat

When a boat is forced onto a mark through, her helmsman believes, a rule infringement by another boat, the helmsman need not take any penalty for hitting the mark provided he protests (rule 52). He can either accept his penalty for hitting the mark and not protest against the other boat, or lodge a protest against this other boat, or both. If the protest committee finds that the collision with the mark was a result of an infringement by the other boat, the collision with the mark is forgiven and the other boat disqualified. However, if the offending boat immediately retires (or does a 360) the mark hitter may sail on without taking a penalty. If the offending yacht does not retire (or do a 360) the mark hitter must protest (rule 52.3).

In the rare event of a mark being submerged by a boat sailing over it, then shooting out of the water to hit a following boat, this boat need not be penalised. She can't protest against the mark, but she can protest against the boat that caused its irregular behaviour. However, she is still obliged to go the correct side of it, no matter where it surfaces (IYRU case 18).

Rights of a boat which has just hit a mark

It can happen that a boat misjudges the course to a mark, hits it and then collides with another boat over which, ignoring the brush with the mark, she would have had right-of-way. What are her rights after touching the mark?

She retains all her normal rights until it is obvious that she is working to get clear of other boats in order to do her turn (rule 34); once it is obvious, she must keep clear of other boats whilst she continues to get clear, and does her turn (rule 45). As soon as she touches the mark, in addition to any normal obligations she might have (like port tack keeps clear of starboard tack) she is, of course, obligated to sail well clear of all other boats as soon as possible (rule 52.2(a)).

Rounding a mark in the wrong direction

After rounding a mark the wrong way, the mistake can be corrected by unwinding. To do this correctly, a string representing the boat's wake would, when drawn tight, have to lie on the required side of the mark (rule 51.2 and 51.4). You don't lose any rights, just because you're going back to unwind or are in the process of unwinding.

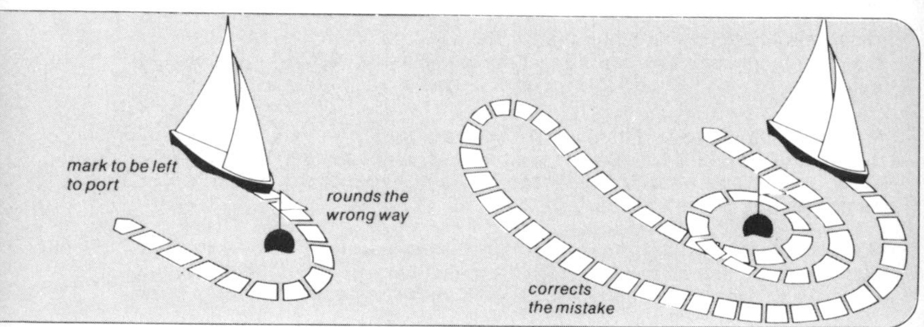

A mark is only a mark of the course for the leg it defines

A mark is only a mark of the course for a particular boat when it defines the leg of the course which that boat is sailing (rule 52.1(a)(ii)). So on leg 5-1 mark 1 is a mark of the course and may not be hit without penalty, but on leg 3-4 mark 1 can be hit without penalty, and between a boat rounding mark 1 on her way to mark 2, and a boat coming down from mark 3 to mark 4, rule 42 (Rounding or passing marks . . .) does not apply, and the boat rounding has no special rights.

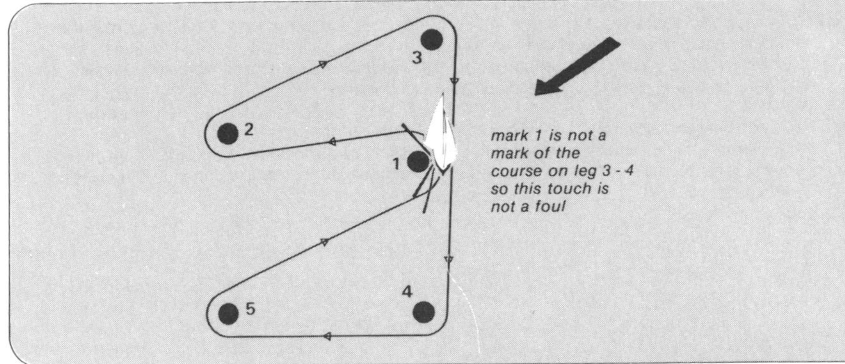
3
2
1
5
4
mark 1 is not a mark of the course on leg 3 - 4 so this touch is not a foul

Mark missing or moved

The race committee should return a drifting mark to its stated position if possible. If that isn't possible they must replace it by a new one with 'similar characteristics' or a buoy or boat displaying International Code flag 'M' and making repetitive sound signals (rule 8.1). Failing that, the race must be shortened or abandoned (rule 5.4(c)(iii)).

M

ROUNDING AT THE END OF AN OFFWIND LEG

Room at a mark

A boat which is overlapped on others outside her has the right to room at the mark, provided the overlap is established before the *leading* boat enters an imaginary circle round the mark whose radius is two of the leading boat's lengths and provided that when the inside boat establishes the overlap the outside boat is able to give room (rules 42.1(a) and 3(a)(ii)). The explanation of an overlap is on page 16.

If the leading boat is unable to give room, the inside boat is not entitled to it (rule 42.3(a)(i)). In other words she is not expected to do the impossible. Situations in which the leading boat is unable to give room are rare in monohulls but include:

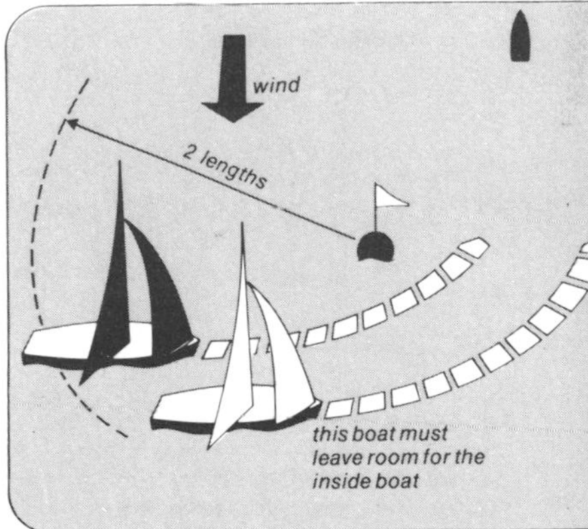
wind
2 lengths
this boat must leave room for the inside boat

1. Situations where groups of boats in the line abreast simply cannot shift aside fast enough to accommodate a late inside overlapper – even though her overlap may have been established outside the two lengths circle.
2. High speed planing or surfing, when the leading boat just isn't able to respond fast enough two lengths from the mark to let anyone in.

The onus of proof here would be with the boat claiming room.

Circumstances where a helmsman isn't able to give room because he isn't properly in control of his boat are not included: a helmsman's incompetence or inexperience is no defence (RYA case 4 1975).

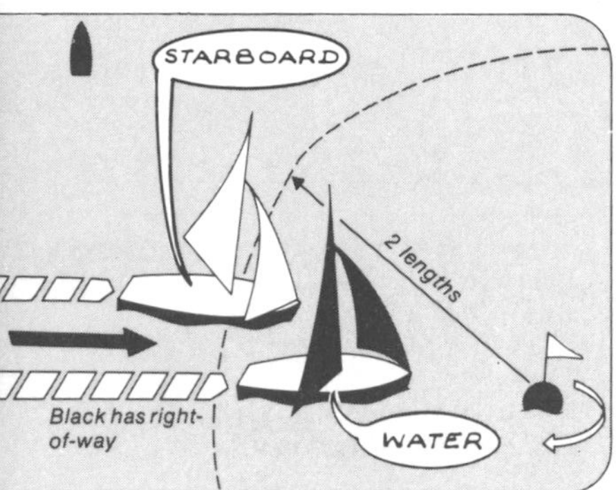

Port and starboard at an offwind mark

The rights of the inside boat take preference over the port and starboard rights, as the note under Section C of the rule book (Part IV) makes clear: 'When a rule of this section applies ... it overrides any conflicting rule of Part IV which precedes it'. The port and starboard rule precedes it.

Before the leader enters the two lengths circle, of course, the starboard boat (white) has right-of-way (rule 36).

The onus in establishing an overlap

A boat which comes from clear astern to claim an inside overlap has the onus of satisfying a protest committee (if the argument gets that far) that the overlap was established in proper time (rule 42.1(d)).

Pusher would find it very difficult to establish that her inside overlap was made soon enough. A witness in another boat or ashore might clinch it, but even so **Pusher** would be foolish in this situation to round on the inside and risk near-certain disqualification. If the outside boat readily concedes the overlap, that's a different matter; then **Pusher** is entitled to round inside.

operate when a boat is carried past a mark by a tide

ters the two lengths circle and leaves it has to establish her overlap n she re-enters the circle (IRYU case 71).

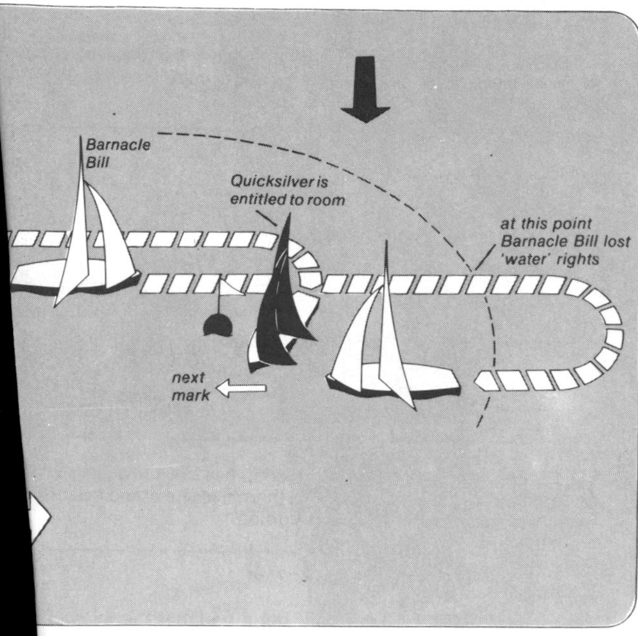
Barnacle
Bill
Quicksilver is
entitled to room
at this point
Barnacle Bill lost
'water' rights
next
mark

applies in really windy conditions when a skipper chooses to tack nd during his tack sails past the mark and outside the two lengths h new rights on re-entering the circle.

ahead of another and a tack is an integral part of the rounding – a reach – the rules that apply are exactly the same as in the he end of windward legs (page 62). When a boat tacks instead bit windy, the tacking in water rules still apply and the overlap to those explained in the section above.

side boat is allowed

er overlapped outside her is not entitled to round as wide as engths circle. To quote the definition: 'Room is the space euvre in a seamanlike manner in the prevailing conditions.' in rough weather. Although an inexperienced helmsman space to allow for his lack of skill, any doubt in a protest will yacht claiming room.

The onus in breaking an overlap

When two overlapped boats are approachin lengths circle the outside one claims that sh of satisfying any protest committee that she two lengths circle (rule 42.1(c)).

If the inside boat – which doesn't h marginal 'clear ahead' claim at the time, th push his luck by going for the inside berth

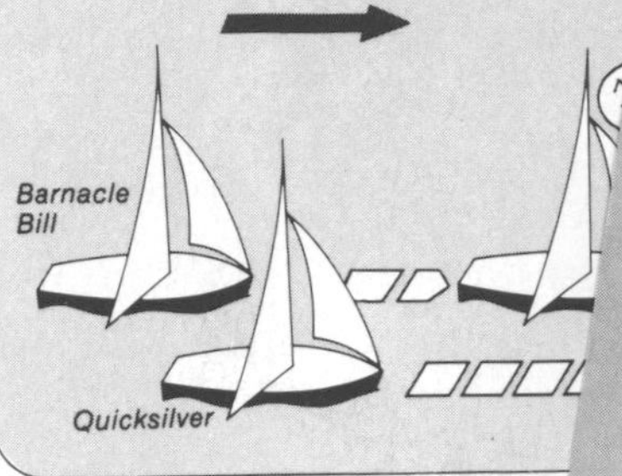

The onus of proof that the ov be foolish to go for the inside be have to avoid her during the rou

Hailing for water

The rules don't insist on a hai broken helps to support the cl before the two lengths 'circle'

How overlaps operate wh boats are making a wide

In a big fleet it often happens mark that boats round very wic a downwind leg so that they c the mark for a good start to th If a boat goes so wide that sh lengths circle at right angles fleet, the whole fleet is entitle are forward of the line at ri aftermost point. They wo make use of their right, b able to, as **Interloper** can

How overlaps

A boat which e rights anew wh

The same principle round instead of gybe a circle. He must establis

Tacking at a mark

When one boat is clear as, say, from a reach to section on rounding at t of gybes because it's a conditions are identical

How much room an in

An inside boat with anoth she likes within the two needed by a yacht to man This means more space cannot count on any extra usually go in favour of the

This definition makes white's rounding here, in which the outside boat is pushed wide for purely tactical reasons, very risky. The dividing line between what is purely a 'seamanlike' rounding and a rounding made primarily for maximum tactical gain is a fine one. The onus of proof here lies with the outside boat to establish that the inside boat has gone unduly wide. In this situation black would win the protest. One and a half lengths here is too wide; one length would probably not be.

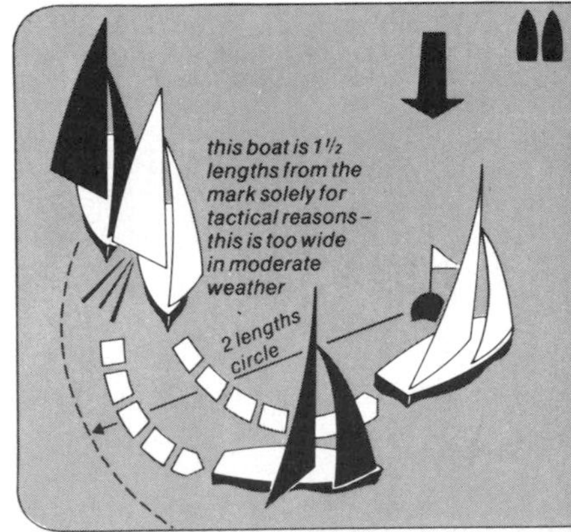
this boat is 1½ lengths from the mark solely for tactical reasons – this is too wide in moderate weather
2 lengths circle

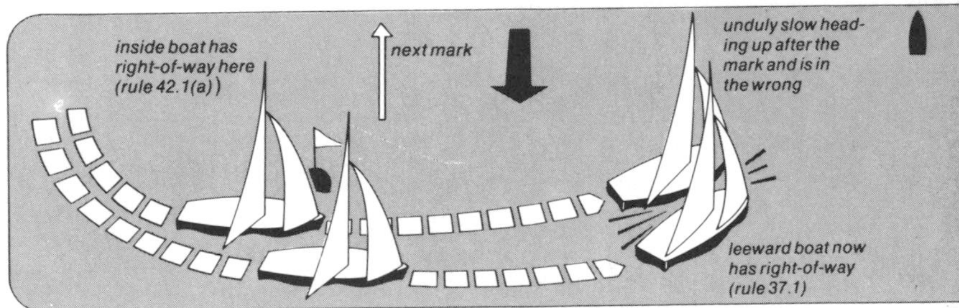
inside boat has right-of-way here (rule 42.1(a))
next mark
unduly slow heading up after the mark and is in the wrong
leeward boat now has right-of-way (rule 37.1)

Once the mark has been passed, the inside boat's right under the mark-rounding rules end and the right-of-way rules that apply for a leg of the course come into play (IYRU case 50).

Breaking an overlap inside the two lengths circle

An outside boat which is required to give room because of an overlap made before entering the two lengths circle is still required to give room if the overlap is subsequently broken (rule 42.1(b)).

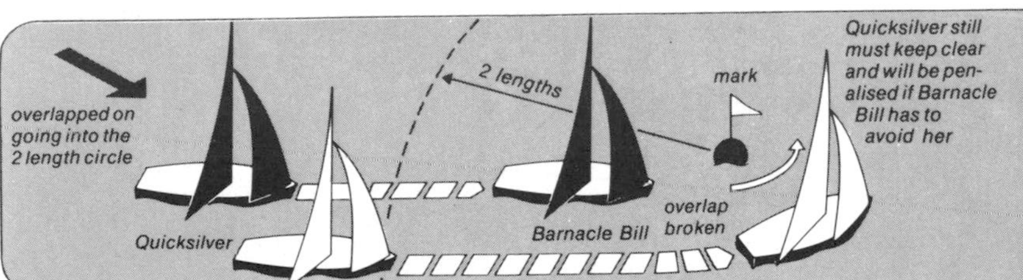
overlapped on going into the 2 length circle
2 lengths
mark
Quicksilver still must keep clear and will be penalised if Barnacle Bill has to avoid her
Quicksilver
Barnacle Bill
overlap broken

Inside boat required to gybe at the first opportunity

An inside boat must gybe at the first reasonable opportunity when a gybe is necessary to get on to the proper course for the next leg, except when the inside boat has luffing rights (rule 42.1(e)).

When the inside boat has luffing rights there is no need for her to gybe. In fact, the inside boat may luff at any time or just sail straight past the mark (rule 42.1(e) does not now apply; rule 39.2 does).

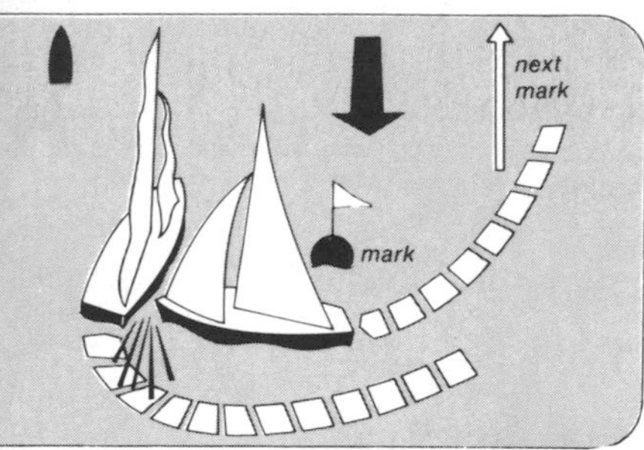

Rounding onto a beat

The port tack boat is in the wrong here, in spite of the right-of-way starboard tack boat altering course. The rule which forbids alteration of course in a way that prevents another boat keeping clear (rule 35) specifically makes an exception of a right-of-way boat rounding a mark. The port and starboard rule (36) governs (USSA case 167).

Luffing another boat the wrong side of a mark

Luffing another boat the wrong side of a mark is rarely wise in normal fleet racing but is sometimes a good tactic in team racing when, by luffing one of the opposition the wrong side of a mark, a team-mate is able to slip by.

For a leeward boat to be allowed to luff a windward boat the wrong side of the mark, the leeward boat must have luffing rights, and neither boat must be 'about to round' the mark. It is difficult to say exactly at what distance from a mark a leading boat is 'about to round', but it would be rare for this distance to be less than two lengths and will sometimes be much more (for example when there is a favourable tide, or when the boats are multihulls).

If, during the luffing process, the luffing boat comes within the 'about to round' distance, then she immediately becomes obliged to bear off to round the mark and if the windward boat is inside, to give room.

No hail is required, though it is often worthwhile to avoid damage.

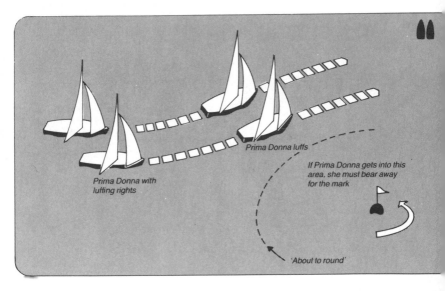

Prima Donna luffs
If Prima Donna gets into this area, she must bear away for the mark
Prima Donna with luffing rights

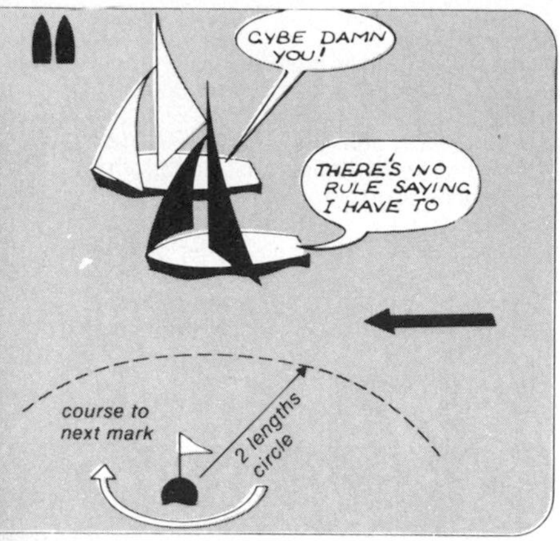

Using starboard rights to sail a boat the wrong side of a mark

When two boats are on opposite tacks the starboard boat may sail any course and the port boat must keep clear (rule 36 and IYRU case 17). This means that provided both boats remain well outside the two lengths circle the starboard boat may sail the port boat the wrong side of the mark. No hail is necessary but any alteration of course by the starboard tack boat towards the port-tack boat must be slow to avoid infringing rule 35 (IYRU case 35).

Rounding a mark in opposite directions

When boats are rounding a mark in opposite directions the port and starboard rule (36) applies even though the starboard boat is rounding the wrong way (IYRU case 37). When a boat is 'unwinding' because she sailed round the mark the wrong way, she maintains her rights.

ROUNDING AT THE END OF A WINDWARD LEG

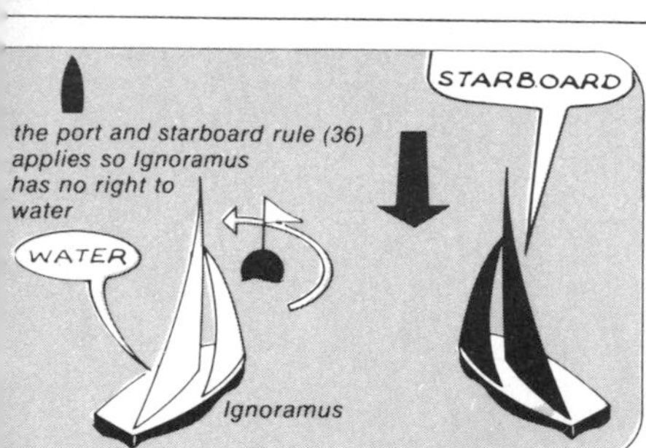

On opposite tacks – port and starboard

When boats on opposite tacks are about to round a windward mark the rules apply essentially as though there were no mark there (rule 42(b)).

A starboard tack boat can sail in a straight line beyond the mark perfectly legitimately to put a port tack boat about (IYRU case 17).

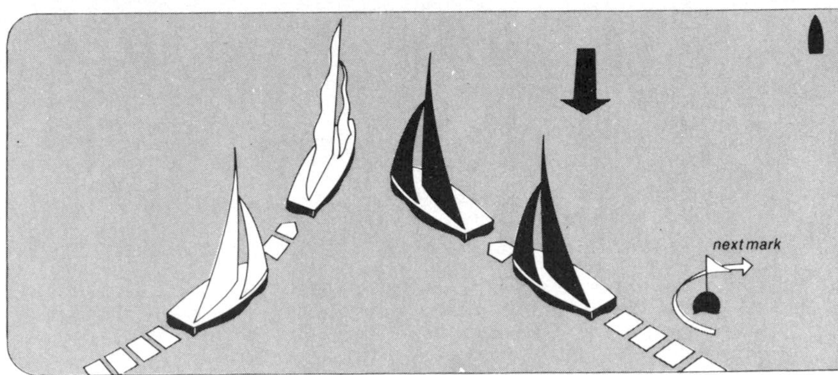

The one time you cannot take the mark away and apply the right-of-way rules to opposite tack boats as in open water is when the starboard tack boat luffs in making the rounding:

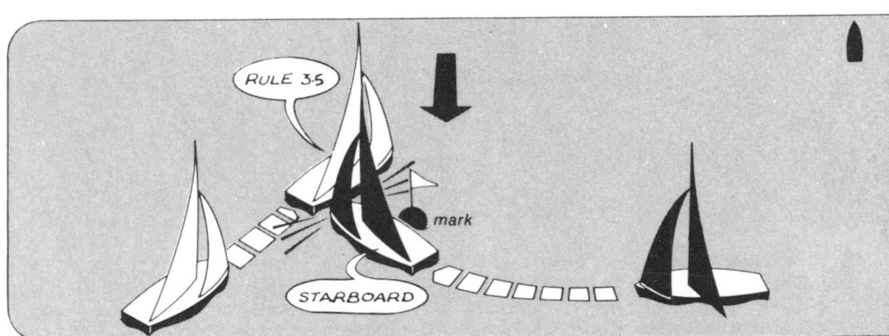

In open water the starboard tack boat would be in the wrong here (except at the start) for altering course when holding right-of-way, in a manner that prevented the other boat keeping clear. When rounding a mark (and at the start) rule 35 specifically allows the right-of-way boat to alter course.

On the same tack – room at the mark

When two boats are overlapped on the same tack the rules apply to room at a mark in the same way as for an offwind mark – rounding (page 51) with only two exceptions (I'll come back to those).

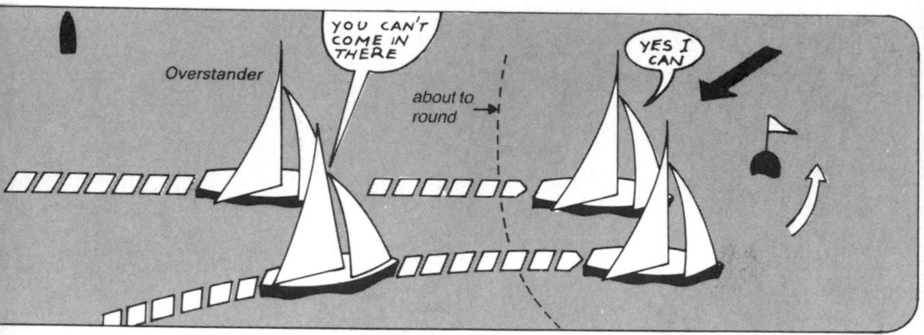

Outside the two lengths circle **Overstander** is required to keep clear as windward boat (rule 37.1), but as soon as the leading boat is 'about to round the mark' the rules that apply to marks come into play and **Overstander** is entitled to room – including room to tack (rule 42.1(a)). 'About to round' is rarely less than two lengths, and could be more.

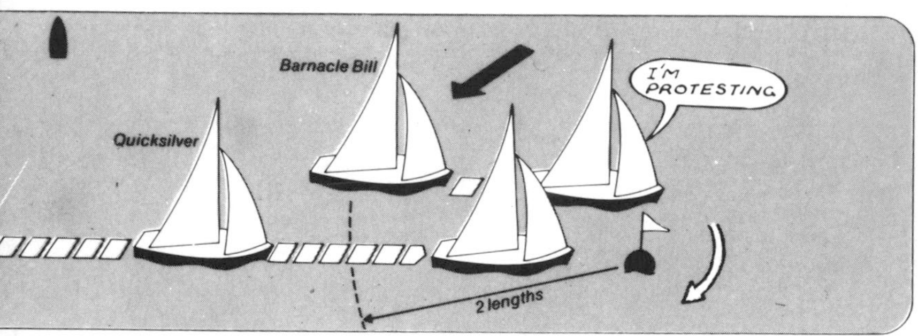

Barnacle Bill is clear ahead on entering the two lengths circle so at the mark **Quicksilver** has no rights. In the two lengths circle it is irrelevant that **Barnacle Bill** is the windward boat – the rules of mark rounding supersede the windward/ leeward rule here (rules of Section C override earlier rules of Section B with which they conflict).

A leeward boat which has an inside overlap on entering the two lengths circle and is below the lay line is entitled to room to luff round the mark (rule 42.1(a) and 35 (b)(ii)).

The two situations where the overlap rules at the end of a windward leg differ from those at the end of an offwind leg are covered in the two sections immediately following: 'Tacking within the two lengths circle' and 'A special case of room to tack when a mark is big'.

Tacking within the two lengths circle

When either of two boats completes a tack within the two lengths circle the usual water rules don't apply and an overlap can be established and room claimed within two lengths of the mark (**rule** 42.3(a)(ii)).

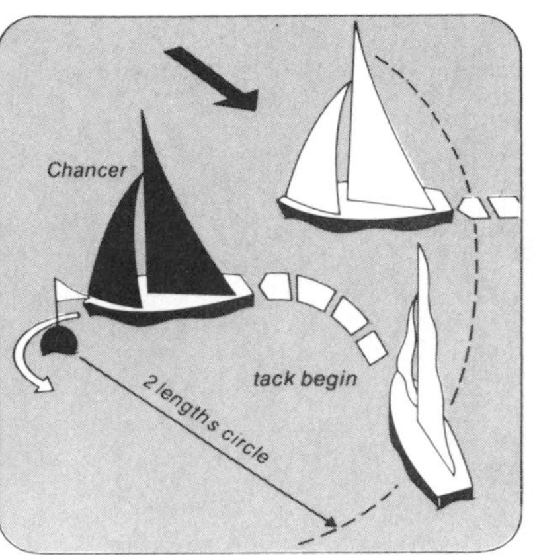
Chancer
tack begin
2 lengths circle

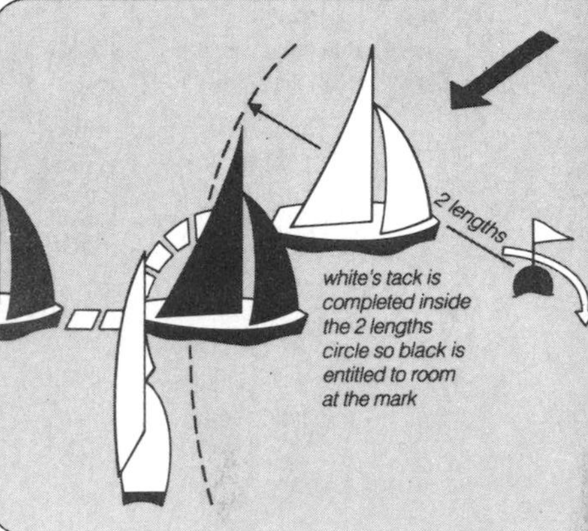
2 lengths
white's tack is completed inside the 2 lengths circle so black is entitled to room at the mark

Chancer completes her tack inside the two lengths circle and so is entitled to room at the mark, provided the other boat is able to give it. **Chancer's** tack is still governed by the usual tacking rules so she must not tack in the other boat's water (rule 41.1, explained on page 43).

These are the only two situations in which a boat is entitled to claim room after an overlap is gained inside the two lengths circle.

A special case of room to tack when a mark is big

This can only crop up when a mark is big enough to rate as an obstruction (rule 43.3).

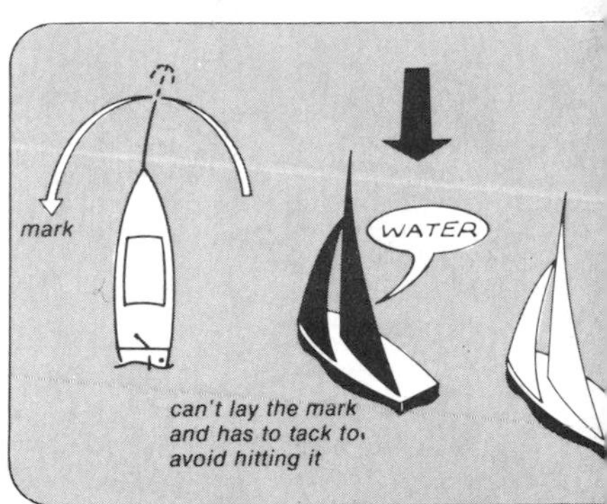
mark
WATER
can't lay the mark and has to tack to avoid hitting it

White must respond to the hail by either:

(a) saying 'I can lay the mark, no water' (or words to that effect) *or*

(b) tacking immediately.

If she tacks, no rules have been broken and there are no grounds for protest.

If white thinks she can lay the mark without tacking (she may luff and squeeze round provided she doesn't go beyond head-to-wind), she may choose to hail 'no water' but if she then fails to lay the mark she must retire (or take a penalty if the sailing instructions allow).

Black should hail early enough to leave room to escape in case white hails

'no water'; if black hits the mark and white succeeds in laying it, black must do a 360 penalty; if black hits the mark and white fails to lay it, black may sail on, but must protest if white doesn't retire or take a penalty.

Tacking at a mark

When two boats approach the mark on opposite tacks and one tacks to round the mark the tacking in water rule (41.1) applies (rule 42.(a)).

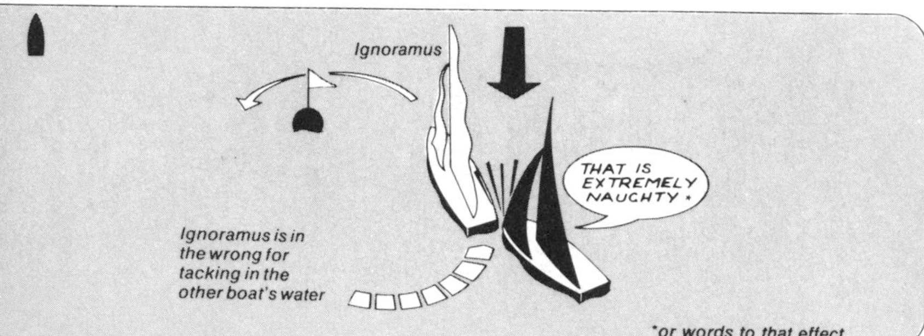

When both boats approach a mark on the same tack with one clear ahead of the other on entering the two lengths circle, the tacking in water rule (41.1) again applies. The white boat on the left is tacking in the other's water (rule 42.2(b)).

It is important to remember, though, that a tack does not start until the instant the boat passes head to wind. So a luff by the leader which doesn't go beyond head to wind is safe – as in the situation below (rule 42.2(a), definition of tacking and USSA case 138).

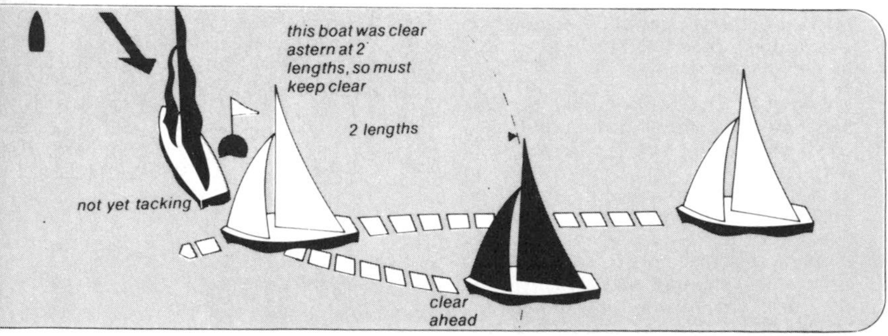

A following boat may not luff higher than close-hauled to prevent the boat ahead tacking (rule 42.2(b) and 35(b)(ii)).

A leading boat which enters the two lengths circle clear ahead may slow down forcing the boat astern onto the outside, then claim room to round once the overlap is made (rule 42.1(a)).

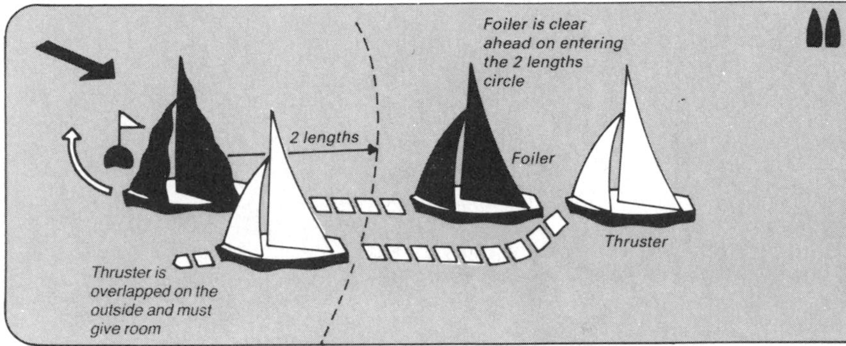
Foiler is clear ahead on entering the 2 lengths circle
2 lengths
Foiler
Thruster
Thruster is overlapped on the outside and must give room

Foiler does nothing wrong here. She is entitled to slow down, and once **Thruster** gets an outside overlap **Foiler** can claim room and, when she's been given it, tack. **Thruster** cannot nudge past **Foiler** to windward, and then call for room at the mark – though that's what two out of three will try.

A special case on a port hand rounding

Both **Complacent** and **Ricochet** must keep clear of **Starboard** under rule 36 while on port tack and under rule 41.1 while tacking. **Ricochet** should have acted sooner when she had the right either to hail **Complacent** for room to tack to keep clear of **Starboard** or to bear away to pass astern of **Starboard**, in which case **Ricochet**, as the outside boat under rule 42.1(a), was required to give **Complacent**, the inside overlapping boat, room to do the same. In the situation shown, **Ricochet** has left it too late to do that. If, in responding to **Ricochet**'s hail, **Complacent** collides with the mark, **Ricochet** will be in the wrong for forcing another boat to infringe a rule.

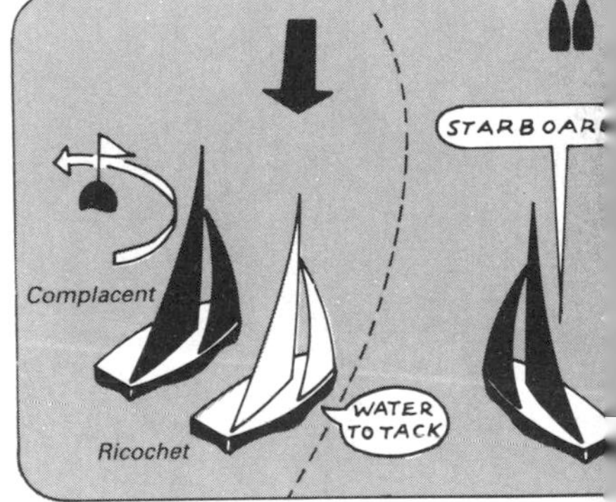
Complacent
Ricochet
WATER TO TACK

Sailing another boat past a mark

This is a manoeuvre used in team racing and accidentally by beginners in individual racing.

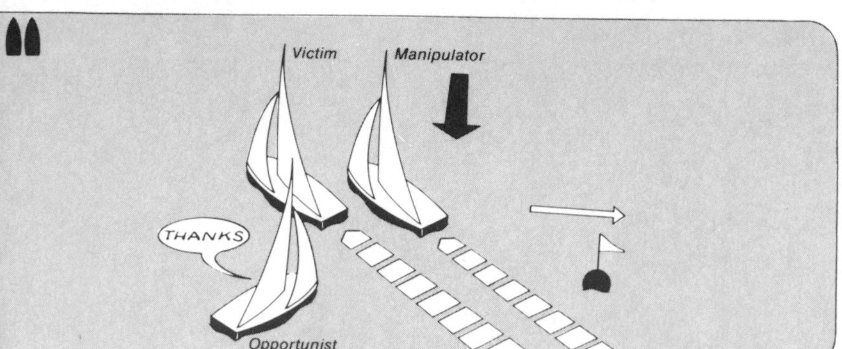

There is no rule to stop **Manipulator** sailing as far beyond the weather mark as she likes, forcing **Victim** to overstand and letting **Opportunist** round ahead (IYRU case 26). This ploy is very common in team racing. **Manipulator** and **Opportunist** would be team mates and **Victim** would be pushed behind **Opportunist.**

OFFWIND LEG

An offwind leg is one that a boat can sail on one tack.

OPPOSITE TACKS

Port and starboard

Port gives way to starboard (rule 36). This is an important rule.

starboard tack boat
has right-of-way
this boat is on
port tack and
must keep clear

Care is sometimes required in applying this rule. It is important to question how long the **relative** rights have existed before any collision. If, for example, the starboard boat gybes into a position which gives her right-of-way, she must do so far enough away to allow the port boat to keep clear without her having to begin to alter course until after the gybe has been completed (rules 41.2 and 35).

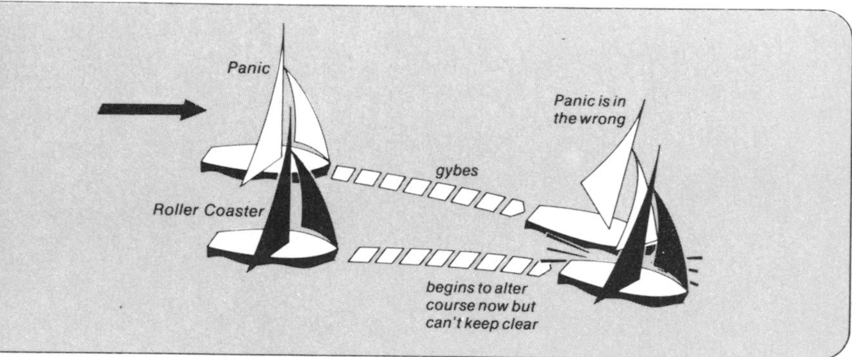
Panic
Roller Coaster
gybes
Panic is in
the wrong
begins to alter
course now but
can't keep clear

Had **Panic** been on starboard tack all along, and made the alteration of course shown in the diagram, **Roller Coaster** would be in the wrong (rule 36). The starboard-tack boat is allowed to sail any course she likes provided she does not prevent the port-tack boat from keeping clear (rule 35, IYRU case 35).

Overtaking

In open water the port and starboard rule (36) applies when boats on opposite tack are overtaking one another. The rule which says that a boat clear astern keeps clear of a boat ahead (rule 37.2) only applies when both are on the same tack.

Room to pass a continuous obstruction

The ruling is reversed when the boats are sailing alongside a continuous obstruction. The rule which governs the passing of marks and obstructions when clear ahead and clear astern (rule 42.2) then overrides the port and starboard rule, so the boat clear astern would have to keep clear (IYRU case 68).

When two boats are overlapped and sailing alongside a continuous obstruction, the inside boat must be given room, regardless of what tacks they are on. (Rule 42.1(a) overrides the port and starboard rule (36) here, IYRU case 68.)

The gaining of the overlap by the inside boat is governed by exactly the same rules as when the boats are on the same tack (page 71). So when a port-tack is ahead and there is insufficient room for a starboard-tack boat to pass in safety between the boat ahead and the shore, the starboard-tack boat must give room – so she'll have to overtake on the outside!

Room at an obstruction which is not continuous

The same as for 'Offwind Same Tack' (page 72).

Starboard tack boat sailing above a proper course

A starboard tack boat may sail any course and the port tack boat is required to keep clear (rule 36, IYRU cases 35 and 17).

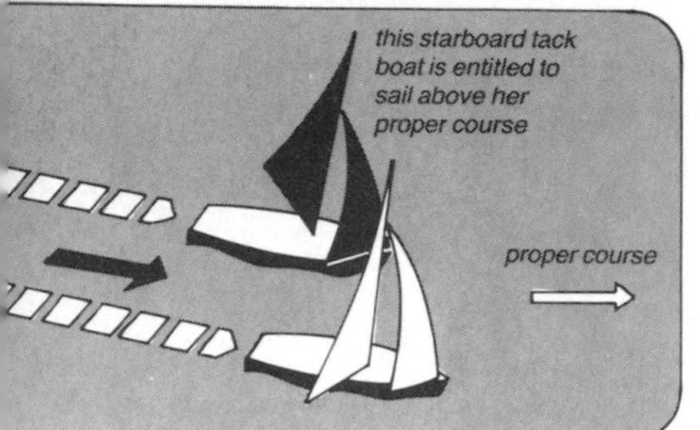
this starboard tack boat is entitled to sail above her proper course
proper course

But the starboard tack boat must establish her rights in sufficient time (as in 'Port and Starboard' above) and not alter course in a way that prevents the other boat from keeping clear (rule 35 and IYRU case 35).

This situation is quite different from the luffing situations described in 'Offwind Same Tack' (page 72); the boats here are on the opposite tacks so the luffing rules do not apply. If white were to gybe the luffing rules would apply and black (without luffing rights) would be required not to sail above her proper course (rule 39.1).

SAME TACK

Windward boat keeps clear

A windward boat is required to keep clear of a leeward boat (rule 37.1).

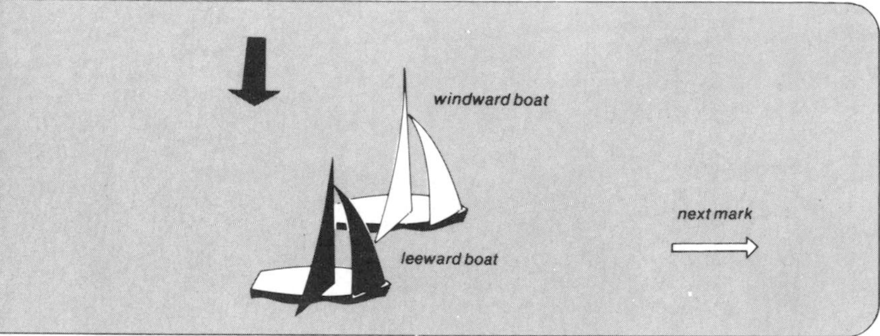
windward boat
next mark
leeward boat

When a leeward boat is sailing her proper course (explained on page 19) and collides with, or has to alter course to avoid, a windward boat the windward boat is in the wrong. The rule is an important one, but in some situations may be overridden, depending on exactly how the two boats approached each other. These overriding situations are dealt with in this section.

Bearing down

A boat within three lengths of another and clear of obstructions must not sail below her proper course when the other boat is steering a course to leeward of the boat ahead, or is overlapped to leeward (rule 39.3 and USSA case 127).

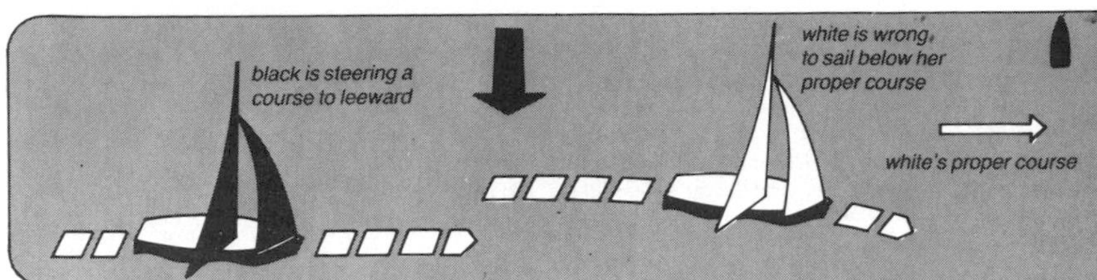

A protest by black here would be successful, provided she could establish that white was sailing below her (white's) proper course. No collision would be necessary to prove the point. It is normal, though not essential, for the leeward boat to give the boat bearing down a warning shout and only protest if the bearing down continues. White could have this protest dismissed, provided white's course could reasonably have been her proper course.

Overtaking one other boat

The boat clear astern is required to keep clear (rule 37.2).

More often an overtaking boat doesn't follow exactly in the wake of the boat ahead, but to leeward.

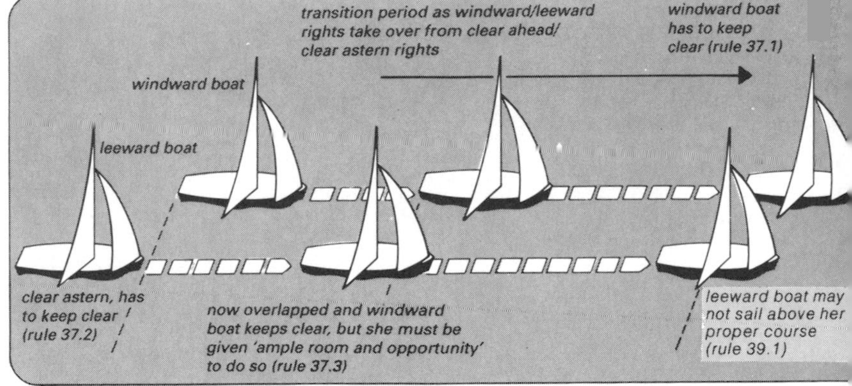

The obligation to keep clear switches as the overlap is gained. First the boat clear astern has to keep clear, then the windward/leeward rule takes over. As soon as the overlap is established the windward boat is required to begin any necessary avoiding action, but the leeward boat must give her 'ample room and opportunity to keep clear' and must not sail 'above her proper course'. 'Ample room and opportunity' (rule 37.3) means more than just 'sufficient' and the benefit of any doubt must go to the windward boat. Even so, the windward boat may well have to sail above her proper course in fulfilling her obligation to keep clear (IYRU case 25).

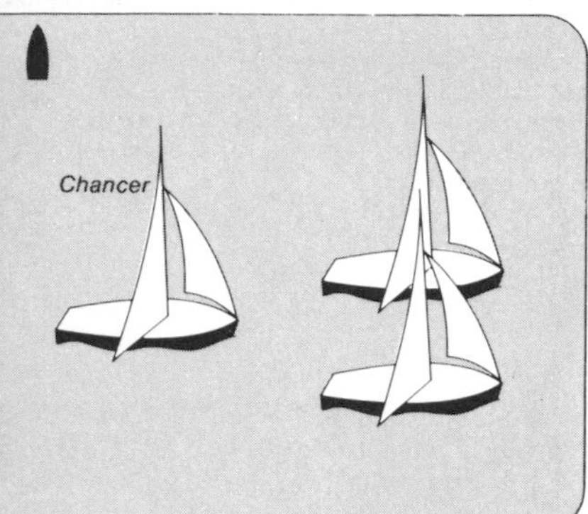
Chancer

Overtaking more than one boat

A following boat is entitled to sail into an overlapped position between two boats ahead only when there is enough room for her to pass between them (rule 42.3(b) and IYRU cases 27, 67 and 69).

The gap is not big enough for **Chancer** to sail right through so she has no right to push her nose in.

Here the gap is wide enough:

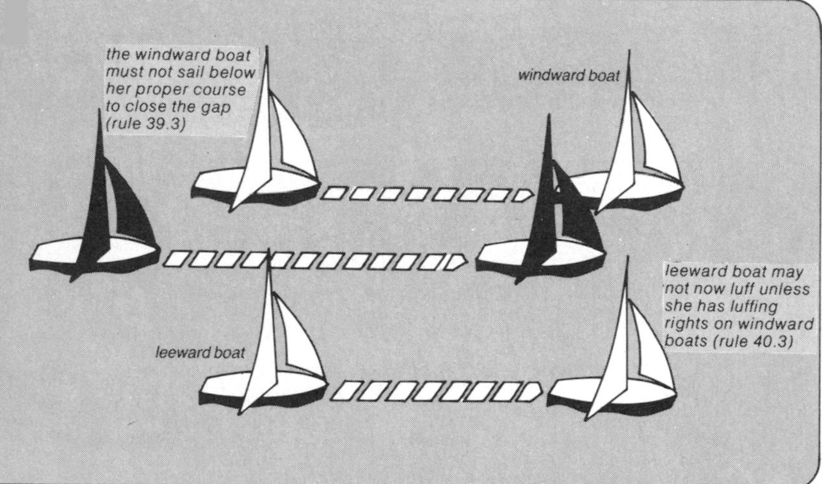
the windward boat must not sail below her proper course to close the gap (rule 39.3)
windward boat
leeward boat may not now luff unless she has luffing rights on windward boats (rule 40.3)
leeward boat

Black is entitled to sail into the gap because there is enough room for her to sail right through (rule 42.3(b)) (IYRU case 67).

In the following situation the rules apply differently. This time the windward boat is slightly back from the leeward boat, though still overlapped. **Prudence** therefore first overlaps the windward boat, without overlapping the leeward boat.

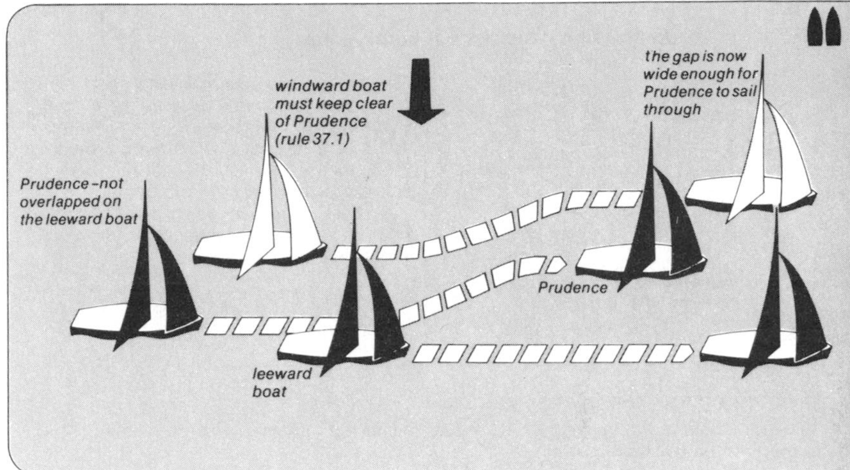
windward boat must keep clear of Prudence (rule 37.1)
the gap is now wide enough for Prudence to sail through
Prudence - not overlapped on the leeward boat
Prudence
leeward boat

The right-of-way between **Prudence** and the windward boat is not now altered by the presence of the leeward boat because **Prudence** does not overlap it. **Prudence** can, therefore, sail her proper course to windward of the boat ahead and the windward boat must widen the gap (her rights before she overlaps the leeward boat are dealt with above in 'Overtaking one other boat').

Room to pass a continuous obstruction

A following boat is only entitled to sail into a gap between a boat ahead and a continuous obstruction, such as a shoreline, when, at the moment the overlap is first established, there is enough room for her to sail safely through the gap (IYRU case 69).

shoreline
this boat was entitled to sail between the other boat and the shore because there was room for her to sail through the gap (rule 42.3 (b))
this boat may not luff, but must give room, since the inside boat gained a legitimate overlap (rule 42.1 (a))

The overtaking boat takes a risk in going for the gap close to the shore unless there is clearly enough room for her to get right through when she first establishes the overlap (IYRU case 69).

Room at an obstruction which is not continuous

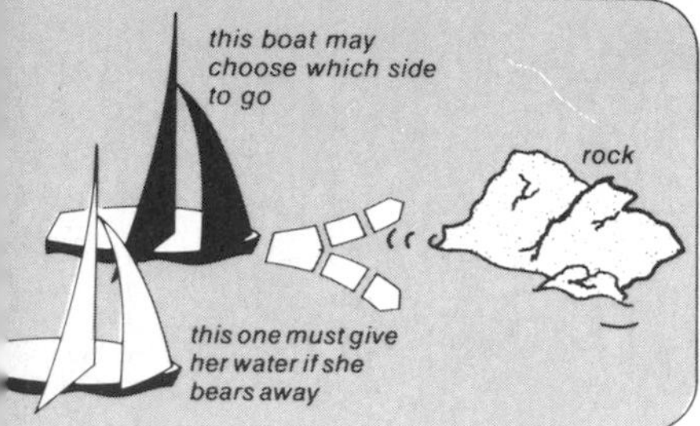
this boat may
choose which side
to go
rock
this one must give
her water if she
bears away

The overlap and room-claiming rights here are similar to those for passing a mark (pages 51 – 53), but with the difference that the boats requiring room may choose to go either side of the obstruction and cannot be penalised for touching it.

There is no rule which dictates that a boat should take the shortest route round an obstruction.

Luffing rights – two boat situations

The idea behind the luffing rule is very simple; its application is unfortunately complicated, so be warned.

A helmsman who is being overtaken to windward, or is about to be overtaken to windward, has considerable powers of retaliation under the rules (rule 39). He can luff as high as head to wind without warning and as suddenly as he likes, provided the other boat is:

1. on the same tack and
2. *either* clear astern
   or overlapped upwind and the helmsman of this windward boat has not been at or forward of a 'mast abeam' position since the establishment of the overlap.

The 'mast abeam' position can most simply be explained as follows:

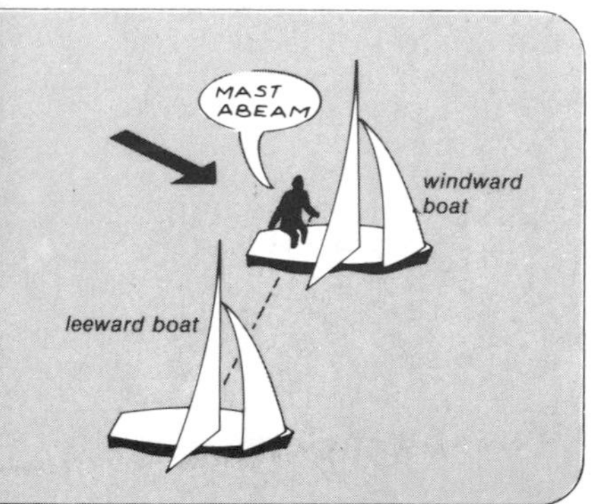
MAST
ABEAM
windward
boat
leeward boat

The windward boat is 'mast abeam' when its helmsman's line of sight abeam from his normal position is forward of the leeward boat's mast, but if the windward boat is sailing a higher course than the leeward boat, then the windward boat's helmsman must also be forward of a line through the leeward boat's mast extending out abeam (ie at right angles to the leeward boat).

There is no restriction on the sharpness of the leeward boat's luff, except that if serious damage is caused in a collision she will be disqualified as well as the windward boat (rule 32).

The way in which the overlap is established is crucial in deciding whether a leeward boat has luffing rights. There are five ways the leeward boat may gain these rights:

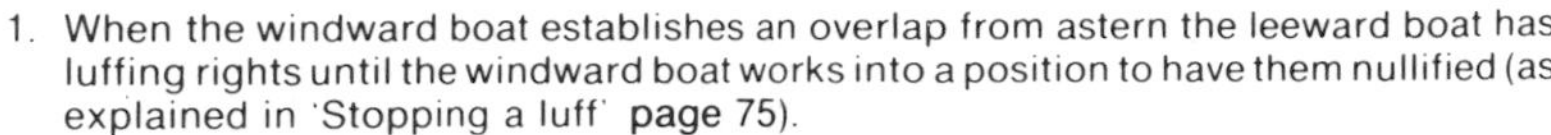

1. When the windward boat establishes an overlap from astern the leeward boat has luffing rights until the windward boat works into a position to have them nullified (as explained in 'Stopping a luff' page 75).

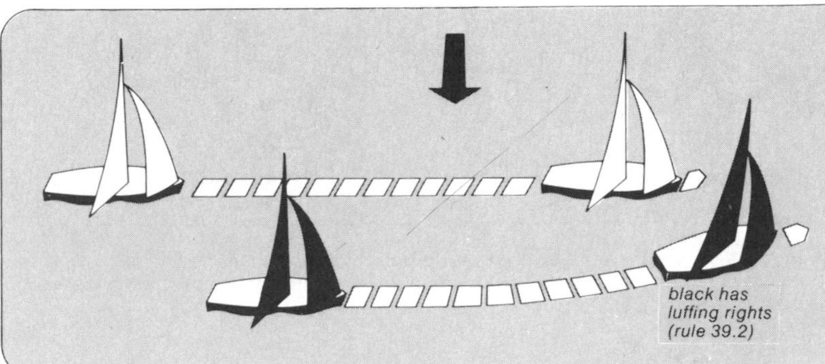
black has
luffing rights
(rule 39.2)

2. Where two boats are converging and neither is clear astern an overlap, for the purposes of luffing, is considered as beginning when they come within two lengths of the longer boat (Definition of Clear Astern and Clear Ahead; Overlap).

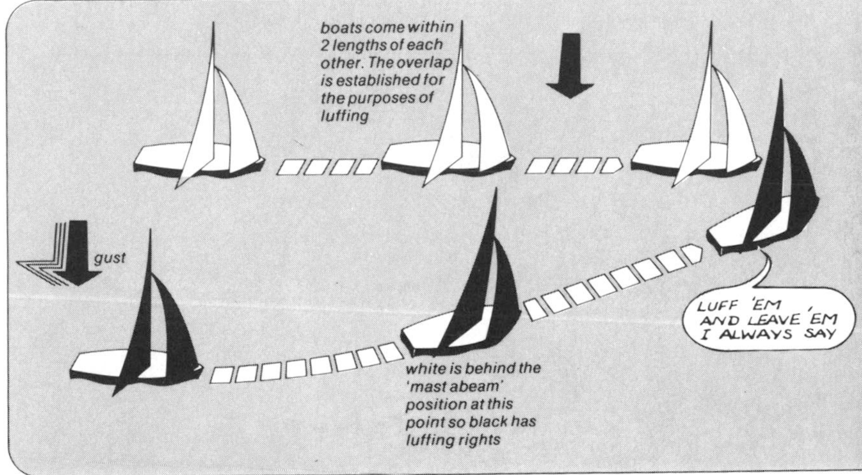
boats come within
2 lengths of each
other. The overlap
is established for
the purposes of
luffing
gust
LUFF 'EM AND LEAVE 'EM I ALWAYS SAY
white is behind the
'mast abeam'
position at this
point so black has
luffing rights

3. At the moment of starting, a leeward boat automatically has luffing rights if the windward boat is aft of the 'mast abeam' position (Definition of Clear Astern and Clear Ahead; Overlap).

4. Luffing rights are also established when either or both boats gybe into a position in which the new windward helmsman is aft of the 'mast abeam' position (Definition of Clear Astern and Clear Ahead; Overlap).

5. A boat which completes a tack to leeward of another automatically has luffing rights if, at the moment the tack is completed, the windward boat is aft of 'mast abeam' position (rule 38.2(b)).

Luffing rights – more than two boats

Before a leeward boat can luff a bunch of overlapping windward boats she must have luffing rights over all of them if she's to luff legitimately (rule 40.3).

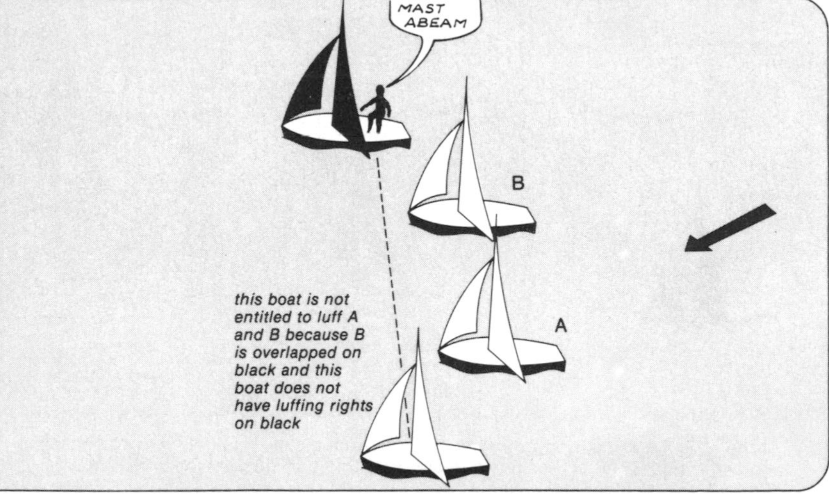

MAST
ABEAM
B
A
this boat is not
entitled to luff A
and B because B
is overlapped on
black and this
boat does not
have luffing rights
on black

Stopping a luff

A leeward helmsman must stop luffing a windward boat when any of the four following cases apply:

1. He is given a 'mast abeam' call by the windward helmsman. If he doesn't like the call he can protest, but he must respond to it nevertheless, because the hail itself removes the leeward yacht's luffing rights. For a 'mast abeam' call by the windward helmsman to be valid, the windward boat must have reached a position in relation to the leeward boat so that if they are on parallel courses (or the windward boat is sailing lower) an imaginary line through the windward boat's helmsman (sitting in his normal position), at right angles to the fore-and-aft line of the windward boat, would pass through the mast of the leeward boat. When the windward boat is sailing higher than the leeward boat, the imaginary line is at right angles to the fore-and-aft line of the leeward boat (rule 40.1). The call is important because without it the leeward helmsman can luff so long as there is doubt about whether the 'mast abeam' position has been reached.
2. There is no doubt that the 'mast abeam' position has been passed (even if there is no call).
3. The windward helmsman hails 'obstruction', or words to that effect, to warn the luffing boat that there is some obstruction to windward (rule 40.2).

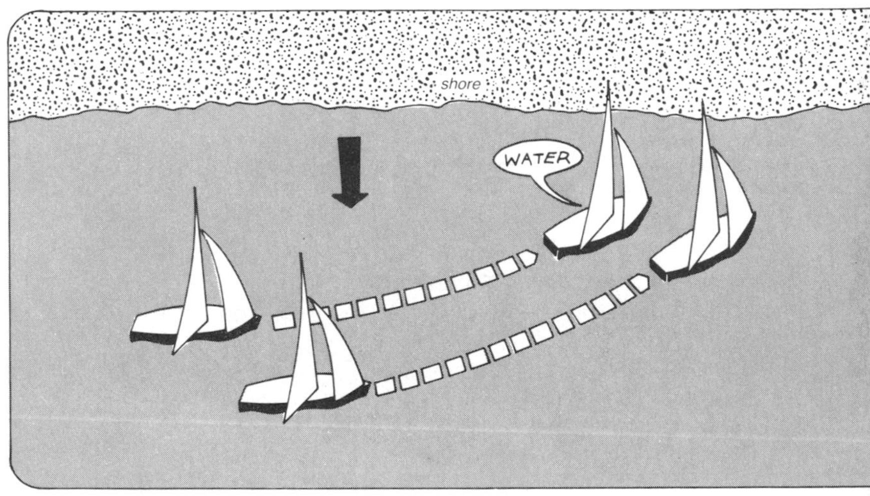

When luffing rights are lost by the hail of 'mast abeam' when there is doubt, or by the mast abeam position having been reached without doubt, then the leeward boat must bear away to her proper course (rules 39.2 and 40.1) – that is the proper course from the point at which the luff ends, not the course that was proper before the luff started – even if she has to gybe to do so (IYRU case 63).

The leeward helmsman is required to respond to the hail immediately. If he does and there is a collision – even between his tiller extension and the windward boat – the windward boat is in the wrong. But when the leeward boat has to gybe to take up her proper course the original leeward boat will be in the wrong if the collision happens while she is actually gybing (RYA case 7 1975). The leeward boat must therefore bear away and gybe quickly to keep out of trouble.

When a leeward helmsman refuses to bear off in response to a legitimate 'mast abeam' hail and the windward helmsman gets upset and collides by bearing away to his proper course, both boats are in the wrong: the leeward boat for not responding to the hail, the windward boat for not keeping clear (USSA case 15).

Sailing above a proper course without luffing rights

A leeward boat which does not have luffing rights over a windward boat is not entitled to sail above her proper course (rule 39.1 and Definition of Mast Abeam).

When the windward boat argues that the leeward boat is sailing above her proper course the onus is on the windward boat to prove her case. The leeward boat must be given the benefit of any doubt (IYRU case 25).

When the leeward boat has to gybe to fulfil her obligation not to sail above her proper course she must gybe (IYRU case 63).

When a leeward boat refuses to go onto her proper course the windward boat would be wise not to bear off and cause a collision – better to keep clear and protest.

GYBING

A boat which is gybing keeps clear

A boat which is gybing is required to keep clear of a boat which isn't (rule 41.1).

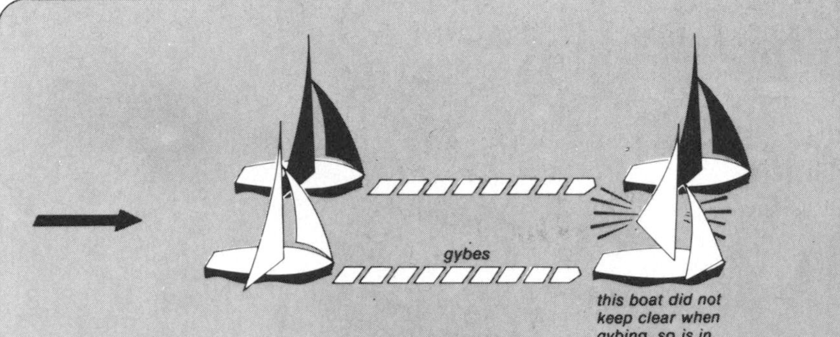
gybes
this boat did not keep clear when gybing, so is in the wrong.

Simultaneous gybing

When two boats are both gybing at the same time the one on the other's port side keeps clear (rule 41.4). The easy way to remember simultaneous gybing and tacking onus is quoted in *Elvström Explains* – 'If you're on the right, you're in the right'.

WHO'S WRONG?
both gybe
YOU ARE

THE FINISH

The finish ends racing; it is also the beginning of the protest period – when this book may be useful.

Finishing

A boat finishes when any part of her crew, hull or equipment in normal position crosses the finish line (definition) after fulfilling any penalty obligations under rule 52.2 (that is, sailing clear and doing a 360 degree turn).

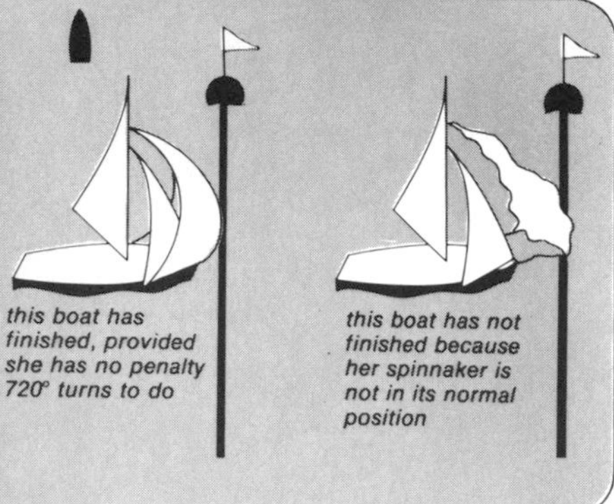

this boat has finished, provided she has no penalty 720° turns to do
this boat has not finished because her spinnaker is not in its normal position

A boat which has finished is still racing until she has cleared the finish line, so a boat which infringes a rule before she has cleared the finish line, but after she has finished, must take her penalty for the infringement.

In the incident below, the port tack boat (white) would not have been penalised if she had been clear of the finish line – that is, no longer intersecting any part of it – since she would not have been racing. Neither boat would then have been penalised (USSA case 99).

To clear the finish line it is not necessary to sail right across it. The boat below has finished and cleared the line quite legitimately (rule 51.3 and 5).

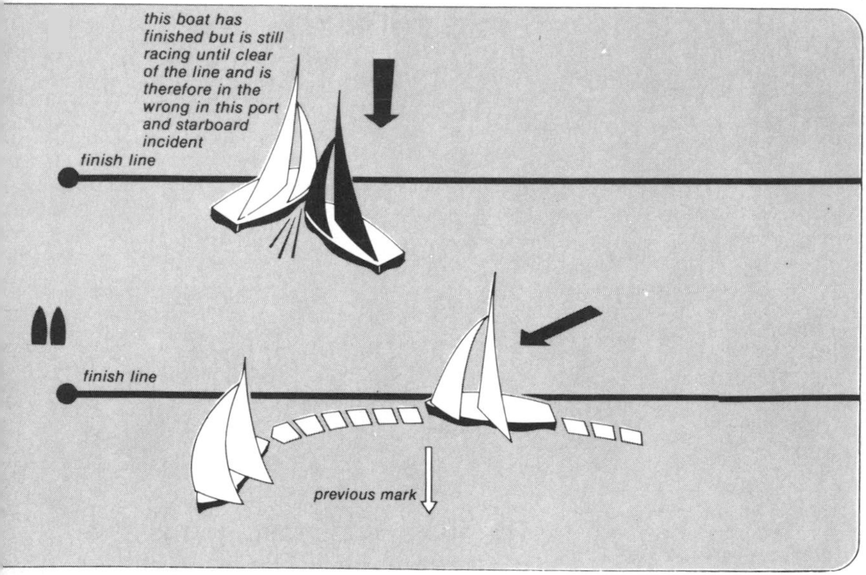

this boat has finished but is still racing until clear of the line and is therefore in the wrong in this port and starboard incident

finish line

finish line

previous mark

A boat also finishes correctly when capsized and the tide carries her across the finish line – provided all the crew are with the boat. But the crew may not swim the capsized boat to the finish line (rule 54).

Hitting a finishing mark

Hitting a finishing mark without having cleared the finish line is exonerated by sailing clear of other boats and doing a 360 degree turn. The finishing position is counted from the moment the first part of the boat, crew or equipment crosses the finish line thereafter.

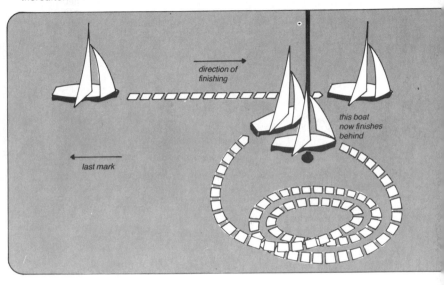

When a boat has crossed and clears the finish line and sailed clear of the marks, but then drifts or sails back and hits a finishing mark she is not penalised for the collision because she is no longer racing (definition). The right-of-way rules apply only to boats which are racing (RYA case 8 1972 and USSA case 136).

Finish lines

Hook finishes of the kind shown here cannot be enforced by the sailing instructions. Sailing instructions may only override parts of Sections II and III.

They don't override the definition of finishing, which says that a boat finishes when she 'crosses the finish line from the direction of the course from the last mark' – which is clearly the opposite direction to that shown in my diagram, since the last mark is taken to be the last turning mark and not a mark used as a finishing mark (IYRU case 102 and USSA case 84).

now finishes

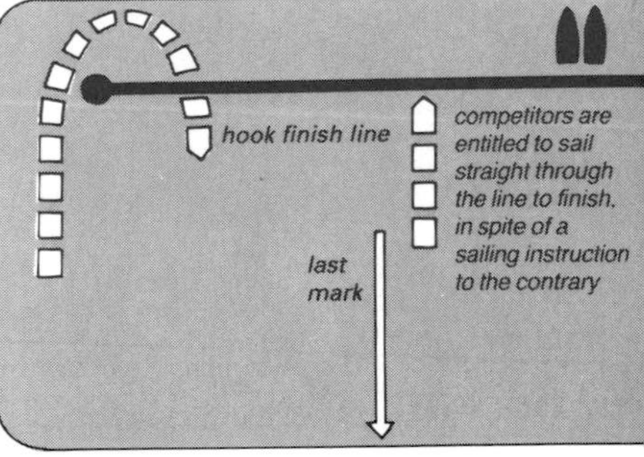

straight through
the line to finish,
in spite of a

to the contrary

A boat sailing a hook finish doesn't actually finish according to the definition, no matter what the sailing instructions say.

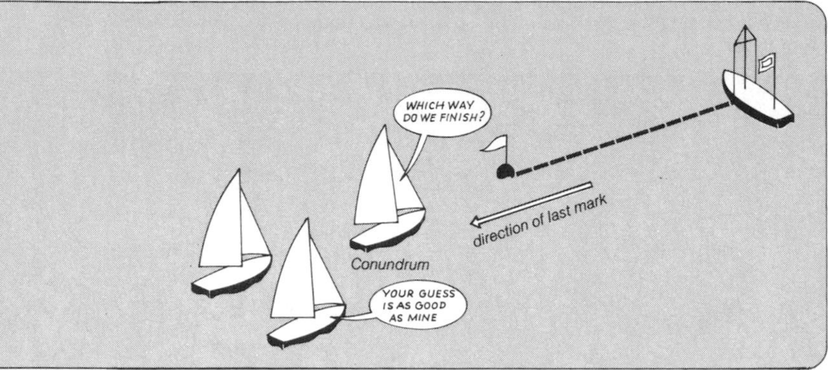

Conundrum will have difficulty knowing which way to finish on this badly set shortened-course finishing line, and the race committee will have to count as finished all the boats, whichever way they cross. Some will have finished correctly (according to the definition) and the others will have to be given redress (by way of finishing places) for the error of the race committee in setting such an impossible finishing line.

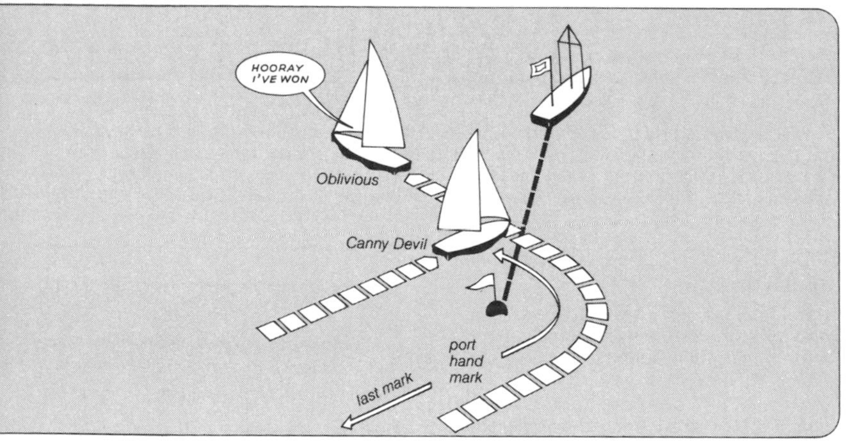

Canny Devil wins the race by being the first boat to finish in accordance with the definition (even if the sailing instructions said she must finish the way **Oblivious** did); **Oblivious** hasn't really finished but she could unwind and finish correctly or she might succeed in getting redress if she can convince a protest committee that the race committee confused her into thinking she was finishing correctly; but in giving redress, the protest committee cannot take away **Canny Devil**'s victory.

OTHER IMPORTANT SAILING RULES, ENFORCEMENT AND PENALTIES

Competitive sailors are their own umpires. If we want rules in our racing, every one of us has an interest in taking our penalties when we ourselves break rules and protesting when someone else does. Otherwise, anarchy.

OTHER IMPORTANT SAILING RULES

Rights of a boat anchored

A boat which is anchored has right-of-way over one which is not. However, an anchored boat must let any boats liable to foul her know that she is at anchor. When two boats are anchored close to one another, the one which anchored last keeps clear, except that a boat dragging keeps clear of one that is not (rule 46.4).

Anchoring includes lowering any weight to the bottom, or the crew standing on the bottom holding onto the boat. Anchoring does not mean tying up to or holding onto a mooring, moored boat or jetty. Nor does it mean standing on a jetty to hold the boat (rule 53.2).

Rights of a boat capsized or aground

A capsized or grounded boat is still racing (rule 46.1), but is not penalised for a collision with another boat. Nor is the other boat penalised if the grounding or capsize happens immediately in front of her (rule 46.2). However, a boat aground must tell any boats which might foul her that she is aground. This is one of only three situations where a collision between two boats racing does not necessarily mean that a protest committee has to disqualify someone (rule 46). One is when a boat has just capsized; another is assisting a boat in distress (see below).

Assisting a boat in distress

When in a position to do so, every boat must help any boat or person in peril (fundamental rule A). Note also rule 46.2. A boat may have any disadvantage she suffers in assisting a boat in distress rectified (rule 69 explained on page 90).

The contact rule

This rule (33) was brought in to tighten up rule observance by placing an onus on people to protest after a collision. The rule places a joint obligation on two boats involved in a collision to ensure that one of them (or a third boat if he's to blame for the collision) retires (or takes a penalty when a penalty system is in force). If no one retires or takes a penalty, and neither of the two involved lodges a valid protest, then both of them have infringed rule 33 and will be disqualified if there is a hearing, no matter who was to blame for the incident.

Notice that both boats may be disqualified under this rule for any kind of contact, so when a boom of one boat collides with a sail of the other, both boats would be disqualified under rule 33 on protest if neither had protested or taken an appropriate penalty.

A third boat which protests that two others collided and that neither took their penalties nor flew protest flags is herself required to fly a protest flag. But when the two boats come ashore and no protest is lodged, although a protest flag was flown by one (or both) of them, a third helmsman witnessing the collision may then lodge a protest, even after the normal time limit has expired and if he didn't display a flag (rule 68.3(b)).

When a race committee sees a collision which did not result in a protest or voluntary penalty they may call a protest hearing of both boats involved (rule 70.2(a), (b), (c), (d) and the final paragraph of the rule). The race committee are not *obliged* to act under rule 70 (although they must if a protest is properly lodged on the same incident by a competitor). Even if the collision happened right in front of the race officer they need do nothing, though in that case they would be wise to act.

But if they do decide to act, any protest brought under this rule must be given a formal hearing. The boats cannot be summarily disqualified on the say-so of a witness to the collision, even if he's the race officer.

When a protest is lodged claiming an infringement only of rule 33 (that is, claiming there was a collision and no one took a penalty or retired), and it is found as a fact at the hearing that there was no contact, or that there was contact but it was minor and unavoidable (which is possible only in light drifting conditions), then neither boat can be penalised (rule 33).

Fair sailing

The fair sailing rule is designed to catch people who have done something naughty which has somehow not been covered by the complex net of the main rules. It only applies when no other rule can be invoked. So any protest hearing in which the fair sailing rule is used must be long if the case is to be properly considered: the protest committee is required to scour the rule book for any other rule which might apply instead.

Unfair sailing is one of those terms which cannot be precisely defined, since what is unfair to one sailor may be perfectly fair and all part of the game to another. This rule has tended, recently, to be used to catch out people whose ingenuity has lent itself to novel ways of disqualifying opponents. Intent is important here. A boat was disqualified when her crew deliberately stretched out an arm to hit a windward boat which was keeping clear (RYA case 6 1971). Another was disqualified for deliberately heeling the boat to windward so that the mast would collide with an overtaking windward boat (IYRA case 23). (This rule is used extremely rarely.)

Illegal propulsion

The basic principle of the revised rule 54 is set out in the definition of sailing and rule 54.1: 'a yacht shall compete only by *sailing*'; sailing is using 'no source of power other than wind and water to increase, maintain or decrease speed.'

In general terms, this means that you can move the crew's bodyweight to trim the boat, but not to impart energy into the boat to drive it forward. You can move the sails to adjust for a change in wind strength or direction, but the move itself must not drive the boat forward.

There are some exceptions: you can propel your boat in any way you like if you are going to help someone in distress, or recovering a person overboard, or rendering assistance. When surfing or planing conditions exist, you may pump (i.e. rapidly trim and release) any sail, or all sails, once, in order to initiate surfing or planing.

You can roll tack, provided that the tacking manoeuvre itself does not advance you in the race, and that the rolling action 'facilitates steering' (rule 54.3(a)).

At well organised regattas, a Jury or protest committee will be on the water and will protest competitors it sees infringing the rule. Most competitors applaud such action, which if taken early in the series inevitably results in suppressing the problem of competitors using 'kinetics' to increase their speed.

PENALTIES AND RULE ENFORCEMENT

Disqualification and retirement

A boat which is found by a protest committee to have infringed a rule or a sailing instruction is disqualified from the race in which the infringement happened. One exception is a boat that retired promptly after the incident, but still protested the other boat: if she lost the protest she would not be disqualified but would be counted as having retired. Another exception is a boat which protests but also takes a 720 degree penalty (when the option has been provided in the sailing instructions).

Retirement for a rule infringement has to happen promptly after the incident or the retiring boat may be disqualified (Fundamental rule D). Promptly does not mean immediately. A reasonable time is allowed to work out whether to retire, exonerate herself (if permitted), protest or do nothing. Two minutes may be too short a time to reach a decision; five minutes I would say is usually too long.

If the sailing instructions specify one of the alternative penalty systems, then a boat that infringes a rule of part of IV can take the penalty rather than having to retire. The two most common alternative penalty systems are the 720 degree turns and the scoring penalty.

Alternative penalties (Appendix B1)

The standards of rule observance have fallen in recent years. This is partly attributable to a widespread feeling, expressed by a refusal to retire after infringing a rule or to protest against other wrong-doers, that retirement from a race is too harsh a penalty for breaking a rule. The alternative penalty systems were introduced to make it easier for people to acknowledge their errors by paying a lesser price. And generally the systems work well. The 720 degree penalty works best for one design boats, especially the smaller ones, and is explained below. The scoring penalty works best for offshore racing and larger boats.

Alternative penalties apply only to infringements of rules in Part IV (the right-of-way rules), and use of either system must be specified in the sailing instructions, otherwise retirement and disqualification are in force (rule 3.2(b)(xxv)).

720 degree turns (Appendix B1)

A boat which breaks a rule of Part IV may exonerate herself by making two full 360 degree turns. She may then carry on with the race.

If she does not acknowledge her error, she may be disqualified after a protest (under rule 68) by another boat or by the race committee (rule 70.2) (Appendix B1, clause 1.5).

The boat which is fouled has to hail the wrongdoer that she intends to protest. The wrongdoer must do her turns at the first reasonable opportunity (clause 1.1). This means as soon as she can work into a clear enough patch of water to gyrate without colliding with other boats, and that may sometimes be on the following leg (clause 1.1 does not say 'same leg'). Clear water must be actively sought; it is not good enough to sail on for five minutes waiting for a space to appear (IYRU case 105).

The turns must both be done in the same direction, one immediately after the other, and must be full turns. That means that on windward leg a helmsman may not go into his turns from close-hauled starboard and leave them close-hauled on port as often happens (clause 1.1).

Before the starting signal, the infringing boat must do her turns as soon as she can. If the turns are not properly done and a valid protest is lodged, she will be disqualified.

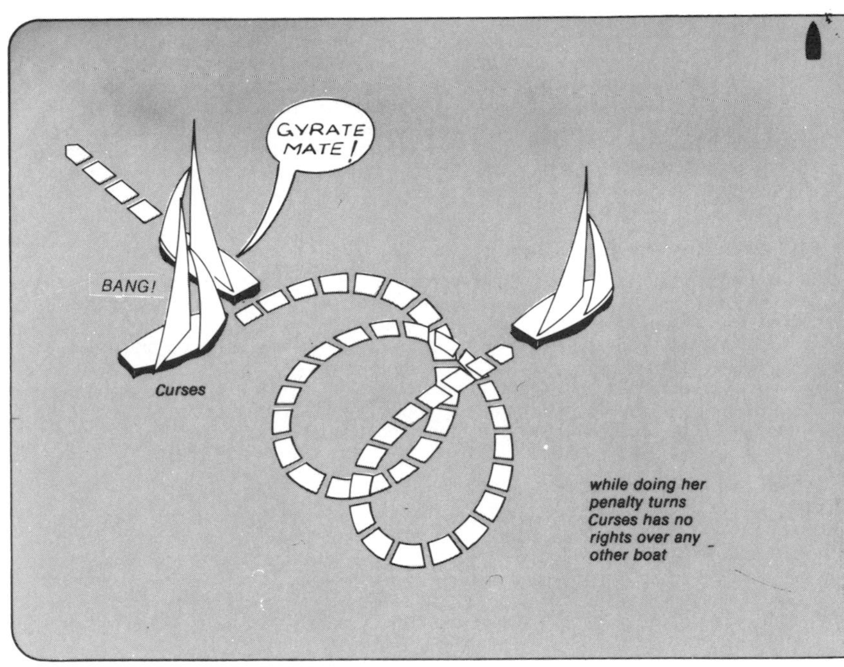
GYRATE MATE!
BANG!
Curses
while doing her penalty turns Curses has no rights over any other boat

When serious damage is caused in a collision the boat in the wrong may be disqualified, even though she may have done her turns properly (clause 1.4).

It is possible under the 720 degree rule for a helmsman very occassionally to deliberately infringe a rule, do the turns and end up better off after the incident than he would have by obeying the rules. A port tack boat beating to a windward mark, for example, against a strong tide in light air might lose less ground by refusing to give way to a starboard boat and take the penalty turns after rounding the mark than by tacking for the starboard boat and failing to lay the mark.

The port boat then could be disqualified on protest (Appendix B1, clause 1.4 and rules 68 or 70), even though she might have done her turns immediately after the incident.

After a collision and when the turns aren't properly carried out – either through some technicality or only one turn being done – the right-of-way boat is protected by clause 1.5 of Appendix B1 from being disqualified under rule 33 (Contact between yachts, explained on page 84).

Penalty points in team racing

Appendix B5 now includes the 'green flag penalty system'. A helmsman who infringes a rule and acknowledges his infringement continues racing and takes a 2.5 point penalty. If he infringes a second or third time in that race, he takes another 2.5 point penalty for each infringement he acknowledges. A lost protest costs him 6 points.

An acknowledged infringement is signalled by tying a green flag to the shroud and a protest is signalled by tying on a red flag. Once a helmsman flies a green flag he may not take it down and fly a red one to protest over the incident. But if he first puts up a red one with the intention of protesting, then thinks better of it, he may take it down and fly the green one – provided the switch happens promptly after the incident.

The advantage of this system is that the balance of a team race is not destroyed either by losing a boat from one team or by the excessive points penalty of a well-placed boat being disqualified. Its provisions must be stated clearly in the sailing instructions. The 720 degree penalty has also been found to work well in team races.

The penalty for not protesting

After a collision with another boat, failure to protest may mean disqualification. If the other boat doesn't protest, either a third boat or anyone else who saw the incident may have both boats disqualified after a protest hearing (rule 33, explained on page 84).

When a rule infringement does not result in a collision there is little risk of disqualification in failing to lodge a protest.

A boat which hits a mark must either retire (or do a 360 penalty turn) or protest – even if she was forced onto the mark – although when the boat that forced her onto the mark takes the penalty for the infringement, no protest is necessary (rule 52.3).

Making the rules work

Except in match races (just two boats), there can be no effective umpires or referees in sailing as there are in games like football and cricket. With sometimes over a hundred competitors but no ball to blaze a trail of fouls, the practical difficulties of even seeing fouls on the water are enormous. To make matters worse, the complexity of the sailing rules would make any instant decisions by an untrained referee extremely unreliable. We sailors are therefore our own umpires. When people foul us and don't take their voluntary penalty we should protest; when we break a rule we should take our penalty voluntarily.

In a fleet where nobody ever protests or retires, the rules cease to exist. The racing is then decidedly less satisfactory than when behaviour on the water is controlled – at least approximately – by a known code, the IYRU rules.

Protest by one competitor against another

When a helmsman thinks he has been fouled by another boat – whether there is a collision or not – or when he thinks any other competitor has broken a rule or infringed one of the sailing instructions, he is entitled to protest (rule 68.1). A protest is decided ashore by a protest committee, which is usually a sub-committee of the race committee. It acts in much the same way as a court of law, first hearing the evidence and then giving its verdict as to which boats, if any, are disqualified.

A helmsman who decides to protest must fly a protest flag (rule 68.3). Code flag B or a red rectangular flag is always acceptable, but any flag will usually do. In one case a piece of red cellophane was allowed (USSA case 88 and IYRU case 147).

A protest flag must be permanently displayed for the rest of the race, except in a singlehander where it may be waved by the protesting helmsman soon after the incident and waved again on finishing.

A protest committee is only allowed to hear a protest for which no flag was flown when:

1. The facts of the incident were not known until after the finish – for example, when a boat is alleged to have touched another and her crew was unaware of any collision at the time. But ignorance of a rule interpretation or a sailing instruction does not rate as

a reason for failing to fly a protest flag at the time of an incident (rule 68.4, IYRU case 47).

2. Seeking redress about some action or omission of the race committee (rule 69).
3. The boat protesting is dismasted (USSA case 153), capsized or sunk.
4. A boat sees a collision between two others and neither of the colliding boats goes through with a protest, although one or both flew flags soon after the incident (rules 33 and 68.4).

Otherwise a protest flag must be displayed, and it must be displayed 'conspicuously', and unless there is some reason concerned with safety, it must be displayed immediately after the incident.

The protester must also hail '"protest" or words to that effect' immediately after the incident, or if the protester is not involved in the incident and is some distance from it, then as soon as the protestee is close enough to hear the hail.

On coming ashore the boat protesting must put in a written protest to the race committee (rule 68.5 and IYRU case 29). The protest must be delivered within two hours of the time the last boat finishes, although when a race committee feel that particular circumstances justify them in extending the time limit they may do so (rule 68.6). Sailing instructions often set different time limits which override the standard IYRU ruling.

The defendant is entitled to see and study the protest. If he asks for it and is not given it, the protest would be dismissed on appeal (USSA case 82). If he doesn't ask for it, that would not be grounds on which an appeal would be dismissed (USSA case 133).

The practice of charging a protest fee returnable only to the helmsman who is not disqualified is decidedly not recommended; it discourages protests, which in turn encourages greater rule abuse. If race committees fine well-meaning people for losing protests, who is ever going to protest? And without protests there is no such thing as rule observance.

Protest by a race committee or protest committee

A race committee can call on its own initiative for a protest hearing to deal with a possible rule infringement by a competitor (rule 70.2). The hearing is carried out as though a protest has been made against the infringing boat by another competitor (rule 70.2(d) and (e)).

A race committee can start its own proceedings in the following circumstances:

1. A member of the race committee may have seen the infringement.
2. The infringement is reported the same day by a disinterested non-competitor.
3. The race committee may have grounds for believing that an infringement resulted in serious damage.
4. A boat in a protest may have committed some other infringement (rule 70.2).
5. The race committee may have learned from a written or oral statement from a boat that she may have infringed a rule. A 'written statement' includes an invalid protest form (rule 70.2(b)).

But except for a starting or finishing infringement, the race committee (or protest committee) is not allowed to penalise any boat without lodging a protest and holding a proper hearing (unless they have made some special provision for doing so in the sailing instructions). However, even when penalised for not starting or finishing properly, a competitor has the right to hearing if he asks for one (rule 70.1).

Disqualification without a hearing

Unless the sailing instructions have extended the power of the race committee to disqualify without a hearing (which they often do in major championships for infringements of rule 54 (Propulsion)), the only infringements for which a race committee may disqualify a boat without a hearing are failing to start or finish correctly. Even then, a competitor who is disqualified without a hearing is entitled to one if he simply asks the race committee (rule 70.1(c)).

Seeking redress from the race committee

This is difficult to win, partly because the protest committee, being a sub-committee of the race committee, is often inclined to regard the point of view of a hard-worked race officer more sympathetically than a trouble-making, self-interested competitor. A good protest committee will guard against this tendency and weigh the evidence fairly.

The request is not strictly against the race committee, but is a plea by a helmsman that his finishing position has been 'materially prejudiced . . . by an improper action or omission of the race committee' (rule 69). The protest committee must proceed in accordance with rule 74.2. From 74.2(c), the arrangements which the race committee may make include the following:

The protest committee must proceed in accordance with rule 74.2. From 74.2(c), the arrangements which the race committee may make include the following:

(i) to let the results of the race stand; or
(ii) to award the prejudiced yacht points according to her recorded position at the rounding mark before the incident; or
(iii) when the incident occurs close enough to the finishing line to enable the race committee to determine the prejudiced yacht's probable finishing position, to award her the points she would have scored if she had finished in that position; or
(iv) to award the prejudiced yacht breakdown points when rule 69(c) applies; or
(v) to award the prejudiced yacht points in accordance with Appendix B2 The Bonus Points Scoring System; or
(vi) in a single race for prizes, assuming that the prejudiced yacht qualifies for one, to award an additional prize to her; or
(vii) to *abandon* or cancel the race; or
(viii) to adopt any other means,

provided that the race committee's arrangement is as equitable as possible to all the yachts concerned.

The rule also covers giving assistance to someone in distress while racing, and being physically damaged by a boat that is in the wrong. Any doubt about the anticipated finishing position of the boat giving assistance, should be resolved in favour of that boat.

A race abandoned or cancelled is unfair to the people who were up front that day; if there is a different solution which is reasonably fair to everybody, that's the one the committee should go for. If not, the race must be abandoned.

When there is reasonable doubt about whether a competitor was prejudiced, the doubt must be resolved in favour of the competitor (USSA case 66).

Composition of a protest committee

A protest committee is appointed by the race committee and is, strictly, part of the race committee. No-one may be on a protest committee who might benefit from that committee's decision. Interpreted strictly, this would bar competitors from protest committees (USSA case 124), but in practice competitors can be included provided both protester and defendant agree to it. So at the start of the hearing, the protester and defendant should be asked whether they object to any member of the protest committee, those members who competed in the race or the series being pointed out. If there are no objections, any right of appeal on that score is automatically invalid (USSA case 175).

Extra care in the appointment of a protest committee is called for when a competitor seeks redress from the race committee for some error or oversight in the running of a race (rule 69). The race committee is then sitting in judgement on itself through its protest committee. Ideally the protest committee should consist of people who were neither involved in the race as competitors nor as organisers.

At major events a jury is appointed which is independent of the race committee; its decisions are usually open to appeal (even by the race committee if it doesn't agree with a decision to which it was a party).

The right to appeal

The final arbiter in a dispute over the IYRU rules is the national sailing authority of the country in which the event is sailed. However, a formal appeal to the national authority can only be considered on questions of rule interpretation, not on questions of fact, the final arbiter of fact is the protest committee (rule 74.1).

For some major events like World Championships, an international jury is appointed which is competent enough for there to be no right of appeal. This waiving of appeal is also common in two day team racing events where teams must be eliminated from early rounds before there can be a final and winners. An appeal on a first round result would dislocate the whole event.

Permission for an organising authority to waive the right of appeal is given only by a national or the international sailing authority; it is not given lightly. However, there is no right to appeal against a decision by an International Jury acting in accordance with Appendix A5.

Counter-protest

It often happens that both boats involved in an incident lodge a protest. If both protests are valid, they may be heard simultaneously. The onus of proof will in no way change. However, if one boat in a collision fails to protest, or fails to fly a protest flag properly, and the other boat does not lodge a valid protest, neither boat may have her protest heard (USSA case 49).

The protest hearing

The procedure for hearing a protest is well explained in Appendix C1 of the IYRU rules. It is important to follow this carefully, because a hearing in which there are major errors of procedure may invalidate a protest (USSA case 54). But if either the protester or defendant (referred to as 'protestee' in the rule book) feels that procedural errors are being made, these should be pointed out at the time. Failure to complain at the time, or as soon afterwards as the wrong procedure became known, would mean that an appeal based on the procedural errors would be dismissed (USSA case 176).

The defendant and the protester have the right to be present at the hearing and throughout the taking of evidence (rule 73.1). When either the defendant or protester has made a reasonable attempt to be present he should be allowed to be present. So if a committee has several protests to hear, it should hear those where both parties are present first (USSA case 104). But if an interested party fails to make an effort to be at the hearing, a committee may deal with the case without a full hearing (rule 73.5 and USSA case 54).

The protester and defendant may call as many witnesses as they choose (rule 73.1) unless witnesses re-iterate facts that have already been established (USSA case 54).

A protest committee should put its findings in writing in the form 'facts found: . . .' and 'decisions: . . .' quoting the rule numbers that apply. There is no obligation to do it this way though, unless asked to do so (USSA case 54). Otherwise it may give its decision orally but a copy of a written decision may be requested by any party to the protest within seven days of the oral decision being given (rule 74.6(b)).

Appeals

A party to a protest may appeal against a decision of a protest committee solely on a question of its interpretation of the rules, and a race or protest committee may refer its own decision for confirmation or correction of its interpretation of the rules.

The appeal or reference must comply with the requirements of rule 78, and any prescriptions which a National Authority may have attached to rule 78.

THE 1993-1996 INTERNATIONAL YACHT RACING RULES

Introduction

The International Yacht Racing Rules have been established by the International Yacht Racing Union for the organisation, conduct and judging of the sport of yacht racing. They are amended and published every four years by the IYRU in accordance with its Regulations.

This edition of the International Yacht Racing Rules becomes effective on 1 April 1993 and supersedes all previous editions. Marginal markings indicate the changes made to the 1989-1992 edition except changes of rule numbers, rule order, rule titles and punctuation. A change of words does not necessarily imply a change of meaning. No changes are contemplated before 1997, except that Appendices A1 and A2 may be changed annually.

The IYRU publishes *Interpretations of the International Yacht Racing Rules* and recognises them as authoritative interpretations and explanations of the rules.

In translating and interpreting these rules, it shall be understood that the word 'shall' is mandatory, and the words 'can' and 'may' are permissive

CONTENTS

Part III—GENERAL REQUIREMENTS

Part IV—RIGHT-OF-WAY RULES

SECTION A—Obligations and Penalties

SECTION B—Basic Right-of-Way Rules and their Limitations

SECTION C—Rules that Apply at Marks and Obstructions and Other Exceptions to the Rules of Section B

Part V—OTHER SAILING RULES

Part VI—PROTESTS, PENALTIES AND APPEALS

SECTION A—Initiation of Action

SECTION B—Protest Procedure

SECTION C—Special Rules

Part I—Fundamental Rules, Definitions and Alterations

Fundamental Rules

A Rendering Assistance

Every yacht shall render all possible assistance to any vessel or person in peril, when in a position to do so.

B Competitors' Responsibilities

It shall be the sole responsibility of each yacht to decide whether or not to *start* or to continue to *race*. By participating in a race conducted under these rules, each competitor and yacht owner agrees:

(i) to be governed by the *rules*;

(ii) to accept the penalties imposed and other action taken in accordance with the *rules*, subject to the appeal and review procedures provided in them, as the final determination of any matter arising under the *rules*; and

(iii) with respect to such a determination, not to resort to any court or tribunal not provided by the *rules*.

C Fair Sailing

A yacht, her owner and crew shall compete only by *sailing*, using their speed and skill, and, except in team racing, by individual effort, in compliance with the *rules* and in accordance with recognised principles of fair play and sportsmanship. A yacht may be penalised under this rule only in the case of a clear-cut violation of the above principles and only when no other *rule* applies, except rule 75.

D Accepting Penalties

A yacht that realises she has infringed a *rule* while *racing* shall either retire promptly or accept an alternative penalty when so prescribed in the sailing instructions.

Definitions

When a term is used in its defined sense, it is printed in ***italic*** *type.*

Abandonment

An *abandoned* race is one that is declared void at any time and that may be re-sailed.

Bearing Away
Altering course away from the wind until a yacht begins to *gybe*.

Clear Astern and Clear Ahead; Overlap
A yacht is *clear astern* of another when her hull and equipment in normal position are abaft an imaginary line projected abeam from the aftermost point of the other's hull and equipment in normal position. The other yacht is *clear ahead*.

The yachts *overlap* when neither is *clear astern*, or when, although one is *clear astern*, an intervening yacht *overlaps* both of them.

The terms *clear astern, clear ahead* and *overlap* apply to yachts on opposite *tacks* only when they are subject to rule 42. For the purposes of rules 39.1, 39.2 and 40 only: an *overlap* does not exist unless the yachts are clearly within two overall lengths of the longer yacht, and an *overlap* that exists when the *leeward yacht starts,* or when one or both yachts completes a *tack* or a *gybe*, shall be regarded as beginning then.

Close-hauled
A yacht is *close-hauled* when *sailing* by the wind as close as she can lie with advantage in working to windward.

Finishing
A yacht *finishes* when any part of her hull, or of her crew or equipment in normal position, crosses the finishing line in the direction of the course from the last *mark*, after fulfilling any penalty obligations under rule 52.2(b).

Gybing
A yacht begins to *gybe* at the moment when, with the wind aft, the foot of her mainsail crosses her centre line, and completes the *gybe* when the mainsail has filled on the other *tack*.

Interested Party
Anyone who stands to gain or lose as a result of a decision of a *protest committee* or who has a close personal interest in the result.

Leeward and Windward
The *leeward* side of a yacht is that on which she is, or, when head to wind, was, carrying her mainsail. The opposite side is the *windward* side.

When neither of two yachts on the same *tack* is clear *astern*, the one on the *leeward* side of the other is the *leeward yacht*. The other is the *windward yacht*.

Luffing
Altering course towards the wind.

Mark
A *mark* is any object specified in the sailing instructions that a yacht must

round or pass on a required side. Ground tackle and any object accidentally or temporarily attached to the *mark* are not part of it.

Mast Abeam

A *windward yacht sailing* no higher than a *leeward yacht* is *mast abeam* when her helmsman's line of sight abeam from his normal station is forward of the *leeward yacht's* mainmast.

A *windward yacht sailing* higher than a *leeward yacht* is *mast abeam* when her helmsman's line of sight abeam from his normal station would be, if she were *sailing* no higher, forward of the *leeward yacht's* mainmast.

Obstruction

An *obstruction* is any object, including a vessel under way, large enough to require a yacht, when more than one overall length away from it, to make a substantial alteration of course to pass on one side or the other, or any object that can be passed on one side only, including a buoy when the yacht in question cannot safely pass between it and the shoal or the object that it marks. The sailing instructions may prescribe that a specified area shall rank as an *obstruction*.

On a Tack; Starboard Tack; Port Tack

A yacht is *on a tack* except when she is *tacking* or *gybing*. A yacht is on the *tack (starboard* or *port)* corresponding to her *windward* side.

Overlap

See *Clear Astern* and *Clear Ahead*; *Overlap*

Parties to a Protest

(a) The protesting yacht, the protested yacht and any other yacht involved in the incident that might be penalised as a result of the *protest*;
(b) a yacht that has requested redress;
(c) the race commitee when it is involved in a *protest* under rules 69(a) or 70; and
(d) a competitor who has been or is liable to be penalised.

Postponement

A *postponed* race is one that is not started at its scheduled time and that can be sailed at any time the race committee may decide.

Proper Course

A *proper course* is any course that a yacht might *sail* after the starting signal, in the absence of the other yacht or yachts affected, to *finish* as quickly as possible. There is no *proper course* before the starting signal.

Protest

An action taken by a yacht, race committee or *protest committee* to initiate a hearing on a possible infringement of a *rule* or a consideration of redress in accordance with rules 68, 69 or 70.

Protest Committee

The body appointed to hear and decide *protests* in accordance with rule 1.4.

Racing

A yacht is *racing* from her preparatory signal until she has either *finished* and cleared the finishing line and finishing *marks* or retired, or until the race has been *postponed* or *abandoned*, or a general recall has been signalled.

Room

Room is the space needed by a yacht to manoeuvre in a seamanlike manner in the prevailing conditions.

Rules

(a) These racing rules, including the definitions, preambles and the rules of an appendix when it applies;
(b) the prescriptions of the national authority concerned, when they apply;
(c) the sailing instructions;
(d) the class rules; and
(e) any other conditions governing the event.

Sailing

A yacht is *sailing* when using only the wind and water to increase, maintain or decrease her speed, with her crew adjusting the trim of sails and hull and performing other acts of seamanship.

Starting

A yacht *starts* when, after fulfilling her penalty obligations, if any, under rule 51.1(c), and after her starting signal, any part of her hull, crew or equipment first crosses the starting line in the direction of the course to the first *mark*.

Tacking

A yacht is *tacking* from the moment she is beyond head to wind until she has *borne away* to a *close-hauled* course.

Windward

See *Leeward* and *Windward*.

Alterations

A national authority may alter these rules by prescription, with the exception of the rules of Parts I and IV, rules 1, 3.1, 16, 17, 18, 61 and 75, and the appendices of Group A, unless permitted in the rule or appendix itself. The sailing instructions may alter a rule only in accordance with rule 3.1.

The appendices to these rules contain alternative or additional rules, guidance, or both. When the rules of an appendix apply, they override any conflicting racing rule.

Part II—Organisation and Management

1 Organising, Conducting and Judging Races

1.1 GOVERNING RULES

The organising authority, race committee, *protest committee* and all other bodies and persons concerned with the organisation, conduct and judging of a race, regatta or series shall be governed by these rules, the prescriptions of the national authority when they apply, the class rules, except when they conflict with these rules, the sailing instructions and any other conditions governing the event. Hereinafter the term 'race' shall, when appropriate, include a regatta or a series of races.

1.2 ORGANISING AUTHORITY

Races shall be organised by:

(a) the IYRU; or

(b) a member national authority of the IYRU; or

(c) a club or regatta committee affiliated to a national authority; or

(d) a class association either with the approval of a national authority or in conjunction with an affiliated club or regatta committee; or

(e) an unaffiliated body in conjunction with an affiliated club or regatta committee;

which will hereinafter be referred to as the organising authority.

The organising authority shall appoint a race committee and publish a notice of race in accordance with rule 2.

1.3 RACE COMMITTEE

The race committee shall publish sailing instructions in accordance with rule 3 and conduct the race, subject to such direction as the organising authority may exercise. The term 'race committee' whenever it is used shall include any person or committee that is responsible for performing any of the duties or functions of the race committee.

1.4 PROTEST COMMITTEE

The receiving, hearing and deciding of *protests* and other matters arising under the rules of Part VI shall be carried out by a *protest committee*, which may be:

(a) the race committee itself; or

(b) a sub-committee thereof appointed by the race committee and consisting of its own members, or others, or a combination of both; or

(c) a jury, which is a *protest committee* separate from and independent of the race committee, appointed by the organising authority or the race committee; or

(d) an international jury appointed by the organising authority in accordance with Appendix A5. A national authority may prescribe that its approval is required for the appointment of international juries for events within its jurisdiction other than those of the IYRU.

A *protest committee* shall not supervise the conduct of the race, or direct the race committee, except when so directed by the organising authority.

1.5 RIGHT OF APPEAL
Decisions of a *protest committee* may be appealed in accordance with rule 77.1, except that:

(a) there shall be no appeal from the decisions of an international jury constituted in accordance with Appendix A5;

(b) when the notice of race and the sailing instructions so state, the right of appeal may be denied when:

(i) it is essential to determine promptly the result of a race that will qualify a yacht to compete in a later stage of the event or a subsequent event (a national authority may prescribe that its approval is required for such a procedure); or

(ii) a national authority so prescribes for a particular event open only to entrants under its own jurisdiction.

1.6 EXCLUSION OF YACHTS AND COMPETITORS
Unless otherwise prescribed by the national authority, the organising authority or the race committee may, before the start of the first race, reject or rescind the entry of any yacht or exclude a competitor without stating the reason. However, at all world and continental championships, no entry within established quotas shall be rejected or rescinded without first obtaining the approval of the IYRU or the relevant international class association or the Offshore Racing Council.

2 Notice of Race

(a) The notice of race shall contain the following information:

(i) The title, place and dates of the event and name of the organising authority.

(ii) That the race will be governed by the International Yacht Racing Rules, the prescriptions of the national authority when they apply, the rules of each class concerned, and such other *rules* as are applicable.

(iii) The class(es) to race, conditions of entry and any restrictions on entries.

(iv) The times of registration and starts of the practice race or first race, and succeeding races when known.

(b) The notice of race shall, when appropriate, include the following:

(i) IYRU approval and eligibility requirements in accordance with Appendix A1.

(ii) The category of the event in accordance with Appendix A3 and, when required, the additional information prescribed by Appendix A3.

(iii) The scoring system.

(iv) The time and place at which the sailing instructions will be available.

(v) Any alterations to the racing rules in accordance with rule 3.1.

(vi) Alteration of class rules, referring specifically to each rule and stating the alteration.

(vii) The procedure for advance registration or entry, including closing dates when applicable, fees and the mailing address.

(viii) Measurement procedures or requirements for measurement or rating certificates.

(ix) The courses to be sailed.

(x) Alternative penalties for rule infringements.

(xi) Prizes, including any cash, cashable prize and/or appearance payments totalling more than US $10,000 that may be received by any one yacht.

(xii) Denial of the right of appeal, subject to rule 1.5.

(xiii) An entry form, to be signed by the yacht's owner or owner's representative, containing words such as: 'I agree to be bound by the racing rules of the IYRU and by all other rules that govern this event.'

3 Sailing Instructions

3.1 STATUS

(a) These rules shall be supplemented by written sailing instructions that may, subject to rule 3.1(b), alter a rule by referring specifically to it and stating the alteration.

(b) Except in accordance with rule 3.2(b)(xxxii), the sailing instructions shall not alter:

(i) Parts I and IV; or

(ii) rules 1, 2, 3, 16, 17, 18, 51.1(a) and 61; or

(iii) Sections C and D of Part VI; or

(iv) the appendices of Group A; or

(v) the provision of rule 68.3(a) that Code flag 'B' or a red rectangular flag is always acceptable as a protest flag; or

(vi) any rule of an appendix that alters a rule listed in rule 3.1(b).

(c) When so prescribed by the national authority, these restrictions shall not preclude the right of developing and testing proposed rule changes in local races. A national authority may also prescribe that its approval is required for such changes.

3.2 CONTENTS

(a) The sailing instructions shall contain the following information:

(i) That the race will be governed by the International Yacht Racing Rules, the prescriptions of the national authority when they apply (for international events, a copy in English of prescriptions that apply shall be included in the sailing instructions), the rules of each class concerned, the sailing instructions, and such other rules as are applicable.

(ii) The schedule of races, the classes to race and times of warning signals for each class.

(iii) The course to be sailed or a list of *marks* from which the course will be selected, describing the *marks*, stating their order and, for each, whether it is to be rounded or passed and on which side. A diagram or chart is recommended.

(iv) Descriptions of the starting and finishing lines, the starting system and any special signals to be used.

(v) The time limit, if any, for *finishing*.

(vi) The scoring system, stated in full or by reference to Appendix B2, class rules or other rules governing the event, and including the method, if any, for breaking ties.

(b) The sailing instructions shall, when appropriate, include the following:

(i) IYRU approval and eligibility requirements in accordance with Appendix A1.

(ii) The category of the event in accordance with Appendix A3, and, when required, the additional information prescribed in Appendix A3.

(iii) A complete statement of any alterations to the racing rules, in accordance with rule 3.1.

(iv) Alteration of class rules, referring specifically to each rule and stating the alteration.

(v) The registration procedure.

(vi) Location(s) of official notice board(s).

(vii) Procedure for changing the sailing instructions.

(viii) Restrictions controlling alterations to yachts when supplied by the organising authority.

(ix) Signals to be made ashore and location of signal station(s).

(x) Class flags.

(xi) The racing area; a chart is recommended.

(xii) The starting area.

(xiii) Course signals.

(xiv) Approximate course length; approximate length of windward legs.

(xv) Information on tides and currents.

(xvi) Any special procedures or signals for individual or general recalls.

(xvii) Any special procedure for shortening the course or for finishing a shortened course.

(xviii) Mark boats; lead boats.

(xix) Procedure for changes of course after the start and related signals.

(xx) The time limit, if any, for yachts other than the first yacht to *finish*.

(xxi) Whether races *postponed* or *abandoned* for the day will be re-sailed, and, if so, when and where.

(xxii) The number of races required to complete the regatta.

(xxiii) Safety, such as requirements and signals for personal buoyancy, check-in at the starting area, and check-out and check-in ashore.

(xxiv) Any measurement or inspection procedure.

(xxv) Alternative penalties for rule infringements.

(xxvi) Whether declarations are required.

(xxvii) Protest procedure and times and place of hearings.

(xxviii) Restrictions on use of support boats, plastic pools, radios, etc., and limitations on hauling out, and on outside assistance provided to a yacht that is not *racing*.

(xxix) Substitute competitors.

(xxx) Prizes, including any cash, cashable prize and/or appearance payments totalling more than US $10,000 that may be received by any one yacht.

(xxxi) Time allowances.

(xxxii) Replacement of the relevant rules of Part IV with the International Regulations for Preventing Collisions at Sea or other government right-of-way rules, the time(s) or place(s) they will apply, and any night signals to be used by race committee.

(xxxiii) Disposition to be made of a yacht appearing at the start alone in her class.

(xxxiv) Denial of the right of appeal, subject to rule 1.5.

(xxxv) Other commitments of the race committee and obligations of yachts.

3.3 DISTRIBUTION
The sailing instructions shall be available to each yacht entitled to race.

3.4 CHANGES
Changes in sailing instructions shall be made in writing before a race by:

(a) posting in proper time on the official notice board; or

(b) being communicated to each yacht on the water before the warning signal, except that oral instructions may be given only on the water in accordance with procedure prescribed in the sailing instructions.

4 Race Committee Signals

4.1 VISUAL SIGNALS
Unless otherwise prescribed in the sailing instructions, the following International Code flags (or boards) and other visual signals shall have the meanings stated in this rule. When displayed alone, they shall apply to all classes; when displayed over a class flag, they shall apply to the designated class only.

'AP', Answering Pennant — Postponement Signal

(a) 'All races not started are *postponed*. The warning signal will be made one minute after this signal is lowered.'
(One sound signal shall be made with the lowering of 'AP'.)

(b) **Over one of the numeral pennants 1 to 9**
'All races not started are *postponed* one hour, two hours, etc.'

(c) **Over Code flag 'A'**
'All races not started are *postponed* to a later day.'

(d) **Over Code flag 'H'**
'All races not started are *postponed*. Further signals will be made ashore.'

'C' — Change of Course while Racing

When displayed at or near a rounding *mark*:
'After rounding this *mark*, the course to the next *mark* has been changed.'

'I' — Round-the-Ends Starting Rule

When displayed before or with the preparatory signal:
'Rule 51.1(c) will be in effect for this start.'

When lowered, accompanied by one long sound signal, one minute before the starting signal:
'The one-minute period of rule 51.1(c) has begun.'

'L' — Notification Signal

(a) When displayed ashore:
'A notice to competitors has been posted on the official notice board.'

(b) When displayed afloat:
'Come within hail' or 'Follow me.'

'M' — Mark Signal

When displayed on a buoy, vessel, or other object:
'Round or pass the object displaying this signal instead of the *mark* that it replaces.'

'N' — Abandonment Signal

(a) 'All races are *abandoned*. Further signals will be made in the starting area. This signal will be lowered one minute before the next signal is made.'
(One sound signal shall be made with the lowering of 'N'.)

(b) **Over Code flag 'H'**
'All races are *abandoned*. Further signals will be made ashore.'

'P' — Preparatory Signal

'The class designated by the warning signal will start in five minutes exactly.'

'S' — Shorten Course Signal

(a) Before or with the warning signal at the starting line:
'*Sail* the shortened course as prescribed in the sailing instructions.'

(b) At the finishing line:
'*Finish* the race either:
(i) at the prescribed finishing line at the end of the round still to be completed by the leading yacht; or
(ii) as prescribed in the sailing instructions.'

(c) At a rounding *mark*:
'*Finish* between the rounding *mark* and the committee boat.'

'X' — Individual Recall

When displayed promptly after the starting signal, accompanied by one sound signal:
'One or more yachts are recalled in accordance with rule 7.1.'

'Y' — Life-Jacket Signal

'The life-jacket requirement of rule 60 is in effect.'

'First Substitute' — General Recall Signal

'The class is recalled for a new start. The preparatory signal (including the class signal when System 1 of rule 4.3(a) is in use) will be made one minute after this signal is lowered.'
(One sound signal shall be made with the lowering of 'First Substitute'.)

Red Flag

When displayed by a committee boat:
'Leave all rounding *marks* to port.'

Green Flag

When displayed by a committee boat:
'Leave all rounding *marks* to starboard.'

Blue Flag or Shape — Finishing Signal

When displayed by a committee boat:
'The committee boat is on station at the finishing line.'

4.2 CALLING ATTENTION TO VISUAL SIGNALS
Whenever the race committee makes a signal, except a course signal displayed before the warning signal or a blue flag or shape when on station at the finishing line, it shall call attention to its action with these sound signals:

(a) three guns or other sound signals when displaying 'N' or 'N over H';

(b) two guns or other sound signals when displaying 'AP', 'S' or 'First Substitute';

(c) repetitive sound signals while displaying 'C' or 'M';

(d) one gun or other sound signal when making any other signal, including the lowering of 'AP', when the length of the *postponement* is not signalled, 'I', 'N' or 'First Substitute'.

4.3 VISUAL SIGNALS FOR STARTING RACES

(a) Unless otherwise prescribed in the sailing instructions, the signals for starting a race shall be made at five-minute intervals exactly, and shall be either System 1 or System 2.

System 1	Warning Signal -	Class signal displayed.
	Preparatory Signal -	Code flag 'P' displayed.
	Starting Signal -	Both warning and preparatory signals lowered.

In System 1, when classes are started:

(i) at ten-minute intervals, the warning signal for each succeeding class shall be displayed at the starting signal of the preceding class.

(ii) at five-minute intervals, the preparatory signal for the first class to *start* shall be left displayed until the last class *starts*. The warning signal for each succeeding class shall be displayed at the preparatory signal of the preceding class.

When a start is recalled, the warning signal of the next class shall be lowered after the general recall has been signalled.

System 2	Warning Signal -	White or yellow shape or flag displayed.
	Preparatory Signal -	Blue shape or flag displayed.
	Starting Signal -	Red shape or flag displayed.

In System 2, each signal shall be lowered one minute before the next is made. Class flags when used shall be displayed not later than the preparatory signal for each class.

When classes are started:

(i) at ten-minute intervals, the starting signal for each class shall be the warning signal for the next.

(ii) at five-minute intervals, the preparatory signal for each class shall be the warning signal for the next.

(b) A warning signal shall not be made before its scheduled time, except with the consent of all yachts entitled to race.

4.4 VISUAL STARTING SIGNALS TO GOVERN
Times shall be taken from the visual starting signals, and a failure or mistiming of a gun or other sound signal calling attention to starting signals shall be disregarded.

5 Designating the Course, Altering the Course or Race

5.1 Before or with the warning signal for a class that has not *started*, the race committee:

(a) shall either signal or otherwise designate the course;

(b) may remove and substitute a new course signal.

5.2 Before the preparatory signal, the race committee may shift a starting *mark*.

5.3 Before the starting signal, the race committee may:

(a) *postpone* to designate a new course before or with the new warning signal, or for any other reason; or

(b) *postpone* to a later day; or

(c) *abandon* the race for any reason.

5.4 After the starting signal, the race committee may:

(a) signal a general recall; or

(b) *abandon* and re-sail the race because of an error in the starting procedure; or

(c) when prescribed in the sailing instructions, change the course at any rounding *mark* subject to proper notice being given to each yacht before she begins the changed leg; or

(d) *abandon* the race or shorten the course:

(i) because of foul weather; or

(ii) because of insufficient wind making it improbable that the race will finish within the time limit; or

(iii) because a *mark* is missing or has shifted; or

(iv) for any other reason directly affecting the safety or fairness of the competition.

5.5 After one yacht has *sailed* the course in accordance with rule 51 within the prescribed time limit, the race committee shall not *abandon* the race without taking the action required of a *protest committee* by rule 74.2(b).

6 Start of a Race

6.1 STARTING AREA

The sailing instructions may define a starting area that may be bounded by buoys; such buoys are not *marks*.

6.2 TIMING THE START

The start of a yacht shall be timed from her starting signal.

7 Recalls

7.1 INDIVIDUAL RECALL

Unless otherwise prescribed in the sailing instructions, when, at her starting signal, any part of a yacht's hull, crew or equipment is on the course side of the starting line, or she has not complied with rule 51.1(c), the race committee shall promptly display Code flag 'X', accompanied by one sound signal, until all such yachts are wholly on the pre-start side of the starting line or its extensions and have complied with rule 51.1(c) when applicable, or for four minutes after the starting signal, whichever is the earlier. The sailing instructions may prescribe that the race committee will also hail the yacht's sail number.

7.2 GENERAL RECALL

(a) When there is a number of unidentified premature starters, the race committee may make a general recall signal in accordance with rules 4.1, 'First Substitute', and 4.2.

(b) Except for infringements of rule 30.1, rule infringements before the preparatory signal for the new start shall be disregarded for the purpose of competing in the race to be restarted.

8 Marks

8.1 MARK MISSING

When any *mark* either is missing or has shifted, the race committee shall, when possible, replace it in its stated position, or substitute a new one with similar characteristics or a buoy or vessel displaying Code flag 'M'.

8.2 MARK UNSEEN

When races are sailed in fog or at night, dead reckoning alone need not necessarily be accepted as evidence that a *mark* has been rounded or passed.

9 Finishing Within a Time Limit

Unless otherwise prescribed in the sailing instructions, in races where there is a time limit, one yacht *sailing* the course in accordance with rule 51 and *finishing* within the prescribed limit shall make the race valid for all other yachts in that race. When no yacht *finishes* within the prescribed time limit, the race shall be *abandoned*.

10 Ties

When there is a tie at the end of a race, either actual or on corrected times, the points for the place for which the yachts have tied and for the place immediately below shall be added together and divided equally. When yachts have equal scores at the end of a series and a tie remains unbroken by the scoring system prescribed in the sailing instructions, it shall stand as part of the final results. Yachts tied for a prize shall share it or receive equal prizes.

11 Races to be Re-sailed

When a race is to be re-sailed:

(a) all yachts entered in the original race shall be eligible to *start* in the race to be re-sailed;

(b) new entries may be accepted subject to the entry requirements of the original race, and at the discretion of the race committee;

(c) rule infringements in the original race shall be disregarded for the purpose of competing in the race to be re-sailed; and

(d) the race committee shall notify the yachts concerned when and where the race will be re-sailed.

(Numbers 12, 13, 14 and 15 are spare numbers)

Part III—**General Requirements**

Competitors' Eligibility and Qualification of Yachts

Competitors and yachts shall comply with the rules of Part III before the preparatory signal and, when applicable, while ***racing****.*

16 Competitors' Eligibility

Competitors shall comply with an event's competitor eligibility requirements when prescribed by or in accordance with Appendix A1. A yacht shall compete only with eligible crew members.

17 Banned Substances and Banned Methods

17.1 (a) A competitor shall neither take a substance nor use a method banned by the current edition of the IYRU *Medical Lists.*

(b) A competitor selected for testing shall not refuse to be tested and shall appear at a control centre when required by a sampling officer.

(c) Competitors are subject to the control, procedures and penalties prescribed in Appendix A2 and the IYRU *Doping Control Procedures.*

17.2 Notwithstanding rules 68 and 70, an alleged infringement of this rule shall not be grounds for a *protest.*

17.3 No control or testing shall be initiated at any event without the written authority of the IYRU or of the national authority having jurisdiction over the event.

18 Advertising and Event Categories

A yacht and her crew shall compete in conformity with Appendix A3.

19 Entries

A yacht shall enter a race as prescribed by the organising authority of the event.

20 Measurement or Rating Certificates

20.1 Every yacht entering a race shall hold such valid measurement or rating certificate as is required by the national authority or other duly authorised body, by her class rules, by the notice of race, or by the sailing instructions.

20.2 An owner shall be responsible for maintaining his yacht in accordance with her class rules and for ensuring that her certificate is not invalidated by alterations. Deviations in excess of tolerances specified in the class rules caused by normal wear or damage and that do not affect the performance of the yacht shall not invalidate the measurement or rating certificate of the yacht for a particular race, but shall be rectified before she *races* again, unless in the opinion of the race committee there has been no practicable opportunity to rectify the wear or damage.

20.3 (a) The owner of a yacht who cannot produce such a certificate when required may be permitted to sign and lodge with the race committee, before the yacht *starts*, a statement in the following form:

UNDERTAKING TO PRODUCE CERTIFICATE

To the Secretary ....Club

The yacht ....competes in the .... race on condition that a valid certificate previously issued by the authorised administrative body, or a copy of it, is submitted to the race committee before the end of the series, and that she competes in the race(s) on the measurement or rating of that certificate.

Signed ....
(Owner or owner's representative)
Date...

(b) In this event the sailing instructions may require that the owner shall lodge such a deposit as may be required by the organising authority, which may be forfeited when such certificate or copy is not submitted to the race committee within the prescribed period.

21 Ownership of Yachts

21.1 A yacht shall be eligible to compete only when she is either owned by or on charter to and has been entered by a yacht or sailing club recognised by its national authority or a member thereof.

21.2 Two or more yachts owned or chartered wholly or in part by the same body or person shall not compete in the same race without the previous consent of the race committee.

21.3 An owner shall not steer any yacht other than his own in a race in which his own yacht competes without the previous consent of the race committee.

22 Member on Board

Every yacht shall have on board a member of a yacht or sailing club recognised by its national authority to be in charge of the yacht as owner or owner's representative.

23 Shifting Ballast

23.1 GENERAL RESTRICTIONS
Floorboards shall be kept down; bulkheads and doors left standing; ladders, stairways and water tanks left in place; and all cabin, galley and forecastle fixtures and fittings kept on board. All movable ballast shall be properly stowed under the floorboards or in lockers and no dead weight shall be shifted.

23.2 SHIPPING, UNSHIPPING OR SHIFTING BALLAST; WATER
From 2100 on the day before the race until she is no longer *racing*, a yacht shall not ship, unship or shift ballast, whether movable or fixed, or take in or discharge water, except for ordinary ship's use and the removal of bilge water. This rule shall not apply to wearing or carrying clothing, equipment or ballast in compliance with rule 61.

24 Life-saving Equipment

Unless otherwise prescribed by her class rules, every yacht shall carry adequate life-saving equipment for all persons on board, one item of which shall be ready for immediate use.

25 Identification — Class Insignia, National Letters and Numbers

25.1 Each yacht shall comply with the requirements of Appendix B3 and her class rules in respect of class insignia, national letters and numbers.

25.2 When a yacht infringes rule 25.1 or any other *rule* governing numbers or letters on sails, hull or equipment, she shall be either warned and given adequate opportunity to make correction or, at the discretion of the *protest committee*, penalised.

26 Forestays and Jib Tacks

Unless otherwise prescribed by the class rules, forestays and jib tacks (not including spinnaker staysails when not *close-hauled*) shall be fixed approximately in the centre-line of the yacht.

(Numbers 27, 28 and 29 are spare numbers)

Part IV—**Right-of-Way Rules**

Rights and Obligations when Yachts Meet

The rules of Part IV apply to yachts that intend to ***race****, are* ***racing*** *or have been* ***racing*** *in the same or different races, from the time they begin to sail in the vicinity of the starting line until they leave the vicinity of the course after* ***finishing*** *or retiring, except when the sailing instructions prescribe that the International Regulations for Preventing Collisions at Sea (IRPCAS) or applicable government right-of-way rules apply. All other vessels shall be treated in accordance with the IRPCAS or the government right-of-way rules applicable to the area.*

SECTION A—**Obligations and Penalties**

30 Hindering Another Yacht

30.1 Before or after she is *racing*, a yacht shall not seriously hinder a yacht that is *racing*.

30.2 Except when *sailing* a *proper course*, a yacht shall not interfere with a yacht that is exonerating herself in accordance with rule 52.2(a) or accepting a 720° turns penalty in accordance with Appendix B1.

31 Penalty Limitations

A yacht shall not be penalised for infringing a rule of Part IV, other than rule 30.1, unless the infringement occurs while she is *racing*.

32 Serious Damage

When serious damage results from a collision, a yacht that had the opportunity but failed to make a reasonable attempt to avoid the collision shall be penalised.

33 Contact between Yachts Racing

When there is contact between yachts *racing* that is not both minor and unavoidable, the yachts shall be penalised unless:

(a) one of them lodges a valid *protest*; or

(b) one of them, or a third yacht, retires (or exonerates herself by accepting an alternative penalty when so prescribed in the sailing instructions) in acknowledgement of an infringement in that incident.

34 Retention of Rights

A yacht that may have infringed a *rule* but that is not obviously retiring or exonerating herself retains her rights under the rules of Part IV, and other yachts shall treat her accordingly.

SECTION B—**Basic Right-of-Way Rules and their Limitations**

These rules apply except when overridden by a rule in Section C.

35 Limitations on Altering Course

When one yacht is required to keep clear of another, the right-of-way yacht shall not alter course so as to prevent the other yacht from keeping clear, or so as to obstruct her while she is keeping clear, except:

(a) when *luffing* as permitted by rule 39.2; or

(b) when assuming a *proper course* either:

(i) to *start*, when she is on the *starboard tack* and the other yacht is on the *port tack*; or

(ii) when rounding a *mark*.

36 Opposite Tacks — Basic Rule

A *port-tack* yacht shall keep clear of a *starboard-tack* yacht.

37 Same Tack — Basic Rules

37.1 OVERLAPPED
A *windward yacht* shall keep clear of a *leeward yacht*.

37.2 NOT OVERLAPPED
A yacht *clear astern* shall keep clear of a yacht *clear ahead*.

37.3 ESTABLISHING AN OVERLAP
A yacht that establishes an *overlap* to *leeward* from *clear astern* shall initially allow the *windward yacht* ample *room* and opportunity to keep clear.

38 Same Tack — Before Clearing the Starting Line

38.1 SAILING ABOVE A CLOSE-HAULED COURSE
Before she *starts* and clears the starting line, a *leeward yacht* shall not

sail above her *close-hauled* course when the *windward yacht* is *mast abeam* and would have to alter course to keep clear.

38.2 LUFFING
Before she *starts* and clears the starting line, when a *leeward yacht* or a yacht *clear ahead luffs* so that another yacht will have to alter course to keep clear, she shall *luff* only slowly, and initially in such a way as to give the *windward yacht room* and opportunity to keep clear.

39 Same Tack — After Clearing the Starting Line

39.1 SAILING ABOVE A PROPER COURSE
After *starting* and clearing the starting line, when a *windward yacht* has been *mast abeam* at any time during the *overlap*, the *leeward yacht* shall not *sail* above her *proper course* unless she *luffs* and *tacks* without interfering with the *windward yacht*.

39.2 LUFFING
After *starting* and clearing the starting line, subject to rule 32, a yacht *clear ahead* or a *leeward yacht* may *luff* as she pleases unless the *windward yacht* has been *mast abeam* at any time during the *overlap*.

39.3 SAILING BELOW A PROPER COURSE
A yacht on a free leg of the course shall not *sail* below her *proper course* when she is within three of her overall lengths of a *leeward yacht* or of a yacht *clear astern* that is steering a course to *leeward* of her, unless she *bears away* and *gybes* onto another *proper course* without interfering with the other yacht.

40 Other Limitations on a Leeward Yacht

40.1 DOUBT ABOUT MAST ABEAM
When there is doubt that a *windward yacht* is *mast abeam* and her helmsman hails 'Mast abeam' or words to that effect, the *leeward yacht* shall promptly comply with rule 38.1 or rule 39.1. When she believes the hail is improper, her only remedy is to protest.

40.2 SAFETY LIMITATION
When a *windward yacht* hails that an *obstruction*, a third yacht or other object limits her ability to keep clear when a *leeward yacht luffs*, the *leeward yacht* shall give the *windward yacht room* to pass the object.

40.3 LUFFING TWO OR MORE YACHTS
A *leeward yacht* shall not *luff* unless she has the right to luff all yachts that would be affected, in which case they all shall respond, including any intervening yacht that does not otherwise have the right to *luff*.

41 Changing Tacks - Tacking and Gybing

41.1 BASIC RULE

A yacht that is either *tacking* or *gybing* shall keep clear of a yacht *on a tack*.

41.2 TRANSITIONAL

A yacht shall neither *tack* nor *gybe* into a position that will give her right of way unless she does so far enough from a yacht *on a tack* to enable that yacht to keep clear without having to begin to alter her course until after the *tack* or *gybe* has been completed.

41.3 ONUS

A yacht that *tacks* or *gybes* has the onus of satisfying the *protest committee* that she completed her *tack* or *gybe* in accordance with rule 41.2.

41.4 TACKING OR GYBING AT THE SAME TIME

When two yachts are both *tacking* or both *gybing* at the same time, the one on the other's port side shall keep clear. When one yacht is *tacking* and another is *gybing* at the same time, the one that is *tacking* shall keep clear.

SECTION C—**Rules that Apply at Marks and Obstructions and Other Exceptions to the Rules of Section B**

When a rule of this section conflicts with a rule of Section B, it overrides the conflicting part of that rule, except that rule 35 always applies.

42 Rounding or Passing Marks and Obstructions

Rule 42 applies when yachts are about to round or pass a *mark* on the same required side or an *obstruction* on the same side, except that it shall not apply:

(a) at a starting *mark* surrounded by navigable water (including such a *mark* that is also an *obstruction*) when approaching the starting line to *start* until clearing the starting *marks*. However, after her starting signal, a *leeward yacht* shall not deprive a *windward yacht* of *room* at such a *mark* by *sailing* either:

(i) to windward of the compass bearing of the course to the next *mark*; or

(ii) above *close-hauled*.

(b) between two yachts on opposite *tacks*:

(i) when they are on a beat; or

(ii) when one, but not both, of them will have to *tack* either to round or pass the *mark* or to avoid the *obstruction*.

42.1 WHEN OVERLAPPED

An Outside Yacht

(a) Except as provided in rule 42.3, an outside yacht shall give each inside *overlapping* yacht *room* to round or pass the *mark* or *obstruction*, including *room* to *tack* or *gybe* when either is an integral part of the rounding or passing manoeuvre.

(b) An outside yacht *overlapped* when she comes within two of her overall lengths of a *mark* or *obstruction* shall give *room* as required, even though the *overlap* may thereafter be broken.

(c) An outside yacht that claims to have broken an *overlap* has the onus of satisfying the *protest committee* that she became *clear ahead* when she was more than two of her overall lengths from the *mark* or *obstruction*.

An Inside Yacht

(d) A yacht that claims an inside *overlap* has the onus of satisfying the *protest committee* that she established the *overlap* in accordance with rule 42.3.

(e) When an inside yacht of two or more *overlapped* yachts, either on opposite *tacks* or on the same *tack* without luffing rights, will have to *gybe* in order most directly to assume a *proper course* to the next *mark*, she shall *gybe* at the first reasonable opportunity.

42.2 WHEN NOT OVERLAPPED

(a) When a yacht *clear ahead* comes within two of her overall lengths of a *mark* or *obstruction*, a yacht *clear astern* shall keep clear until the yachts complete the rounding or passing manoeuvre, provided the yacht *clear ahead* remains on the same *tack* or *gybes*. A yacht *clear ahead* is not required to give *room* to a yacht *clear astern* before an *overlap* is established.

(b) A yacht *clear ahead* that *tacks* to round a *mark* is subject to rule 41, but a yacht *clear astern* shall not *luff* above *close-hauled* so as to prevent her from *tacking*.

42.3 LIMITATIONS

(a) Limitation on Establishing an Overlap
A yacht that establishes an inside *overlap* is entitled to *room* under rule 42.1(a) only when, at that time, the outside yacht:

(i) is able to give *room*; and

(ii) when the *overlap* is established from *clear astern*, is more than two of her overall lengths from the *mark* or *obstruction*.

However, when a yacht completes a *tack* within two of her overall lengths of a *mark* or *obstruction*, she shall give *room* as required by rule 42.1(a) to a yacht that, by *luffing*, cannot thereafter avoid establishing a late inside *overlap*.

(b) Limitation When an Obstruction is a Continuing One
When yachts are passing a continuing *obstruction*, such as a shoal or the shore or another vessel, rule 42.3(a)(ii) does not apply, and a yacht *clear astern* may establish an *overlap* between a yacht *clear ahead* and the *obstruction*, provided, at that time, there is *room* for her to pass between them in safety.

43 Close-hauled, Hailing for Room to Tack at Obstructions

43.1 HAILING
When two yachts are on the same *tack* and the yacht *clear ahead* or the *leeward yacht* is *close-hauled*, and safe pilotage requires her to make a substantial alteration of course to clear an *obstruction*, and when she intends to *tack*, but cannot *tack* without colliding with the other yacht, she shall hail the other yacht for *room* to *tack* and clear the other yacht, but she shall not hail and *tack* simultaneously.

43.2 RESPONDING
The hailed yacht at the earliest possible moment after the hail shall either:

(a) *tack*, in which case the hailing yacht shall begin to *tack* as soon as she is able to *tack* and clear the other yacht; or

(b) reply 'You *tack*' or words to that effect, in which case:

(i) the hailing yacht shall immediately *tack* and
(ii) the hailed yacht shall give the hailing yacht *room* to *tack* and clear her.
(iii) The onus of satisfying the *protest committee* that she gave sufficient *room* shall lie on the hailed yacht that replied 'You *tack*'.

43.3 WHEN AN OBSTRUCTION IS ALSO A MARK

(a) When an *obstruction* is a starting *mark* surrounded by navigable water, or the ground tackle of such a *mark*, and when approaching the starting line to *start* and after *starting*, the yacht *clear ahead* or the *leeward yacht* shall not be entitled to *room* to *tack*.

(b) At other *obstructions* that are *marks*, when the hailed yacht can fetch the *obstruction*, the hailing yacht shall not be entitled to *room* to *tack* and clear the hailed yacht, and the hailed yacht shall immediately so inform the hailing yacht. When the hailed yacht then fails to fetch, she shall retire or accept an alternative penalty when so prescribed in the sailing instructions.

44 On the Course Side of the Starting Line

After her starting signal, a yacht that has not *started* and is sailing toward the pre-start side of the starting line or its extensions shall, until wholly on its pre-start side, keep clear of yachts that have *started* or are on the pre-start side. She shall then give any newly obligated yacht ample *room* and opportunity to keep clear.

45 Keeping Clear after Touching a Mark

A yacht that has touched a *mark* and is exonerating herself shall keep clear of all other yachts until she has completed her exoneration and, when she has *started*, is on a *proper course* to the next *mark*.

46 Person Overboard; Yacht Anchored, Aground or Capsized

46.1 A yacht under way shall keep clear of another yacht *racing* that:

(a) is manoeuvring or hailing for the purpose of rescuing a person overboard; or

(b) is anchored, aground or capsized.

46.2 A yacht shall not be penalised when she is unable to avoid fouling a yacht that she is attempting to assist or that goes aground or is capsized.

46.3 A yacht is capsized from the time her masthead is in the water until her masthead is clear of the water and she has steerage way.

46.4 A yacht anchored or aground shall indicate the fact to any yacht that may be in danger of fouling her. Under normal conditions, a hail is sufficient indication. Of two yachts anchored, the one that anchored later shall keep clear, except that a yacht dragging shall keep clear of one that is not.

(Numbers 47, 48, 49 and 50 are spare numbers)

Part V—**Other Sailing Rules**

Obligations in Handling a Yacht

A yacht is subject to the rules of Part V only while she is ***racing.***

51 Sailing the Course

51.1 (a) A yacht shall *start* and *finish* only as prescribed in the starting and finishing definitions.

(b) When any part of a yacht's hull, crew or equipment is on the course side of the starting line or its extensions at her starting signal, she shall thereafter *start* in accordance with the definition.

(c) When Code flag 'I' has been displayed, and when any part of a yacht's hull, crew or equipment is on the course side of the starting line or its extensions during the minute before her starting signal, she shall *sail* to the pre-start side of the line across one of its extensions and *start*.

(d) Failure of a yacht to see or hear her recall signal shall not relieve her of her obligation to *start* correctly.

51.2 A yacht shall *sail* the course so as to round or pass each *mark* on the required side in correct sequence, and so that a string representing her wake, from the time she *starts* until she *finishes*, would, when drawn taut, lie on the required side of each *mark*, touching each rounding *mark*. When she fails to do so, she may correct her error before she *finishes* by making her course conform to this rule.

51.3 A *mark* has a required side for a yacht as long as she is on a leg that it begins, bounds or ends, except that a starting *mark* begins to have a required side when she is approaching the starting line from its pre-start side to *start*, and a finishing *mark* ceases to have a required side when she *finishes*.

51.4 It is not necessary for a yacht to cross the finishing line completely; after *finishing*, she may clear it in either direction.

52 Touching a Mark

52.1 A yacht shall neither:

(a) touch:

(i) a starting *mark* before *starting*; or

(ii) a *mark* that begins, bounds or ends the leg of the course on which she is *sailing*; or

(iii) a finishing *mark* after *finishing* and before clearing the finishing line and *marks;* nor

(b) cause a *mark* or *mark* vessel to shift to avoid being touched.

52.2 (a) When a yacht infringes rule 52.1, she may exonerate herself by, as soon as possible, *sailing* well clear of all other yachts and, while remaining clear, immediately making one complete 360° turn including one *tack* and one *gybe*.

(b) When a yacht touches a finishing *mark*, she shall not be recorded as having *finished* until she completes her turn and returns wholly to the course side of the line, and then *finishes*.

52.3 When a yacht is wrongfully compelled by another yacht to infringe rule 52.1, she shall be exonerated:

(a) by the retirement of the other yacht (or by the other yacht accepting an alternative penalty when so prescribed in the sailing instructions) in acknowledgement of the infringement; or

(b) in accordance with rule 74.4(a)(ii) after lodging a valid *protest*.

53 Anchoring, Making Fast and Hauling Out

53.1 LIMITATIONS ON MAKING FAST AND HAULING OUT
When *racing*, a yacht may anchor, but shall neither make fast or be made fast by means other than anchoring, nor be hauled out, except for the purpose of rule 55, or to effect repairs, reef sails or bail out.

53.2 MEANS OF ANCHORING
Means of anchoring may include the crew standing on the bottom or any weight lowered to the bottom. A yacht shall recover any anchor or weight used before continuing in the race, unless, after making every effort, she fails to do so. In this case she shall report the circumstances to the race committee, which shall penalise her when it considers the loss due either to inadequate gear or to insufficient effort to recover it.

54 Propulsion

54.1 BASIC RULE
Except when permitted by rule 54.3, a yacht shall compete only by *sailing*, and her crew shall not otherwise move their bodies to propel the yacht. Fundamental Rule A and rule 55 override rule 54.

54.2 PROHIBITED ACTIONS
Without limiting the application of rule 54.1, these actions are prohibited:

(a) pumping: repeated fanning of any sail either by trimming and releasing the sail or by vertical or athwartships body movement;

(b) rocking: repeated rolling of the yacht, induced either by body movement or adjustment of the sails or centreboard, that does not facilitate steering;

(c) ooching: sudden forward body movement, stopped abruptly;

(d) sculling: repeated movement of the helm not necessary for steering;

(e) repeated *tacks* or *gybes* unrelated to changes in the wind or to tactical considerations.

54.3 EXCEPTIONS

(a) A yacht's crew may move their bodies to exaggerate the rolling that facilitates steering the yacht through a *tack* or a *gybe*, provided that, at the moment the *tack* or *gybe* is completed, the yacht's speed is not greater than it would have been in the absence of the *tack* or *gybe*.

(b) On a free leg of the course, when surfing (rapidly accelerating down the leeward side of a wave) or planing is possible, the yacht's crew may, in order to initiate surfing or planing, pump the sheet and the guy controlling any sail, but only once for each wave or gust of wind.

54.4 CLASS RULES
Class rules may alter rule 54.

55 Aground or Foul of an Obstruction

A yacht, after grounding or fouling another vessel or other object, is subject to rule 56 and may, in getting clear, use her own anchors, boats, ropes, spars and other gear; may send out an anchor in a boat; may be refloated by her crew going overboard either to stand on the bottom or to go ashore to push off; but may receive outside assistance only from the crew of the vessel fouled. When a yacht fails to recover all her own gear, she shall report the circumstances to the race committee, which shall penalise her when it considers the loss due to insufficient effort to recover it.

56 Manual and Stored Power

A yacht's standing rigging, running rigging, spars and movable hull appendages shall be adjusted and operated by manual power only, and no device shall be used for these operations that derives assistance from stored energy for doing work. A power winch or windlass may be used in weighing anchor or in getting clear after running aground or fouling any object, and a power pump may be used in an auxiliary yacht.

57 Boarding

Unless otherwise prescribed in the sailing instructions, no person shall board a yacht, except for the purposes of Fundamental Rule A or to attend an injured or ill member of the crew or temporarily as one of the crew of a vessel fouled.

58 Leaving, Crew Overboard

Unless otherwise prescribed in the sailing instructions, no person on board a yacht when she begins *racing* shall leave, unless injured or ill, or for the purposes of Fundamental Rule A, except that any member of the crew may fall overboard or leave her to swim, stand on the bottom as a means of anchoring, haul her out ashore to effect repairs, reef sails or bail out, or to help her to get clear after grounding or fouling another vessel or object, provided that this person is back on board before the yacht continues in the race.

59 Outside Assistance

Except as permitted by Fundamental Rule A and rules 55 and 57, a yacht shall neither receive outside assistance nor use any gear other than that on board when her preparatory signal was made.

60 Personal Buoyancy

60.1 It shall be the individual responsibility of each competitor to wear adequate personal buoyancy when conditions warrant. A wet-suit is not adequate personal buoyancy.

60.2 Unless otherwise prescribed in the sailing instructions, when Code flag 'Y' is displayed before or with the warning signal, life-jackets or other adequate personal buoyancy shall be worn while *racing* by all competitors.

61 Clothing and Equipment

61.1 (a) Except as permitted by rule 61.2, a competitor shall not wear or carry clothing or equipment for the purpose of increasing his weight.

(b) Furthermore, the total weight of clothing and equipment worn or carried by a competitor shall not be capable of exceeding 15 kilograms when weighed as provided in Appendix A4, unless class rules or the sailing instructions prescribe a lesser or greater weight, in which case such weight shall apply, except that it shall not exceed 20 kilograms.

61.2 When so prescribed by the class rules, weight jackets of non-metallic material (excepting normal fasteners), with or without pockets, compartments or containers, shall be permitted, provided that the jacket:

(a) is permanently buoyant;

(b) does not extend more than 30 mm above the competitor's shoulders;

(c) is worn outside all other clothing and equipment; and

(d) can be removed by the competitor in less than ten seconds;

and that ballast carried in the pockets, compartments or containers shall only be water. For the purpose of rule 61.1(b), the pockets, compartments and containers shall be filled completely with water and included in the total weight.

61.3 When protested or selected for inspection, a competitor shall produce all containers referred to in rule 61.2 that were carried while *racing*.

61.4 Unless otherwise prescribed by the sailing instructions, rule 61.1(b) shall not apply in events for cruiser-racer type yachts required to be equipped with lifelines.

62 Increasing Stability

(a) Unless otherwise prescribed by the class rules, a yacht shall not use any device, such as a trapeze or plank, to project outboard the weight of any of the crew.

(b) When lifelines are required by the class rules or the sailing instructions, no crew member shall station any part of his torso outside them, except when it is necessary to perform a task, and then only temporarily. On yachts equipped with upper and lower lifelines of wire, a crew member sitting on the deck facing outboard with his waist inside the lower lifeline may have the upper part of his body outside the upper lifeline.

63 Skin Friction

A yacht:

(a) shall not eject or release from a container any substance (such as polymer); or

(b) unless otherwise prescribed by her class rules, shall not have specially textured hull or appendage surfaces;

the purpose of which is, or could be, to reduce the frictional resistance of her surface by altering the character of the flow of water inside the boundary layer.

64 Setting and Sheeting Sails

64.1 CHANGING SAILS
While changing headsails and spinnakers, a replacing sail may be fully set and trimmed before the sail it replaces is taken in, but only one mainsail and, except when changing, only one spinnaker shall be carried set.

64.2 SPINNAKER POLES AND WHISKER POLES
Only one spinnaker pole or whisker pole shall be used at a time and, when in use, shall be attached to the foremost mast.

64.3 USE OF OUTRIGGERS

(a) No sail shall be sheeted over or through an outrigger, except as permitted in rule 64.3(b). An outrigger is any fitting or other device so placed that it could exert outward pressure on a sheet or sail at a point from which, with the yacht upright, a vertical line would fall outside the hull or deck planking. For the purpose of this rule: bulwarks, rails and rubbing strakes are not part of the hull or deck planking. A boom of a boomed headsail that requires no adjustment when *tacking* is not an outrigger.

(b) (i) Any sail may be sheeted to or led above a boom regularly used for a working sail and permanently attached to the mast from which the head of the working sail is set.

(ii) A headsail may be sheeted or attached at its clew to a spinnaker pole or whisker pole, provided that a spinnaker is not set.

64.4 HEADSAILS
The following distinction shall apply between spinnakers and headsails. A headsail is a sail in which the mid-girth, measured from the mid-points of the luff and leech, does not exceed 50% of the length of the foot, and in which any other intermediate girth does not exceed a value similarly proportional to its distance from the head of the sail. A sail tacked down abaft the foremost mast is not a headsail.

64.5 CLASS RULES
Class rules may alter rule 64.

65 Fog Signals and Lights

When safe pilotage requires, every yacht shall sound fog signals and exhibit lights as required by the International Regulations for Preventing Collisions at Sea or applicable government rules.

(Numbers 66 and 67 are spare numbers)

Part VI—**Protests, Penalties and Appeals**

SECTION A—**Initiation of Action**

68 Protests by Yachts

68.1 RIGHT TO PROTEST

A yacht can protest any other yacht, except that a *protest* for an alleged infringement of the rules of Part IV can be made only by a yacht directly involved in or witnessing an incident.

68.2 INFORMING THE PROTESTED YACHT

During a race, a yacht that is directly involved in an incident and intends to protest shall immediately inform the other yacht by hailing 'Protest' or words to that effect. In all other cases, a yacht intending to protest shall try at the first reasonable opportunity so to inform the other yacht.

68.3 PROTEST FLAG REQUIREMENTS

(a) During a race, a yacht intending to protest another yacht shall conspicuously display Code flag 'B' or a red rectangular flag. Either flag is acceptable, irrespective of any alteration to this rule made in the sailing instructions.

(b) The flag shall be displayed at the first reasonable opportunity, which normally is immediately after the incident.

(c) (i) Except as provided in rule 68.3(c)(ii), the flag shall be displayed until the yacht *finishes* or, when the first opportunity occurs after *finishing*, until acknowledged by the race committee.

(ii) In the case of a yacht sailed single-handed, it will be sufficient to display the flag at the first reasonable opportunity after the incident and to have it acknowledged by the race committee when the protesting yacht *finishes*.

(d) When the yacht retires, the flag shall be displayed until she has informed the race committee or has left the vicinity of the course.

68.4 EXCEPTION TO PROTEST REQUIREMENTS

A yacht may protest another yacht without having displayed a protest flag or hailed when either:

(a) she has no knowledge of the facts justifying a *protest* until she has *finished* or retired; or

(b) having been a witness not directly involved in the incident, she learns that a yacht that displayed a protest flag has failed to lodge a valid *protest* in accordance with rule 33(a) or rule 52.3(b).

request is lodged before 1800 on the day following the decision, unless the *protest committee* has reason to extend this time limit.

(b) When the hearing of a *protest* is reopened, a majority of the members of the *protest committee* shall, when possible, be members of the original *protest committee*.

74 Decisions and Penalties

74.1 FINDING OF FACTS

The *protest committee* shall determine the facts and base its decision upon them. The finding of facts shall not be subject to appeal.

74.2 CONSIDERATION OF REDRESS

(a) When consideration of redress has been initiated as provided in rule 69 or rule 70.3, the *protest committee* shall decide whether the finishing place of a yacht has been materially prejudiced through no fault of her own in any of the circumstances set out in rule 69.

(b) If so, the *protest committee* shall satisfy itself by taking appropriate evidence, especially before *abandoning* the race, that it is aware of the relevant facts and of the probable consequences of any arrangement to all yachts concerned for that particular race and for the series, if any, as a whole.

(c) The *protest committee* shall then make as equitable an arrangement as possible for all yachts concerned. This may be to let the results of the race stand, to adjust the points score or the finishing time of the prejudiced yacht, to *abandon* the race or to adopt some other means.

74.3 MEASUREMENT PROTESTS

(a) A *protest* under rule 20 or class rules that a measurement, scantling or flotation rule has been infringed while *racing*, or that a classification or rating certificate is invalid, may be decided by the *protest committee* immediately after the hearing, provided that it is satisfied there is no reasonable doubt as to the interpretation or application of the rules. When the *protest committee* is not so satisfied, it shall refer the question, together with the facts found, to an authority qualified to resolve such questions. The *protest committee*, in making its decision, shall be governed by the report of the authority.

(b) In addition to the requirements of rule 74.6, the body that issued the certificate of the yacht concerned shall also be notified.

(c) When an appeal under rule 77 is lodged, the yacht may compete in further races, but subject to the results of that appeal.

74.4 PENALTIES AND EXONERATION

(a) When the *protest committee* after finding the facts, or the race committee or *protest committee* acting under rule 70.1, decides that:

(i) a yacht has infringed any of the *rules*; or

(ii) as a consequence of her infringement of any of the *rules*, a yacht has compelled other yachts to infringe any of the *rules*;

she shall be disqualified, unless the sailing instructions applicable to that race provide some other penalty, and, in the case of (ii), the other yachts shall be exonerated. Such disqualification or other penalty shall be imposed irrespective of whether the *rule* that led to the disqualification or penalty was mentioned in the *protest*, or the yacht that was at fault was mentioned or protested; e.g. the protesting yacht or a third yacht may be disqualified and the protested yacht exonerated.

(b) When a yacht infringes a *rule* when not *racing*, her penalty shall apply to the race sailed nearest to the time of the infringement.

74.5 SCORING

(a) A yacht whose entry has been accepted and that *starts* or *sails* about in the vicinity of the starting line between her preparatory and starting signals shall be scored as a competing yacht.

(b) When a yacht either is disqualified or has retired after *finishing*, the following yachts shall each be moved up one place.

(c) When a yacht is penalised by being removed from a series or a part of a series, no races are to be re-scored and no changes are to be made in the scores of other yachts, except that, when the incident from which the penalty resulted occurred in a particular race, she shall be disqualified from that race and the yachts *finishing* behind her in that race shall each be moved up one place.

(d) When a scoring system provides that one or more scores are to be excluded in calculating a yacht's total score, a disqualification under Fundamental Rule C, Fundamental Rule D or rule 54 shall not be excluded.

74.6 THE DECISION

(a) After making its decision, the *protest committee* shall promptly communicate the following to the *parties to the protest*:

(i) the facts found;

(ii) the *rule* or *rules* judged applicable;

(iii) the decision and grounds on which it is based;

(iv) the yacht or yachts penalised, if any; and

(v) the penalty imposed, if any, or the redress granted, if any.

(b) A *party to the protest* may request, in writing, a written decision within seven days of the oral decision. The *protest committee* shall promptly transmit to the party the above details and, unless irrelevant, its endorsed diagram of the incident.

SECTION C—**Special Rules**

75 Gross Infringement of Rules or Misconduct

75.1 PENALTIES BY THE RACE COMMITTEE OR PROTEST COMMITTEE

(a) The race committee or *protest committee* may call a hearing when it has reasonable grounds for believing that a competitor has committed a gross infringement of the *rules* or a gross breach of good manners or sportsmanship.

(b) When the *protest committee* finds that there has been a gross infringement of the *rules* or a gross breach of good manners or sportsmanship, it may exclude a competitor, and a yacht when appropriate, either from further participation in a series, or from the whole series, or take other disciplinary action within its jurisdiction. The committee shall report any penalty imposed to its national authority, to that of the competitor, and to that of the yacht.

(c) No action shall be taken under this rule without a written statement of allegation and a hearing held in accordance with the rules of Part VI, Section B, by a *protest committee* consisting of at least three members.

75.2 PENALTIES BY THE NATIONAL AUTHORITY

(a) Upon a receipt of a report of gross infringement of the *rules* or a gross breach of good manners or sportsmanship, or a report of a penalty imposed under rule 75.1(b), a national authority may conduct an investigation and, when appropriate, a hearing and take such disciplinary action as it deems appropriate against the persons or yachts involved. Such action may include:

(i) suspension of eligibility to compete in any event held in its juridiction for any period; and

(ii) suspension of IYRU eligibility in accordance with Appendix A1, paragraph 5.1(a).

(b) The national authority shall promptly report all suspensions of eligibility under this rule to the IYRU and, when the competitor or the owner of the yacht is not a member of the suspending national authority, to the national authority of the competitor and that of the owner. The IYRU shall inform all national authorities, which may also suspend the competitors' eligibility for events held in their jurisdictions.

75.3 PENALTIES BY THE IYRU

Upon receipt of a report of suspension of a competitor's eligibility by a national authority under rule 75.2(a)(i), the IYRU Executive Committee shall suspend the competitor's IYRU eligibility in accordance with Appendix A1, paragraph 5.1(a).

76 Liability

76.1 DAMAGES
The question of damages arising from an infringement of any of the *rules* shall be governed by the prescriptions, if any, of the national authority.

76.2 MEASUREMENT EXPENSES
Unless otherwise prescribed by the *protest committee*, the fees and expenses entailed by a *protest* on measurement or classification shall be paid by the unsuccessful party.

SECTION D—**Appeals**

77 Right of Appeal and Decisions

77.1 RIGHT OF APPEAL
Except when the right of appeal has been denied in accordance with rule 1.5(a) or (b), a *party to a protest* may appeal a decision of a *protest committee* to the national authority concerned. A race committee that is a *party to a protest* may appeal only the decision of a jury.

77.2 RIGHT OF REFERENCE
A *protest committee* may refer its own decision to the national authority for confirmation or correction of its interpretation of the *rules*. A reference shall contain the *protest committee's* decision and the relevant documents listed in rule 78.1(b).

77.3 QUESTIONS OF INTERPRETATION
When no *protest* that may be appealed is involved, a national authority may answer questions from a club or other organisation affiliated to the national authority. A question shall contain sufficient detail for an interpretation to be made.

77.4 INTERPRETATION OF RULES
Appeals, references and questions shall be made only on interpretations of the *rules*. The national authority shall accept the *protest committee's*

finding of facts, except that, when it is not satisfied with the facts presented, it may direct the *protest committee* to provide additional information or to reopen the hearing and report any new finding of facts.

77.5 INTERESTED PARTIES

No *interested party* or member of the *protest committee* shall take any part in the discussion or decision upon an appeal or reference.

77.6 DECISIONS

(a) A national authority may uphold, alter or reverse a *protest committee's* decision, declare the *protest* invalid or return the *protest* for a new hearing and decision by the same or a different *protest committee*.

(b) When, from the facts found by the *protest committee*, it believes that any yacht that was a *party to the protest* infringed a *rule*, it shall penalise her, irrespective of whether that yacht or that *rule* was mentioned in the decision.

(c) The decision of the national authority shall be final, and shall be transmitted in writing by the national authority to all *parties to the protest* and the *protest committee*, who shall be bound by the decision.

78 Appeal Procedures

78.1 APPELLANT'S RESPONSIBILITIES

(a) Within 15 days of receiving the *protest committee's* written decision or its decision not to reopen a hearing, the appellant shall transmit to the national authority the dated appeal, which shall include the grounds for the appeal, i.e. why the appellant believes the *protest committee's* interpretation of the *rules* to be incorrect, a copy of the *protest committee's* decision and any fee required under rule 78.6.

(b) Any of the following documents in the appellant's possession shall be sent with the appeal or as soon as possible thereafter:

(i) the protest form(s);

(ii) a diagram, prepared or endorsed by the *protest committee*, showing the force and direction of the wind; the set and rate of the current or tidal stream, if any; the course to the next *mark*, or the *mark* itself, and the required side; the positions and tracks of all yachts involved; and, if relevant, the depth of the water;

(iii) the notice of race, the sailing instructions, any other conditions governing the event, and any amendments thereto;

(iv) any written statements submitted by the *parties to the protest* to the *protest committee*;

(v) any additional relevant documents; and

(vi) the names and addresses of all *parties to the protest* and the protest committee chairman.

78.2 NOTIFICATION OF THE PROTEST COMMITTEE
Upon receipt of a valid appeal, the national authority shall transmit a copy of the appeal and of the decision to the *protest committee*, informing the *protest committee* of the documents supplied by the appellant.

78.3 PROTEST COMMITTEE'S RESPONSIBILITIES
The *protest committee* shall transmit to the national authority the documents listed in rule 78.1(b) that were not supplied by the appellant.

78.4 NATIONAL AUTHORITY'S RESPONSIBILITIES
The national authority shall transmit copies of the appeal and of the decision to the other *parties to the protest*. It shall transmit to any *party to the protest* upon request any of the documents listed in rule 78.1(b). It shall transmit to the appellant copies of documents that were not supplied by the appellant.

78.5 COMMENTS
All *parties to the protest* and the *protest committee* may submit comments on the appeal to the national authority within a reasonable time. The national authority shall transmit such comments to all *parties to the protest* and to the *protest committee*.

78.6 FEE
A national authority may prescribe that a fee be paid for it to consider an appeal, reference or question.

78.7 WITHDRAWING AN APPEAL
An appellant may withdraw an appeal, at any time, by accepting the decision of the *protest committee*.

APPENDICES

The appendices to the rules have been divided into three groups, A, B and C. Group A appendices are those which always apply and which shall not be altered by national authority prescriptions, sailing instructions or class rules except insofar as each appendix permits. Appendices B1 and B2 apply when prescribed in the sailing instructions; Appendix B3 always applies, other Group B appendices apply when appropriate. All Group B appendices may be altered in accordance with rule 3.1. Group C appendices are advisory. When the rules of an appendix apply, they override any conflicting rule.

Appendix A1—Competitors' Eligibility Code

Actions by competitors before 1 January 1992 shall not affect their eligibility except those for which penalties were imposed before that date under rule 75.2.

1 Eligibility Rules of Class Associations and Organising Authorities

Subject to paragraphs 2 and 3, a class association or an organising authority may prescribe eligibility rules for its events, which shall be included in the notice of race and the sailing instructions.

2 Eligibility Rules of National Authorities

Subject to paragraph 3, a national authority may prescribe eligibility rules for events within its jurisdiction.

3 IYRU Eligibility Rules

To be eligible to compete in an event listed in paragraph 4, a competitor shall:

(a) be governed by the regulations and rules of the IYRU;

(b) be a member of a member national authority or one of its affiliated organisations. Such membership shall be established by the competitor:

- (i) being entered by the national authority of the country of which the competitor is a national or ordinarily a resident; or
- (ii) presenting a valid membership card or certificate, or other satisfactory evidence of identity and membership;

(c) not be under suspension of IYRU eligibility.

4 Events Requiring IYRU Eligibility

4.1 IYRU eligibility is required for the following:

(a) the yachting regatta of the Olympic Games;

(b) the yachting regattas of regional games recognised by the International Olympic Committee;

(c) events including 'IYRU' in their titles;

(d) the world and continental championships of IYRU international classes and of the Offshore Racing Council; and

(e) any other event approved by the IYRU as a world championship and so stated in the notice of race and sailing instructions.

4.2 IYRU eligibility may be required for any other event when so prescribed in the notice of race and sailing instructions with specific reference to Appendix A1.

5 Suspension of IYRU Eligibility

5.1 A competitor's IYRU eligibility shall be promptly suspended with immediate effect, permanently or for a specified period of time, after proper inquiry by the national authority of the competitor or by the IYRU Executive Committee:

(a) for any suspension of eligibility in accordance with rule 75.2;

(b) for infringing rule 17.1; or

(c) for competing, within the two years preceeding the inquiry, in an event that the competitor knew or should have known was a prohibited event.

5.2 A prohibited event is an event:

(a) allowing or requiring advertising beyond that permitted for Category B under Appendix A3 that is not approved as required by that appendix;

(b) in which cash or cashable prizes and/or appearance payments totalling more than US $10,000 (or its equivalent) may be received by any one yacht, that is not approved by the national authority of the venue or, for events conducted in more than one country, the IYRU; or

(c) that is described as a world championship, either in the title of the event or otherwise, and that is not approved by the IYRU. (IYRU approval is not required for world championships of IYRU international classes or of the Offshore Racing Council.)

5.3 When an event described in paragraph 5.2 has been approved as required, that fact shall be stated in the notice of race and sailing instructions.

6 Reports, Reviews, Notification and Appeals

6.1 When a national authority suspends a competitor's IYRU eligibility under paragraph 5.1, it shall promptly report the suspension and reasons therefor to the IYRU. The IYRU Executive Committee may revise or annul the suspension with immediate effect. The IYRU shall promptly notify all national authorities, international class associations, the Offshore Racing Council and other IYRU affiliated organisations of any suspension of a competitor's IYRU eligibility, or of its revision or annulment by the Executive Committee.

6.2 A competitor whose suspension of IYRU eligibility has been either imposed by a national authority, or imposed or revised by the IYRU Executive Committee, shall be advised of the right to appeal to the IYRU Review Board and be provided with a copy of the Review Board Rules of Procedure.

6.3 A national authority or the IYRU Executive Committee may request a review of its decision by the IYRU Review Board by complying with the Review Board Rules of Procedure.

6.4 The Review Board Rules of Procedure shall govern all appeals and requests for review.

6.5 Upon an appeal or request for review, the IYRU Review Board may confirm, revise or annul a suspension of eligibility, or require a hearing or re-hearing by the suspending authority.

6.6 Decisions of the Review Board are not subject to appeal.

6.7 The IYRU shall promptly notify all national authorities, international class associations and the Offshore Racing Council of all Review Board decisions.

7 Reinstatement of IYRU Eligibility

The IYRU Review Board may reinstate the IYRU eligibility of a competitor who:

(a) applies for reinstatement;

(b) establishes substantial, changed circumstances justifying reinstatement; and

(c) has completed a minimum of three years of suspension.

Appendix A2—**Banned Substances and Banned Methods**

Governmental requirements override any conflicting parts of this appendix.

Doping is the taking or using by a competitor of a substance or a method banned by the IYRU. Doping is governed by rule 17, this appendix, the Medical Lists *(containing the official lists of doping classes and methods, medicines that may be taken, and laboratories accredited for doping control) and* Doping Control Procedures *(the medical procedure leaflet).*

1 General

1.1 The IYRU publishes the *Medical Lists, Doping Control Procedures* and doping control forms which are available to national authorities and competitors on request.

1.2 The IYRU has adopted a schedule of penalties applicable in the event of a positive test or a refusal to be tested. This schedule is available on request.

2 Initiation of Doping Control

The IYRU or a national authority within its own jurisdiction may at any time initiate medical testing to control doping. A sampling officer shall be appointed to execute or supervise the procedure.

3 Selection at Events of Competitors to be Tested

3.1 (a) The *protest committee* shall select the finishing places of competitors to be tested each day. This may be by means of a draw or by such other arrangement as may be decided by the *protest committee*. When there is more than one competitor in each yacht, any or all may be selected.

(b) The IYRU or an initiating national authority may order a named competitor to be tested.

(c) A competitor may be tested more than once during an event.

3.2 The race committee shall give the sampling officer the names of those competitors who finished in the selected places.

4 Procedure

4.1 (a) The sampling officer or his representative shall inform a competitor by written notice, in confidence, that he has been selected for testing and is required to provide a urine sample at the time and place specified in the notice. The notice shall also specify the name of the sampling officer appointed for the event and of the designated laboratory to which specimens will be sent.

(b) The competitor shall acknowledge receipt of the notice, and the time of its delivery shall be recorded by the sampling officer or his representative.

(c) The competitor may be accompanied by one person of his choice.

(d) The *Medical Lists* and *Doping Control Procedures* shall be available to the competitor on request.

(e) A competitor who fails to appear at the appointed time and place or who refuses to provide a sample shall be removed, together with the yacht involved, from the event and all its results. The *protest committee* shall initiate a hearing in accordance with the rules of Part VI, Section B, to investigate the circumstances and report its findings to the IYRU or to the initiating national authority, and to the national authority of the competitor.

4.2 The doping control team shall act in accordance with *Doping Control Procedures* and shall explain the procedures to the competitor.

4.3 The competitor shall be given a copy of the doping control form and shall sign it to indicate that he has been informed of the procedures.

4.4 The competitor shall provide a postal (or fax) address at which, for the next 60 days, he may be informed of the result of the test of sample B.

4.5 Failure by a competitor to acknowledge receipt of the notice, to sign the form or to provide an address will not to be grounds for setting aside any penalty imposed for an infringement of rule 17.1.

5 Sampling and Results

5.1 The competitor shall provide a urine sample which will be divided into two samples, A and B, and sent to the designated laboratory.

5.2 When sample A is negative, the sampling officer shall so inform the competitor immediately and no further action shall be taken.

5.3 When sample A is positive:

(a) the initiating authority shall so inform the competitor and his national authority immediately. No race results shall be altered at this stage; and

(b) the laboratory will proceed to test sample B. The competitor or his representative may be present at the testing.

5.4 (a) When sample B is negative, the initiating authority shall so inform the competitor and his national authority, and no further action shall be taken.

(b) When no result has been obtained from sample B after 60 days from the date of the race, the test shall be considered void and no further action shall be taken.

5.5 When sample B is positive, the IYRU or the initiating national authority will, in writing, inform the competitor at the address provided (see paragraph 4.4) and his national authority. The IYRU will inform the national authority having jurisdiction over the event.

5.6 (a) Any positive result of a medical test shall be reported promptly by the initiating national authority to the IYRU.

(b) Any penalties imposed by the national authority for infringements of rule 17.1(a) or (b) shall promptly be reported to the IYRU.

6 Appeal Procedure

6.1 The competitor has 20 days from the date of the communication sent to him in accordance with paragraph 5.5 to appeal to the International Medical Commission (IMC) of the IYRU. When after 20 days the competitor has not appealed, his national authority and that of the event will be notified of this fact.

6.2 Upon expiry of the time for submitting an appeal, penalties will be applied, and the competitor and the yacht in which he was sailing shall be removed from the results of the event.

7 Exemptions

7.1 A competitor may request, in writing, prior approval from the IMC for the use of a banned substance or a banned method for special medical reasons. The reasons shall be stated and supported with medical evidence from a doctor.

7.2 In offshore races of more than 50 nautical miles, the use during the race of any banned substance or banned procedure for emergency medical treatment shall be reported promptly to the *protest committee*, which shall inform the appropriate national authority and the IYRU. The IMC may grant dispensation for such use.

8 Suspension of IYRU Eligibility

8.1 In addition to any penalty imposed under paragraph 1.2, a competitor who has infringed rule 17 may have his IYRU eligibility suspended in accordance with Appendix A1.

8.2 The competitor has the right to appeal as provided in Appendix A1.

9 Competitor's Expenses

Any expenses incurred in connection with this appendix by a competitor shall be his responsibility.

Appendix A3—**Advertising and Event Categories**

When governmental requirements conflict with this appendix, they override the conflicting parts of the appendix.

1 Definition of Advertising

For the purposes of this appendix, advertising is the name, logo, slogan, description, depiction, a variation or distortion thereof, or any other form of communication that promotes an organisation, person, product, service, brand or idea so as to call attention to it or to persuade persons or organisations to buy, approve or otherwise support it.

2 General

2.1 Advertisements and anything advertised shall meet generally accepted moral and ethical standards.

2.2 This appendix shall apply when *racing* and, in addition, unless otherwise prescribed in the notice of race, from 0700 on the first race day of a regatta until the expiry of the time limit for lodging *protests* following the last race of the regatta.

2.3 An event shall be designated Category A, B or C in its notice of race and sailing instructions, but when not so designated shall be Category A. However, at the world and continental championships of Olympic classes, Category B advertising shall be permitted on hulls and, for Olympic sailboard classes, on hulls and sails. After the notice of race has been published, the category shall not be changed within ninety days before the event without prior approval of the national authority of the organising authority.

2.4 The notice of race and sailing instructions for an event or the class rules or the rules of the Offshore Racing Council (ORC) may include rules for advertising that are more restrictive than those of the event's category.

2.5 Advertisements on sails shall be clearly separated from national letters and sail numbers.

2.6 When a *protest committee* after finding the facts decides that a yacht or her crew has infringed this appendix, the *protest committee* shall:

(a) warn the infringing yacht that a further infringement will result in disqualification; or

(b) disqualify the yacht in accordance with rule 74.4; or

(c) disqualify the yacht from more than one race or from the series when it decides that the infringement warrants a stronger penalty; or

(d) act in accordance with rule 75.1 when it decides that there may have been a gross infringement.

2.7 The IYRU, a national authority, a class association or the ORC may, for its events, subject to paragraph 5, authorise categories and may require a fee for doing so.

2.8 The IYRU or a national authority may, for its events, prescribe rules and require a fee for giving consent to individual yachts for advertisements, provided that such consents do not conflict with, when relevant, class rules or the rules of the ORC.

3 Category A

3.1 Advertising on yachts other than sailboards is permitted only as follows:

(a) One sailmaker's mark, which may include the name or mark of the sailcloth manufacturer and the pattern or model of the sail, may be displayed on both sides of any sail and shall fit within a 150 mm x 150 mm square. On sails other than spinnakers, no part of such mark shall be placed farther from the tack than the greater of 300 mm or 15% of the length of the foot.

(b) One builder's mark, which may include the name or mark of the designer, may be placed on the hull and one maker's mark may be displayed on spars and on each side of small equipment. Such marks shall fit within a 150 mm x 150 mm square.

(c) The yacht's type may be displayed on each side of her hull. Lettering shall not be higher than 1% or longer than 5% of the overall length of the yacht, to a maximum of 100 mm or 700 mm respectively.

(d) One maker's mark that fits within a square not exceeding 100 mm x 100 mm may be displayed at all times on each item of competitors' clothing and equipment. Other advertising may be displayed on clothing and equipment ashore.

(e) The organising authority of a sponsored event may permit or require the display of an advertisement of the event sponsor not larger than 2700 cm^2 in the form of a flag, and/or of a decal or sticker attached within the forward 25% of each side of the hull or to a dodger on each side of the yacht. In addition, when a sponsor supplies all hulls and sails at no cost to the organising authority or competitors, one advertisement not larger than 2700 cm^2 may be displayed on each side of the mainsail. For an event of a class association or the ORC, such advertising requires approval by the class association or the ORC and, when it so prescribes, by the national authority concerned. Notice of such permission or requirement shall be included in the notice of race and the sailing instructions.

3.2 Advertising on sailboards is permitted only as follows:

(a) One sailmaker's mark, which may include the name or mark of the sailcloth manufacturer and the pattern or model of the sail, may be displayed on both sides of the sail. No part of such mark shall be placed farther from the tack than 20% of the length of the foot of the sail, including the mast sleeve. The mark may also be displayed on the lower half of the part of the sail above the wishbone but no part of it shall be farther than 50 cm from the clew.

(b) The sailboard's type or manufacturer's name or logo may be placed on the hull in two places and on the upper third of the part of the sail above the wishbone. One maker's mark may be displayed on spars, on each side of small equipment and on a competitor's clothing and harness.

(c) The organising authority of a sponsored event may permit or require the display of an advertisement of the event sponsor on both sides of the sail between the sail numbers and the wishbone and on a bib worn by the competitor. For an event of a class association, such advertising requires approval by the class association and, when it so prescribes, by the national authority concerned. Notice of such permission or requirement shall be included in the notice of race and the sailing instructions.

4 Category B

A yacht competing in a Category B event may display advertising only as permitted for Category A and by paragraph 4.1 (for yachts other than sailboards) or paragraph 4.2 (for sailboards) and shall not display advertising chosen by the yacht of more than two organisations or persons. A Category B advertisement shall be either one or two of the name of an organisation or person, a brand or product name, and a logo.

4.1 ADVERTISING ON YACHTS OTHER THAN SAILBOARDS

(a) The forward 25% of each side of the hull may display not more than two advertisements chosen by the IYRU, the national authority, the class association or the ORC, for its event; or by the organising authority of the event when it wishes to display advertising of an event sponsor. When both the organising authority and one of the other organisations wish to use the space, they shall each be entitled to one-half of the length of the space on each side. The remaining length of the hull shall be free of any advertising except as permitted by paragraph 3.1(b) and except that one-half of that length may be used for advertising chosen by the yacht.

(b) Advertising chosen by the yacht may be displayed on sails as follows:

(i) Advertising on spinnakers is without restriction except as provided in paragraphs 2.5 and 4.

(ii) On other sails, only one advertisement may be carried at any one time, and it may be on both sides of one sail. It shall be placed below the national letters and sail numbers and have a width no greater than two-thirds of the length of the foot of the sail and a height no greater than one-third of that width.

(c) Advertising chosen by the yacht on the mainmast or main boom shall be limited to the name, brand or product name, or logo of one organisation. The space within one-third of the length of the mast and two-thirds of the length of the boom may be used.

(d) In addition to the advertisements carried on the yacht, advertisements limited to the organisation(s) advertising on the yacht and one or two additional organisations may be displayed on the clothing and equipment worn by competitors.

4.2 ADVERTISING ON SAILBOARDS

(a) The forward 25% of the hull may display not more than two advertisements chosen by the IYRU, the national authority or the class association, for its event; or by the organising authority of the event when it wishes to display advertising of an event sponsor. When both the organising authority and one of the other organisations wish to use the space, they shall each be entitled to one-half of the length of the space on each side. Advertising chosen by the competitor may be displayed within the remaining length of the hull.

(b) That part of the sail below the wishbone not used for Category A advertising may display advertising chosen by the competitor.

(c) In addition to the advertisements carried on the sailboard, advertisements limited to the organisation(s) advertising on the sailboard and one or two additional organisations may be displayed on the clothing and equipment worn by competitors.

5 Category C

Rules for an event governing advertising beyond that permitted for Category B shall be prescribed in the notice of race and sailing instructions and be:

(a) approved by the national authority of the event's venue when the event is not international, or is international and held at a single venue; or

(b) approved by the IYRU when the event is conducted in more than one country.

When such an event has been approved, that fact shall be stated in the notice of race and sailing instructions.

Appendix A4—**Weighing of Wet Clothing**

1 To test the weight of clothing and equipment worn by a competitor all items to be weighed shall be taken off and thoroughly soaked in water. Equipment includes items such as trapeze harness, life-jacket and heavy jacket.

2 The manner in which the clothing and equipment are arranged on the rack has a considerable effect on the weight recorded, and it is important that free draining be achieved without the formation of pools of water in the clothing. It is recommended that a rack comprised of 'clothes hanger' type bars be used and that provision be made for suspending boots or shoes in an inverted position.

3 Pockets in clothing that are designed to be self-draining, i.e. those that have drain holes and no provision for closing them, shall be empty during the weighing; however, pockets or equipment designed to hold water as ballast shall be full when weighing takes place. Boots and shoes shall be empty when weighed.

4 Ordinary clothing becomes saturated within a few seconds but 'heavy jackets' of the water-absorbent type require longer and should be immersed for not less than two minutes.

5 On removal from the water the items shall be allowed to drain freely for one minute, at the end of which period the weight shall be recorded.

6 When the weight recorded exceeds the amount permitted, the measurer may allow the competitor to repeat the test twice by rearranging the clothing and equipment on the rack, re-soaking and re-weighing. When a lesser weight results, that weight shall be taken as the actual weight of clothing and equipment.

7 A competitor who is wearing a dry-suit may accept an alternative means of establishing the weight of clothing and equipment as follows:

(a) the dry-suit and any items of clothing and equipment that are worn outside the dry-suit shall be weighed according to paragraphs 1 to 6;

(b) any clothing underneath the dry-suit shall be weighed without draining as it was worn while *racing*; and

(c) the two weights shall be added together for a total weight.

Appendix A5—**International Juries**

An organising authority may appoint an international jury from whose decisions there shall be no appeal, in accordance with rules 1.4 and 1.5, provided that the jury remains constituted as stated herein.

1 Constitution

1.1 An international jury shall consist of a chairman, a vice-chairman, and other members sufficient for a total membership of at least five.

1.2 When the membership is reduced below the required minimum by illness or emergency, and no qualified replacements are available, the jury remains properly constituted provided that it consists of at least three members, all from different countries (in Group M, South and West South America, and Group N, Central and East South America, two may be from one country).

1.3 When it is considered desirable that some members should not participate in the discussion and decision of a *protest*, and at least three members remain, the jury remains properly constituted. For the purpose of rule 71.2, members shall not be regarded as *interested parties* by reason of their nationality.

1.4 When the jury acts while not properly constituted, its decisions shall be subject to appeal.

2 Membership

2.1 The officers and other members of the jury shall be appointed by the organising authority, subject to approval by the national authority when so required in accordance with rule 1.4(d), from amongst experienced yachtsmen having extensive knowledge of the *rules* and *protest committee* experience. In addition, a secretary without vote may be appointed.

2.2 The jury shall be separate from and independent of the race committee and shall not include any member of the race committee.

2.3 A majority shall be international judges certified by the IYRU.

2.4 Not more than two members (three when the event is held in Group M, South and West South America, or Group N, Central and East South America) shall be from the same country, except that, when there is more than one panel, the requirements for the membership of a jury shall apply to each panel and not to the jury as a whole.

3 Functions

3.1 To determine whether *protests* are valid or invalid.

3.2 To conduct hearings and decide *protests* in accordance with the rules of Part VI.

3.3 To penalise yachts in accordance with rule 70.1(b).

3.4 To call hearings in accordance with rule 70.2.

3.5 To initiate considerations of redress in accordance with rule 70.3.

3.6 To reopen hearings in accordance with rule 73.6.

3.7 When requested, to assist the race committee or the organising authority, particularly on such matters as may directly affect the fairness of the competition.

3.8 Unless otherwise specifically directed by the organising authority:

(a) to decide questions of eligibility, measurement or ratings of yachts.

(b) to authorise the substitution of competitors, yachts, sails or equipment.

3.9 When specifically directed by the organising authority:

(a) to initiate or authorise changes in or additions to the sailing instructions.

(b) to supervise or direct the race committee in the conduct of the races.

(c) to deal with such other matters as may be requested.

4 Procedures

4.1 Decisions of the jury shall be made by a simple majority vote, each member having one vote. When there is an equality of votes cast, the chairman of the meeting shall be entitled to an additional vote.

4.2 The jury may be divided into panels of at least five members each, of which a majority shall be international judges certified by the IYRU. When a panel fails to agree on a decision, it may adjourn and refer the *protest* to the full jury.

4.3 When the national authority prescribes that its approval is required for the appointment of an international jury, its approval shall be included in the notice of race or the sailing instructions, or be posted on the official notice board.

Appendix B1—**Alternative Penalties for Infringing a Rule of Part IV**

The 720° turns penalty is most satisfactory for small yachts sailing relatively short races, when the penalty usually will affect a yacht's finishing place. The scoring penalty is satisfactory for any racing because it always affects a yacht's finishing place, with uniform results. Both systems keep yachts ***racing****.*

The 720° turns penalty can be made applicable by including a statement in the sailing instructions such as 'The 720° turns penalty, Appendix B1 of the racing rules, will apply.' The scoring penalty can be made applicable by including a statement such as 'The scoring penalty, Appendix B1 of the racing rules, will apply. The penalty will be ____ places.' or 'The penalty will be the number of places equal to 20% of the number of yachts entered.'

1 720° Turns Penalty

1.1 A yacht that may have infringed a rule of Part IV while *racing* and that wishes to exonerate herself by accepting a 720° turns penalty shall, as soon as possible after the incident, *sail* well clear of all other yachts and, while remaining clear, immediately make two complete 360° turns (720°) in the same direction, including two *tacks* and two *gybes*. When in the same incident she has infringed rule 52.1, she need not make an additional turn to exonerate herself.

1.2 When the incident occurs at the finishing line, she shall not be recorded as having *finished* until she completes her turns and returns wholly to the course side of the line, and then *finishes*.

1.3 When a yacht complies with some but not all of the requirements of paragraph 1.1 or 1.2, other yachts involved in the incident will not be penalised under rule 33.

1.4 A yacht that accepts a 720° turns penalty may protest with respect to the same incident. She shall not be penalised further for an infringement for which she accepted the penalty, except as provided by paragraph 1.5.

1.5 The *protest committee* shall disqualify a yacht that has accepted a 720° turns penalty when it decides that she infringed a rule and that her infringement resulted in serious damage or in her gaining a significant advantage.

2 Scoring Penalty

2.1 A yacht that may have infringed a rule of Part IV while *racing* and that wishes to exonerate herself by accepting a scoring penalty shall:

(a) display Code flag 'I' or a yellow rectangular flag at the first reasonable opportunity, which normally is immediately after the incident;

(b) except for a yacht sailed single-handed, keep it displayed until she has *finished*;

(c) call the race committee's attention to her flag at the finishing line at the first reasonable opportunity; and

(d) identify to the race committee the yacht infringed against at the finishing line if practicable; otherwise, at the first reasonable opportunity within the time limit for lodging *protests*.

When in the same incident she has infringed rule 52.1, she need not make a 360° turn to exonerate herself.

Her penalty score shall be the score for the place worse than her actual finishing place by the number of places prescribed in the sailing instructions, except that she shall not be scored worse than 'Did not finish'. When the sailing instructions do not prescribe the number of places, the number shall be the whole number (rounding 0.5 upward) nearest to 20% of the number of yachts entered. The scores of other yachts shall not be changed; therefore two yachts may receive the same score.

2.2 A yacht that displays a penalty flag shall comply with paragraphs 2.1(b), (c) and (d).

2.3 When a yacht displays a penalty flag, other yachts involved in the incident will not be penalised under rule 33.

2.4 A yacht that accepts a scoring penalty may protest with respect to the same incident, but her penalty shall not be affected, except as provided by paragraph 2.5.

2.5 The *protest committee* shall disqualify a yacht that has accepted a scoring penalty when it decides that she infringed a rule and that her infringement resulted in serious damage or in her gaining a significant advantage.

Appendix B2—**Scoring Systems**

The two scoring systems most often used are the bonus-points (formerly the Olympic) and the low-point. The bonus-points system has been adopted for many class championships; the low-point system is suitable both for championships and for club and other small fleet racing, and is somewhat easier to use for race committees and competitors.

In both systems, lower points designate better finishing places. The low-point system uses a 'straight line' points schedule that rewards performance in direct proportion to finishing place; the bonus-points system uses a 'curved' points schedule that provides an additional reward in the top six finishing places. Although designed primarily for scoring regattas, either system may be used for other series; see paragraph 3.

The sailing instructions may include a complete system verbatim or may incorporate either system by reference, with or without alterations, as explained in the notes following each system. See also Appendix C2, Instruction 19.

1 The Bonus-Points Scoring System

1.1 NUMBER OF RACES, MINIMUM REQUIRED, AND RACES TO COUNT
There will be seven races, of which five shall be completed to constitute a series. Each yacht's total score will be the sum of her scores for all races, excluding her worst score in accordance with rule 74.5(d). The lowest total score wins.

1.2 POINTS
Each yacht *finishing* in a race and not thereafter retiring or being disqualified will be scored points as follows:

Finishing Place	*Points*
First	0
Second	3
Third	5.7
Fourth	8
Fifth	10
Sixth	11.7
Seventh and thereafter	Place plus six

All other yachts, including a yacht that *finishes* and thereafter retires or is disqualified, will be scored points for the finishing place one more than the number of yachts entered in the series. Rule 74.5 also applies.

1.3 TIES

When there is a tie on total points between two or more yachts, the tie will be broken in favour of the yacht or yachts with the most first places, and, when the tie remains, the most second places, and so on, if necessary, for such races as count for total points. When the tie still remains, it shall stand as part of the final results. Rule 10 also applies. |

Notes:

(a) The sailing instructions can incorporate the bonus-points system by stating 'The bonus-points scoring system, Appendix B2.1 of the racing rules, will apply.'

(b) When the number of races is not seven, add 'except that ___ races are scheduled, of which ___ shall be completed to constitute a series'. (Insert the number of races.)

(c) When all races are to be counted, add 'except that each yacht's total score will be the sum of her scores for all races'.

2 The Low-Point Scoring System

2.1 NUMBER OF RACES, MINIMUM REQUIRED, AND RACES TO COUNT

The number of races scheduled and the number required to constitute a series shall be prescribed in the sailing instructions. Each yacht's total score will be the sum of her scores for all races, excluding her worst score in accordance with rule 74.5(d). The lowest total score wins.

2.2 POINTS

Each yacht *finishing* in a race and not thereafter retiring or being disqualified will be scored points equal to her finishing place, minus one-quarter point for first place, as follows:

Finishing Place	*Points*
First	0.75
Second	2
Third	3
Fourth	4
and so on.	

All other yachts, including a yacht that *finishes* and thereafter retires or is disqualified, will be scored points for the finishing place one more than the number of yachts entered in the series. Rule 74.5 also applies. |

2.3 TIES

When there is a tie on total points between two or more yachts, the tie will be broken in favour of the yacht or yachts with the most first places, and, when the tie remains, the most second places, and so on, if necessary, for such races as count for total points. When the tie still remains, it shall stand as part of the final results. Rule 10 also applies. |

Notes:

(d) The sailing instructions can incorporate the low-point system by stating 'The low-point scoring system, Appendix B2.2 of the racing rules, will apply, with ___ races scheduled, of which ___ shall be completed to constitute a series.' (Insert the numbers of races.)

(e) When all races are to be counted, add 'except that each yacht's total score will be the sum of her scores for all races'.

3 Suggested Alterations for a Series that is not a Regatta

3.1 In a regatta all yachts are expected to compete in all races, and the difference between the number of entrants and the number of starters is usually insignificant. However, in a longer series there may be a number of yachts that compete in fewer races than others, in which case it is suggested that the following be substituted for the last paragraph in either 1.2 or 2.2:

> A yacht that cannot be scored as a competing yacht in accordance with rule 74.5(a) will be scored points for the finishing place one more than the number of yachts entered in the series. All other yachts, including a yacht that *finishes* but thereafter retires or is disqualified, will be scored points for the finishing place one more than the number of yachts that were scored as competing yachts in accordance with rule 74.5(a) in that race.

3.2 When it is desired to increase the number of races to be excluded from each yacht's series score, change the second sentence in 1.1 or 2.1 to read: 'excluding her ___ worst scores'. (Insert the number.)

4 Guidance for Race and Protest Committees

4.1 ABBREVIATIONS FOR SCORING RECORDS

The following abbreviations are recommended to record the various occurrences that may determine a particular score:

DNC	Did not compete; i.e. was not scored as a competing yacht in accordance with rule 74.5(a).
DNS	Did not *start*; i.e. was a competing yacht in accordance with rule 74.5(a) but failed to *start*.
PMS	Started prematurely or otherwise failed to comply with the starting procedure.
DNF	Did not *finish*.
RET	Retired after *finishing*.
DSQ	Disqualified.
DND	Disqualification not discardable under rule 74.5(d).
YMP	Yacht materially prejudiced.

4.2 REDRESS

In applying rule 74.2, when it is deemed equitable to adjust the score of the prejudiced yacht by awarding points different from those she received for the race in question, the following possibilities are to be considered:

(a) points equal to the average, to the nearest tenth of a point (round 0.05 upward), of her points in all the races in the series except [her worst race and]* the race in question.

*Delete these words when all scores count for series results, or alter when more than one race is to be excluded.

(b) points equal to the average, to the nearest tenth of a point (round 0.05 upward), of her points in all the races before the race in question.

(c) an arbitrary number of points based on the position of the yacht in the race in question at the time she was prejudiced.

Appendix B3—**Identification — Class Insignia, National Letters and Numbers**

1 International Class Yachts

1.1 IDENTIFICATION

Every yacht of an international class recognised by the IYRU shall carry on her mainsail, and, as provided in paragraph 1.3(c), on her spinnaker:

(a) the insignia denoting the class to which she belongs.

(b) letters showing her nationality in accordance with the 'new' national letters below, except that until 31 March 1997, a sail measured before 1 April 1993 may carry the 'old' national letter or letters. National letters need not be carried in home waters, except in an international championship.

New	Nationality	Old	New	Nationality	Old
AHO	Netherlands Antilles	HA	CRO	Croatia	
ALG	Algeria	AL	CUB	Cuba	RC
AND	Andorra	AND	CYP	Cyprus	CP
ANG	Angola	AN	DEN	Denmark	D
ANT	Antigua	ANU	DJI	Djibouti	DJ
ARG	Argentina	A	DOM	Dominican Republic	DR
ARU	Aruba		ECU	Ecuador	EC
ASA	American Samoa	ASA	EGY	Egypt	AR
			ESA	El Salvador	
			ESP	Spain	E
AUS	Australia	KA	EST	Estonia	EST
AUT	Austria	OE	FIJ	Fiji	KF
BAH	Bahamas	BA	FIN	Finland	L
BAR	Barbados	KBA	FRA	France	F
BEL	Belgium	B	GBR	Great Britain	K
BER	Bermuda	KB	GER	Germany	G
BLS	Belarus		GRE	Greece	GR
BRA	Brazil	BL	GUA	Guatemala	GU
BRN	Bahrain	BH	GUM	Guam	GM
BUL	Bulgaria	BU	HKG	Hong Kong	KH
CAN	Canada	KC	HUN	Hungary	M
CAY	Grand Cayman	CI	INA	Indonesia	RI
CHI	Chile	X	IND	India	IND
CHN	China	CH	IRL	Ireland	IR
COL	Colombia	CB	ISL	Iceland	IL
CRC	Costa Rica	CR	ISR	Israel	IS

ISV	U.S. Virgin Islands	VI	POR	Portugal	P
ITA	Italy	I	PRK	Korea DPR	DK
IVB	British Virgin Islands	KV	PUR	Puerto Rico	PR
JAM	Jamaica	KJ	QAT	Qatar	QA
JPN	Japan	J	ROM	Romania	RM
KEN	Kenya	KK	RSA	Republic of South Africa	SA
KOR	Korea	RK	RUS	Russia	
KUW	Kuwait	Q	SEN	Senegal	SE
LAT	Latvia		SEY	Seychelles	
LIE	Liechtenstein	FL	SIN	Singapore	KS
LTU	Lithuania	LIT	SLO	Slovenia	
LUX	Luxembourg	LX	SMR	San Marino	SM
MAR	Morocco	MA	SRI	Sri Lanka	CY
MAS	Malaysia	MY	SUD	Sudan	
MEX	Mexico	MX	SUI	Switzerland	Z
MLT	Malta	MT	SWE	Sweden	S
MON	Monaco	MO	TAH	Tahiti	T
MRI	Mauritius		TCH	Czechoslovakia	CZ
MYA	Myanmar	BR	THA	Thailand	TH
NAM	Namibia	NA	TPE	Chinese Taipei	TA
NED	Netherlands	H	TRI	Trinidad and Tobago	KT
NOR	Norway	N	TUN	Tunisia	TN
NZL	New Zealand	KZ	TUR	Turkey	TK
PAK	Pakistan	PK	UAE	United Arab Emirates	AE
PAR	Paraguay	PY	UKR	Ukraine	
PER	Peru	PU	URU	Uruguay	U
PHI	Philippines	PH	USA	United States of America	US
PNG	Papua New Guinea	KP	VEN	Venezuela	V
POL	Poland	PZ	ZIM	Zimbabwe	ZB

(c) a sail number allotted to her by her national authority or, when so prescribed by the class rules, by the international class association. Alternatively, when so prescribed by the class rules, an owner may be allotted a personal sail number by the relevant issuing authority, which may be used on all his yachts in that class.

1.2 SPECIFICATIONS

(a) National letters and sail numbers shall be:

(i) clearly visible, legible and, unless otherwise prescribed by the class rules, of a single colour that strongly contrasts with the sail;

(ii) capital letters and arabic numerals with lines that are continuous, without serifs; and

(iii) upright or with a slope of not less than 10:1 (ten vertical to one horizontal) relative to a line through their base;

(iv) thickness requirements shall not apply at junctions of strokes which, when appropriate, shall be chamfered.

(b) The sizes of national letters and sail numbers shall be related to the yacht's overall length as follows:

Overall Length	Minimum Height	Minimum width excluding numeral 1 and Letter I	Thickness Min.	Thickness Max.	Minimum space between adjoining letters and numerals or edge of sail
Under 3.5 m	230 mm	150 mm	30 mm	40 mm	45 mm
3.5 m - 8.5 m	300 mm	200 mm	40 mm	50 mm	60 mm
8.5 m - 11 m	375 mm	250 mm	50 mm	60 mm	75 mm
Over 11 m	450 mm	300 mm	60 mm	70 mm	90 mm

On yachts that carry letters and numerals larger than the minimum requirements, the maximum thickness may be correspondingly larger.

1.3 POSITIONING

Class insignia, national letters and sail numbers shall be positioned as follows:

(a) Unless otherwise prescribed by the class rules, the class insignia, national letters and sail numbers shall be above an imaginary line projecting at right angles to the luff from a point one-third of the distance, measured from the tack, to the head of the sail, and shall be placed at different heights on the two sides of the sail, those on the starboard side being uppermost.

(b) Unless otherwise prescribed by the class rules, the class insignia shall be placed above the national letters. Where the class insignia is of such a design that, when placed back to back on the two sides of the sail, they coincide, they may be so placed.

(c) The national letters and numbers only shall be similarly placed on both sides of the spinnaker, totally below an arc whose centre is the head of the spinnaker, and whose radius is 40% of the mean length of the two leeches and, when possible, totally above an arc of 60% of the mean length of the two leeches.

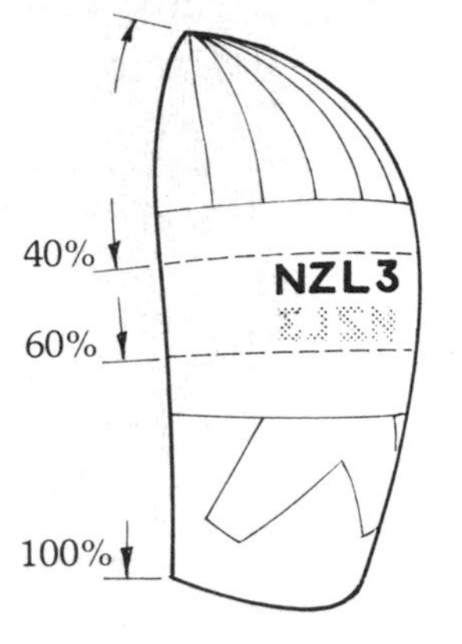

(d) National letters shall be placed in front of or above the sail numbers. When the national letters end in 'I' (e.g. Mauritius, Switzerland) and are placed in front of the numbers, they shall be separated from them by a horizontal line approximately 50 mm long.

2 Other Yachts

Other yachts shall comply with the rules of their national authority or class in regard to the allotment, carrying and size of insignia, letters and numbers, which rules shall, when practicable, conform to the above requirements.

3 Chartered or Loaned Yachts

When so prescribed in the notice of race or in the sailing instructions, a yacht chartered or loaned for an event may carry national letters or sail numbers in contravention of her class rules. In all other respects the sails shall comply with the class rules.

Appendix B4—**Sailboard Racing Rules**

Sailboard races shall be sailed under the International Yacht Racing Rules as altered by this appendix.

1 Part I—Fundamental Rules, Definitions and Alterations

1.1 The definitions of *leeward* and *windward* are deleted and replaced with:

Leeward and *Windward* - The *leeward* side of a sailboard is the side that is, or, when head to wind or directly down wind, was away from the wind. However, when *sailing* by the lee (i.e. with the wind coming over her stern from the side on which she is carrying the clew of her sail), the *leeward* side is the side on which she is carrying the clew. The opposite side is the *windward* side.

When neither of two sailboards on the same *tack* is *clear astern*, the one on the *leeward* side of the other is the *leeward sailboard*. The other is the *windward sailboard*.

1.2 In the definition of *mast abeam*, 'mainmast' is deleted and replaced with 'foot of the mast'.

1.3 Add the following definitions:

Capsized - A sailboard is *capsized* when her sail is in the water or when waterstarting.

Recovering - A sailboard is *recovering* from the time her sail or, when waterstarting, the competitor's body is out of the water, until she has steerage way.

2 Part II—Organisation and Management

Rule 3.4(b) is deleted and replaced with: 'Changes in sailing instructions may be communicated orally, but only in accordance with procedures prescribed in the sailing instructions.'

3 Part III—General Requirements

3.1 Add to Rule 20.1: 'When so prescribed by the national authority, a numbered and dated device on the board, daggerboard and sail shall rank as a measurement certificate.'

3.2 Rule 24 is deleted and replaced with: 'A safety device shall prevent the mast separating from the board.'

4 Part IV—Right-of-Way Rules

4.1 Rule 33 does not apply between sailboards.

4.2 Rule 46.3 does not apply.

4.3 Add to section C of Part IV:

(a) Capsize

A sailboard *recovering* shall not obstruct a sailboard or yacht under way.

(b) Sail out of the Water when Starting

When approaching the starting line to *start*, a sailboard shall have her sail out of the water and in a normal position, except when *capsized* unintentionally.

(c) Moving Astern

A sailboard moving astern shall keep clear of all other sailboards and yachts.

5 Part V—Other Sailing Rules

5.1 Rule 52.1(a) does not apply; however, a competitor shall not hold on to a starting *mark*.

5.2 Rule 54 is deleted and replaced with: 'A sailboard shall be propelled by the action of the wind on the sail, by the action of the water on the hull and by the unassisted actions of the competitor.'

6 Part IV—Protests, Penalties and Appeals

Rule 68.3 is deleted and replaced with:

INFORMING THE RACE COMMITTEE

As soon as possible after she *finishes* or retires, a protesting sailboard shall try to inform the race committee that a *protest* will be lodged.

7 Appendices

7.1 Appendix B1 - 720° Turns Penalty

Unless otherwise prescribed in the sailing instructions, the 720° turns penalty, Appendix B1, shall apply, except that paragraph 1.1 is altered by deleting the requirement to make two *tacks* and two *gybes*.

7.2 Appendix B3—Identification—Class Insignia, National Letters and Numbers

(a) Add to paragraph 1.1(a): 'The class insignia shall not refer to anything other than the manufacturer or class and shall not consist of more than two letters and three numbers or an abstract design.'

(b) Paragraphs 1.3(a), (c) and (d) are deleted and replaced with: 'The class insignia shall be displayed once on each side of the sail in the area above a line projected at right angles from the luff of the sail one third of the distance from the head to the wishbone. The national letters and sail numbers shall be in the central third of the sail above the wishbone and clearly separated from advertising and shall be placed at different heights on the two sides of the sail, those on the starboard side being uppermost.'

8 Rules for Multi-Mast Sailboards

8.1 Add to the definition of *mast abeam*: 'The normal station of the helmsman is the normal station of the crew member controlling the foremost sail, and the mainmast is the foremost mast.'

8.2 Delete paragraph 1.3 of this appendix and replace it with:

Capsized - A multi-mast sailboard is *capsized* when one or more of her sails are in the water or one or more of her crew are waterstarting.

Recovering - A multi-mast sailboard is *recovering* from the time both her sails or, when waterstarting, both the competitors' bodies are raised out of the water, until she has steerage way.

8.3 In paragraph 4.3(b) of this appendix, 'sail' is deleted and replaced with 'sails'.

Alternative Sailboard Racing Rules

Paragraphs 9 - 11 are alternative sailboard rules that apply, either as a whole or in part, only when so prescribed in the notice of race and the sailing instructions.

9 Part IV—Right-of-Way Rules

Add to rule 37.2: 'Exception: a sailboard *clear ahead* shall keep clear of a sailboard *clear astern* that began *racing* at a later time.'

10 Part V—Other Sailing Rules

10.1 Paragraph 5.1 of this appendix is deleted, and the penalty in rule 52.2(a) is altered by deleting the words 'one *tack* and one *gybe*'.

10.2 Paragraph 5.2 of this appendix and rule 54.3 are deleted, and rule 54.3 is replaced with:

(a) Dragging a foot in the water to check way is permissible.

(b) On a free leg of the course, when surfing (rapidly accelerating down the leeward side of a wave) or planing is possible, the rig may be pumped in order to initiate surfing or planing, but only three times for each wave or gust of wind.

11 Part VI—Protests, Penalties and Appeals

Rule 68.1 is altered by removing the right of a sailboard witnessing an incident to protest under the rules of Part IV.

Slalom Sailboard Rules

Paragraphs 12 to 14 apply only to slalom races.

12 Part I - Definitions

Add the following definitions:

(a) *Going Out* and *Coming In* - When *sailing* from the shore against the incoming surf, a sailboard is *going out*. When *sailing* toward the shore with the incoming surf, a sailboard is *coming in*.

(b) *Right-of-Way Line* - The *right-of-way line* is an imaginary line through the bow of a sailboard at 90^0 to the line between the two course marks that bound the leg on which she is *sailing*.

(c) *Inside* and *Outside* - The *inside* of a sailboard is the side on which she shall leave the next course *mark*. The *outside* of a sailboard is her other side.

(d) *Overtaking* - A sailboard is *overtaking* from the time she establishes an *overlap* from *clear astern* until:

(i) when *overtaking* on the *outside*, she is clear *ahead*; or

(ii) when *overtaking* on the *inside*, her *right-of-way line* is ahead of the *right-of-way line* of the overtaken sailboard.

When an *overlap* exists while approaching the starting line to *start*, the *windward sailboard* is the *overtaking* sailboard.

13 Part IV—Right-of-Way Rules

13.1 Rule 35 is deleted and replaced with: 'When one sailboard is required to keep clear of another, the right-of-way sailboard shall not alter course so as to obstruct the other sailboard while she is keeping clear.'

13.2 When the race committee specifies that surf conditions exist, rule 36 is deleted and replaced with:

(a) A sailboard that is *coming in* shall keep clear of a sailboard that is *going out*.

(b) A *port-tack* sailboard that is neither *going out* nor *coming in* shall keep clear of a *starboard-tack* sailboard.

13.3 Rule 41 is deleted and replaced with: 'Except when *gybing* around a *mark*, a sailboard that is either *tacking* or *gybing* shall keep clear of a sailboard *on a tack*.'

13.4 Rules 37 to 40 and rule 42 are deleted and replaced with:

(a) A sailboard *overtaking* on the *inside* shall keep clear of an overtaken sailboard until her *right-of-way line* is ahead of the *right-of-way line* of the overtaken sailboard.

(b) A sailboard *overtaking* on the *outside* shall keep clear of an overtaken sailboard throughout the existence of that *overlap*.

14 Part VI—Protests, Penalties and Appeals

14.1 Rule 68.5 is deleted and replaced with: 'A *protest* may be made orally provided it identifies to the *protest committee* the sailboard protested and the nature of the incident.'

14.2 Rule 77.1 is altered to deny the right to appeal to competitors and sailboards, except for a competitor or sailboard penalised under rule 75.1.

Wave Performance Sailboard Rules

Paragraphs 15 and 16 apply only to wave performance competition.

15 Part IV—Right-of-Way Rules

15.1 Except for rules 37.1, 37.2, 41.1 and 41.4, rules 35 to 42 do not apply.

15.2 Paragraphs 12(a), 13.1 and 13.2 of this appendix apply.

16 Part V—Other Sailing Rules

Rule 59 is deleted and replaced with: 'A sailboard that suffers equipment breakdown may receive outside assistance to repair or replace equipment. When a sailboard receiving outside assistance or the vessel providing the assistance interferes with another competing sailboard, the sailboard receiving assistance shall be penalised.'

Appendix B5—**Team Racing Rules**

Team racing shall be sailed under the International Yacht Racing Rules as altered by this appendix.

1 Sailing Rules

1.1 Except when *sailing* a *proper course*, a yacht shall not act to interfere with another yacht *sailing* on a different leg of the course. Each time a leg is *sailed*, it is a different leg.

1.2 Right of way may be waived between team-mate yachts, provided that doing so does not directly affect a yacht of the other team adversely.

1.3 When contact occurs between team-mate yachts and neither promptly displays a green flag, rule 33 will apply, except that only the lower-scoring yacht shall receive the penalty points prescribed in paragraph 3.1(b). A yacht damaged by a team-mate yacht is ineligible for redress under rule 69(c).

1.4 Except to protect her position or that of a team-mate yacht, a yacht that is *sailing* the last leg of the course shall not act to interfere with a yacht of another team that has no opponent astern of her. A team-mate yacht shall not attempt to render this rule inapplicable by reducing speed or departing from a *proper course*.

1.5 Rule 41.3 does not apply.

1.6 A yacht that receives assistance from a team-mate yacht does not infringe rule 59.

2 Acknowledgement of Infringements; Intention to Protest

2.1 A yacht may acknowledge an infringement of a rule of Part IV, except rule 32, by hailing such acknowledgement to the yacht infringed against immediately, and by promptly displaying a green flag. After displaying the flag, she shall not remove it. She shall display one green flag for each incident, unless all green flags supplied are already displayed.

2.2 A yacht intending to protest shall hail the other yacht immediately and promptly display a red flag. She shall display one red flag for each incident, unless all red flags supplied are already displayed. A yacht that has displayed a red flag and that decides reasonably promptly thereafter that she, and not the other yacht, was at fault shall immediately replace the red flag with a green flag and hail the other yacht accordingly.

2.3 When a yacht displaying a red flag with respect to an incident is satisfied that the other yacht has displayed a green flag in accordance with paragraph 2.1 or 2.2, she shall immediately remove her red flag.

3 Scoring a Race

3.1 Each yacht completing a race will be scored points equal to her finishing place, minus one-quarter point for first place, and all other yachts will be scored points for the finishing place one more than the number of yachts entitled to *race*. In addition, a yacht's score will be increased for:

Infringement	*Penalty Points*
(a) an infringement of a rule of Part IV, other than rule 32, acknowledged in accordance with paragraph 2.1 or paragraph 2.2.	2.5
(b) an infringement of any *rule*, other than rule 32 or rule 51.2, not so acknowledged.	6
(c) an infringement of rule 32.	10

The *protest committee* may further increase a yacht's score when it finds that she gained a significant advantage from an infringement. The team with the lowest total score wins.

3.2 When all yachts of one team have *finished* or retired, the race committee may stop the race. The other team's yachts shall be scored the points they would have been scored had they *finished*.

3.3 When all the yachts of a team fail to *start* in a race, each shall receive points equal to the number of yachts entitled to *race*, and the yachts of the other team shall be scored as if they had *finished* in the best positions.

4 Scoring a Series

4.1 A team racing series shall consist of races or matches. A match shall consist of two races between the same two teams. The team with the lower total points for the race or the match shall be the winner.

4.2 When two or more teams are competing in a series consisting of races or matches, the series winner shall be the team winning the greatest number of races or matches. The other teams shall be ranked in order of number of wins. Tied matches shall count as half a win to each team.

4.3 When there is a tie:

(a) Ties between two teams will be broken in favour of the winner of the match or race when the two teams met, or, failing this, the winner of the second race of that match.

(b) Ties between three or more teams will be broken in favour of the team or teams scoring the lowest aggregate points when the tied teams met, or, failing this, the lowest total points in the series. Failing this, the tie shall be broken by means of a draw.

When the Organising Authority Supplies All Yachts

5 Assignment of Yachts

5.1 The organising authority shall form groups of yachts, and for the first race shall draw lots to assign the groups to the teams. The groups of yachts shall be exchanged between races so that, as far as possible, each team uses each group the same number of times. The organising authority shall identify each yacht within her group by use of special sail numbers or by display of a distinctive colour in her rigging or on her hull or sails.

5.2 In a two-team series after an even number of races, either team may require that the yachts be re-grouped. The groups will be assigned for the next race by the spin of a coin, except that, when there will be a final odd race in a series between a host team and a visiting team, the visiting team shall choose the group it will use.

5.3 Sails and other equipment shall remain with a yacht throughout the event, except when damage or loss requires the race committee to make substitutions. In such case, it shall inform all teams affected thereby.

6 Breakdowns

6.1 A yacht suffering a breakdown shall display a red flag as soon as practicable and, when possible, continue *racing*.

6.2 When the race committee decides that the yacht's finishing position was materially prejudiced, that the breakdown was not the fault of the crew, and that in the circumstances a reasonably competent crew would not have been able to avoid the material prejudice, it shall make as equitable a decision as possible, which may be to order the race to be re-sailed, or, when the yacht's finishing position was predictable, award her points for that position. In case of doubt as to her position when she broke down, the doubt shall be resolved against her.

6.3 A breakdown caused by defective equipment, or by an infringement by an opponent, shall not normally be deemed to be the fault of the crew, but one caused by careless handling, capsizing or by an infringement by a yacht of the same team shall be. When in doubt about the fault of the crew, the race committee shall resolve it in the yacht's favour.

Appendix B6—**Match Racing Rules**

A match is a race between two yachts. Matches shall be sailed under the International Yacht Racing Rules as altered by this appendix. Unless otherwise prescribed in the notice of race and sailing instructions, ***protests*** *will be decided and penalties initiated by umpires during the racing. Some or all of the umpires may also be members of the* ***protest committee*** *appointed to hear* ***protests*** *under paragraph 6.*

1 Alterations to the Racing Rules

1.1 When the yachts are provided by the organising authority, rule 32 is deleted and replaced with: 'A yacht shall attempt to avoid a collision resulting in damage.'

1.2 Rule 35 is deleted and replaced with:

A right-of-way yacht shall not alter course so as to limit the actions of the yacht required to keep clear without giving her *room* and opportunity to do so in a seamanlike manner, except:

(a) when *luffing* as permitted by rule 39.2; or

(b) when assuming a *proper course* either:

(i) to *start*, when she is on the *starboard tack* and the other yacht is on the *port tack*; or

(ii) when rounding a *mark*.

1.3 Rule 39.3 is deleted and replaced with: 'A yacht on a free leg of the course shall not *sail* below her *proper course* when she is within two of her overall lengths of a *leeward yacht*, unless she *bears away* and *gybes* onto another *proper course* without interfering with the other yacht.'

1.4 Except when *sailing* a *proper course*, a yacht shall not interfere with the other yacht in her match when that yacht:

(a) is on another leg of the course; or

(b) has been penalised and is exonerating herself in accordance with paragraph 5.4.

1.5 When a yacht in one match is required to keep clear of a yacht in another match, any alteration of course by either yacht that is not necessary to comply with a rule of Part IV shall be consistent with winning her own match.

2 Additional Alterations to the Racing Rules for Umpired Match Racing

2.1 Fundamental Rule D is deleted and replaced with: 'A yacht is not required to take a penalty unless signalled to do so.'

2.2 The definition of *finishing* is deleted and replaced with: 'A yacht *finishes* when any part of her hull, or of her crew or equipment in normal position, crosses the finishing line in the direction of the course from the last *mark* after fulfilling any penalty obligations signalled for infringements occurring when *racing*.'

2.3 Rule 33 is deleted.

2.4 Rule 40.1 is altered by adding: 'The hail shall be accompanied by the helmsman signalling with his arm by repeatedly and conspicuously pointing toward the foot of the mainmast of the *leeward yacht*.'

2.5 In addition to the hails required by rule 43, the following arm signals by the helmsman are required:

(a) for 'Room to *tack*', repeatedly and conspicuously pointing to windward;

(b) for 'You *tack*', repeatedly and conspicuously pointing to the other yacht and making a waving gesture back toward the *windward yacht*.

2.6 Rule 52.2 is deleted.

2.7 The provision in rule 74.4 for exonerating a yacht overrides any conflicting rule of this appendix.

2.8 Rule 70.2 does not apply to infringements for which penalties are provided in paragraphs 5.2, 7.1 and 7.2.

3 Starting Signals

Rule 4.3 is deleted and replaced with:

The signals for starting a match will be:

Time in Minutes	Signal	Means
10	Code flag 'F' with sound signal	Attention
6	Code flag 'F' lowered	

5	Numeral pennant* with sound signal	Warning signal
4	Code flag 'P' or blue shape with sound signal	Preparatory signal
2	Sound signal**	End of pre-start entry time
0	Lower warning and preparatory signals with sound signal	Starting signal

* or other match-identifying flag prescribed in the sailing instructions.

** See paragraph 4.2. This sound signal will not be made if, at that time, both yachts have complied with paragraph 4.2.

When more than one match is to be started, the warning signal for the succeeding match will be displayed at the starting signal of the preceding match.

4 Requirements before the Start

4.1 At her preparatory signal, a yacht shall be outside a line that is perpendicular to the starting line through the starting *mark* at her assigned end of the line.

4.2 Within the two-minute period following her preparatory signal, a yacht shall first cross and clear the starting line from the course side to the pre-start side.

4.3 Yachts not *racing* shall keep well clear of yachts *racing* (and their umpire boats when the match is umpired).

5 Protests Alleging Infringements of Rules of Sections B and C of Part IV in Umpired Matches

5.1 When a yacht believes that the other yacht in her match has infringed a rule of Section B or C of Part IV or paragraph 1.4 of this appendix, she may protest by immediately:

(a) hailing 'Protest' and

(b) conspicuously displaying Code flag 'Y'.

5.2 As soon as possible after a 'Y' flag is displayed, the umpires shall decide whether a penalty will be imposed on the protested yacht. Only the protested yacht may be penalised. The umpires shall promptly signal their decision by displaying a visual signal accompanied by a sound signal as follows:

(a) A green flag means: 'The umpires are not satisfied that the protested yacht has infringed a rule' and/or 'No penalty is imposed.'

(b) A visual signal identifying a yacht means: 'The designated yacht has infringed a rule, is penalised and shall exonerate herself in accordance with paragraph 5.4.'

5.3 The protesting yacht shall lower Code flag 'Y' before or as soon as possible after the umpires' signal.

5.4 The penalised yacht shall exonerate herself by, as soon as possible, *sailing* clear of the other yacht and taking the appropriate penalty.

(a) When the penalty is signalled before she has *started*, it shall be taken as soon as possible after *starting* in accordance with paragraph 5.4(b).

(b) When a penalty is signalled after she has *started*, it shall be:

(i) when beating to windward, to *gybe*;

(ii) when not beating to windward, to *tack*. However, when the head of her spinnaker is hoisted above the main-boom gooseneck, the penalty may be taken at any time on that leg of the course provided that the spinnaker is first lowered so that its head is below the gooseneck and remains so until the *tack* is completed. (A yacht completes a leg of the course when her bow crosses that part of a line projecting from the previous *mark* through the *mark* she is rounding.)

(c) When the penalty is signalled at or beyond the finishing line, the penalised yacht shall not be recorded as having *finished* until she exonerates herself and returns wholly to the course side of the line, and then *finishes*.

5.5 A yacht required to take more than one penalty shall take the first penalty as prescribed, then, when the penalty requires her:

(a) to *gybe*, she shall *luff* to a *close-hauled* course before taking each subsequent penalty;

(b) to *tack*, she shall return to a *proper course* before taking each subsequent penalty.

5.6 A yacht that is exonerating herself shall keep clear of the other yacht until she has completed her penalty and is on a *proper course*.

6 Protests Alleging Infringements of Other Rules and Requests for Redress in Umpired Matches

6.1 A yacht may protest the other yacht in her match in accordance with rule 68 for an alleged infringement of a sailing instruction or other *rule* except:

(a) the rules of Sections B and C of Part IV;

(b) rules 52 and 54; or

(c) paragraphs 1.4, 2, 4 and 5 of this appendix.

6.2 A yacht may, after an incident with a yacht in another match, protest her under a rule of Section B or C of Part IV.

6.3 A *protest* in accordance with rule 68 shall be signalled by a yacht displaying her protest flag until she has informed the umpires after *finishing* or retiring.

6.4 A yacht requesting redress due to circumstances that arose before she *finished* or retired shall display her protest flag at the first reasonable opportunity after she becomes aware of the circumstances that may justify her request, but not later than five minutes after *finishing*.

6.5 Following the race, the *protest committee* may take testimony in any way it deems appropriate and may communicate its decision orally. When the *protest committee* decides to conduct a hearing ashore, or to re-open or resume a hearing held on the water, it shall so advise the yachts and proceed in accordance with the rules of Part VI.

6.6 When the *protest committee* decides that an infringement has had no significant effect on the outcome of the match, it may:

(a) impose a penalty of one point or part of one point;

(b) order a re-sail; or

(c) make such other arrangement as it thinks equitable, which may be to impose no penalty.

7 Penalties Initiated by Umpires

7.1 When the umpires decide that a yacht has infringed rule 52, rule 54 or paragraphs 4, 5.3 or 5.6 of this appendix, she shall be penalised in accordance with paragraph 5.2.

7.2 When the umpires decide that a yacht has failed to comply with paragraph 5.4 or 5.5, or as a result of an infringement and despite taking her penalty for that infringement, has nevertheless gained an advantage over the other yacht, or has committed a breach of good sportsmanship, she shall be penalised in accordance with paragraph 5.2 or 7.3.

7.3 When the umpires display a black flag and the visual signal designating a yacht, it means: 'The designated yacht is disqualified and the match is terminated and awarded to the other yacht.'

7.4 When the umpires, or non-umpire members of the *protest committee*, decide that a yacht may have infringed a *rule* other than:

(a) those in Sections B and C of Part IV or paragraph 1.4 of this appendix; or

(b) those for which penalties are provided in paragraphs 7.1 and 7.2;

they shall so report to the *protest committee*, which shall proceed in accordance with paragraphs 6.5 and 6.6.

8 Appeals, Redress, Reopened Hearings

8.1 There shall be no appeals, requests for redress or reopened hearings from decisions made in accordance with paragraphs 5 and 7. No approval by a national authority is required.

8.2 No proceedings of any kind may be taken in relation to any action or non-action by the umpires when this appendix applies.

9 Scoring

9.1 The winner of each match scores one point, the loser scores no points. The highest total score wins.

9.2 A yacht that has won a match but is disqualified for an infringement against a yacht in another match shall lose the point for that match. However, the losing yacht shall not be awarded the point.

9.3 Ties between two or more competitors in a round-robin series shall be decided in favour of the competitor who has the most points in the matches between the tied competitors.

9.4 When paragraph 9.3 does not resolve a tie, it shall be decided in favour of the competitor who has won the match against the competitor (excluding the tied competitors) who has the highest score in the round-robin or, when necessary, the second highest score in the round-robin, and so forth until the tie is broken.

9.5 When paragraph 9.4 partially resolves a tie, paragraph 9.3 shall be re-applied to the competitors still tied.

9.6 When paragraphs 9.4 and 9.5 do not resolve a tie, and there has been fleet racing prior to the round-robin, the tie shall be decided in favour of the competitor who has won the match against the competitor (excluding the tied competitors) who has the highest score in the fleet racing or, when necessary, the second highest score in the fleet racing, and so forth until the tie is broken.

9.7 When the preceding paragraphs do not resolve a tie, it shall be decided by means of a draw.

Appendix C1—**Protest Committee Procedure**

In a protest hearing, the *protest committee* should give equal weight to all testimony; should recognise that honest testimony can vary and even be in conflict as a result of different observations and recollections; should resolve such differences as best it can; should recognise that no yacht is guilty until her infringement has been established to the satisfaction of the *protest committee*; should keep an open mind until all the evidence has been submitted as to whether the protestor or the protestee or a third yacht, when one is involved in the incident, has infringed a *rule*.

1 Preliminaries

1.1 Preliminaries are completed by the jury secretary, race committee or *protest committee* as circumstances dictate.

1.2 Note on the protest form the time it is received.

1.3 Notify the representative of each yacht involved, and of the race committee when appropriate, of the time and place of the hearing (rule 72).

1.4 Make available the protest form and any written statement regarding the incident (preferably photocopies) to all *parties to the protest* and each member of the *protest committee* for study before the hearing begins. Allow a reasonable time for the preparation of a defence (rule 72).

2 The Protest Committee

2.1 Make sure that a quorum is present when required by the organising authority. The quorum is not affected when some members of the committee leave the hearing during the discussion and decision at the request of the committee.

2.2 Make sure that no *interested party* is a member of the *protest committee*. When the hearing starts, ask the *parties to the protest* whether they object to any member on the grounds of 'interest' (rule 71.2).

2.3 When the *protest* involves a question of redress under rule 69(a) and involves a member of the race committee, he does not serve as a member of the *protest committee*, but he may appear as a witness.

3 The Validity of the Protest

3.1 At the beginning of the hearing, determine whether the *protest* contains the information called for by rule 68.5, provided it already identifies the incident (rule 68.7). If not, ask the protestor to supply the information (rule 68.7). When the *protest* does not identify the nature of the incident, it is refused (rule 73.2).

3.2 Unless the *protest* already provides the information:

(a) when the protestor was involved in the incident, ask whether the protestor hailed the protested yacht immediately in accordance with rule 68.2; when no hail was required, ask whether the protestor tried to inform the protestee that a protest would be lodged (rule 68.2).

(b) ask whether the protestor displayed a protest flag in accordance with rule 68.3, unless rule 68.4 applies or the protestor is seeking redress under rule 69, and note his answer on the protest form.

3.3 When a protest flag has not been properly displayed or a hail not made, or an attempt not made to inform the protestee when required, the protest is refused (rule 73.2), except when the *protest committee* decides either that:

(a) rule 68.4 applies, or

(b) it was impossible for the yacht to have displayed a protest flag because she was, for example, dismasted, capsized or sunk.

4 Evidence and Statements

4.1 One representative of each *party to the protest* (with a language interpreter when needed) has the right to be present throughout the hearing. When appropriate, make sure that the representative has been on board. Witnesses are excluded except when giving their evidence. Observers may be admitted at the discretion of the *protest committee* (rule 73.1).

4.2 Invite the protestor and then the protestee(s) to give their accounts of the incident. Each may question the other(s). Questions by the *protest committee*, except for clarifying details, are preferably deferred until all accounts have been presented. Models are useful. The positions of the yachts before and after the incident are often helpful.

4.3 Invite the protestor and then the protestee(s) to call witnesses (rule 73). They may be questioned by the parties as well as by the *protest committee*. The *protest committee* may also call witnesses. An *interested party* may give evidence [rule 71.2(a)], but it may be appropriate and prudent to ask a witness to disclose any business or other relationship through which he might have an interest or might stand to benefit from the outcome of the *protest*.

4.4 When any member of the *protest committee* saw the incident, his evidence is given as a witness only in the presence of the *parties to the protest*, and he may be questioned (rule 73.4).

4.5 Invite first the protestor and then the protestee to make a final statement of his case, including any application or interpretation of the *rules* he thinks useful.

4.6 A hearing may be adjourned in order to obtain additional evidence.

4.7 When one of the parties has been notified (rule 72) but has made no effort to attend the hearing (rule 73.5), the *protest* may be heard without him. Make careful notes on any steps taken to try to find him. When the protestee is absent, hear the evidence of the protestor and question him before imposing a penalty.

5 Decision

5.1 After dismissing the *parties to the protest*, decide what the relevant facts are (rule 74.1).

5.2 Apply the *rules* and reach a decision as to which yacht, if any, infringed a *rule* and which *rule* was infringed (rule 74).

5.3 Having reached a decision and recorded it, recall the *parties to the protest* and read them the facts found, the decision and the grounds for it (rule 74.6).

5.4 Any *party to the protest* is entitled to a copy of the decision (rule 74.6). A copy is also filed with the committee records.

6 Reopening a Hearing

When a timely request is made for a hearing to be reopened (rule 73.6), hear how the committee may have made a significant error and investigate the evidence (e.g. see the video tape or question the witness) and decide whether it is material and may change the decision. If none of these, refuse to reopen; otherwise, call the hearing.

7 Rule 75

7.1 An action under this rule is not a *protest,* but the race committee or *protest committee* gives its allegations in writing to the competitor before the hearing, and the hearing is conducted under the rules of Part VI, Section B, [rule 75.1(c)]. Exercise the greatest care to protect the competitor's rights.

7.2 A competitor, or yacht, cannot protest under rule 75, but the protest form of a competitor who tries to do so may be accepted as a report to the race committee or *protest committee*, which can then decide whether to call a hearing or not.

7.3 When it is desired to call a hearing under rule 75 as a result of a Part IV incident, it is important for the *protest committee* to hear any yacht-v-yacht *protest* in the normal way, deciding which, if any, yacht or yachts infringed what rule, before proceeding against the competitor under rule 75.

7.4 Although action under rule 75 is taken against a competitor, not a yacht, the committee's decision may include penalisation of a yacht [rule 75.1(b)].

8 Photographic Evidence

Photographs and video recordings may be accepted as evidence at a hearing and can sometimes be useful. However, there are some limitations and problems, and these should be appreciated by the *protest committee*.

The following points may be of assistance to *protest committees* when video evidence is used, but many of them apply also to still photographs.

8.1 When a video recording is to be replayed to the *protest committee* by a *party to the protest*, he should arrange that the necessary machinery be set up in a private room and an operator (preferably the person who made the recording) be available to operate it.

8.2 The party bringing the video evidence should have seen it before the hearing and have reasons why he believes it will assist the committee.

8.3 It is usually preferable to view the video after the parties have presented their cases.

8.4 Allow the recording to be viewed first without comment, then with the comments of the party bringing the evidence, then with those of the other party. Questions may be asked in the normal way by the parties and the committee members.

8.5 The depth perception of any single-lens camera is very poor; with a telephoto lens it is non-existent. When, for example, the camera's view is at right angles to the courses of two overlapped yachts, it is impossible to assess the distance between them. Conversely, when the camera is directly ahead or astern, it is impossible to see when an overlap begins or even if one exists, unless it is substantial. Keep these limitations firmly in mind.

8.6 Use the first viewing of the tape to become oriented to the scene. Where was the camera in relation to the yachts? What was the angle between them? Was the camera's platform moving? If so, in what direction and how fast? Is the angle changing as the yachts approach the critical point? (Beware of a radical change caused by fast panning of the camera.) Did the camera have an unrestricted view throughout? If not, how much does that diminish the value of the evidence? Full orientation may require several viewings; take the time necessary.

8.7 Since it takes only about 30 seconds to run and re-wind a typical incident, view it as many times as needed to extract all the information it can give. Also, be sure that the other party has an equal opportunity to point out what he believes it shows and does not show.

8.8 Hold the equipment in place until the end of the hearing. It is often desirable, during deliberation, to be able to review the tape to settle questions as to just what fact or facts it establishes. Also, one of the members may have noticed something that the others did not.

8.9 Do not expect too much from the videotape. Only occasionally, from a fortuitous camera angle, will it establish clearly the central fact of an incident. Yet, if it does no more than settle one disputed point, that will help in reaching a correct decision.

Appendix C2—**Sailing Instructions Guide**

This guide provides a set of checked and tested instructions that may be used verbatim for any regatta that will be sailed on a single course. Thus they will be particularly useful for most world, continental and national championships and other principal events. Also, when a regatta will use more than one course, the sailing instructions regarding courses can be altered appropriately; and most, if not all, other instructions will be applicable as they stand.

Some instructions are required or strongly recommended, while others are optional. Those that are required or recommended are shown with an asterisk (*).

The principles on which all sailing instructions should be based are as follows:

1 They should include only two types of statement: the intentions of the race committee and the obligations of competitors.

2 They should be concerned only with racing. Other information should be communicated through other means. For example: measurement regulations, requirements concerning registration of competitors or yachts, assignment of moorings, liability insurance, etc. should be in different documents.

3 They should not alter the racing rules, unless it is clearly desirable.

4 They should not repeat or restate any of the racing rules.

5 They should not repeat themselves.

6 The order of the instructions should reflect the chronological order in which the competitor will use them.

7 When possible, words or phrases used in the racing rules should be used in writing sailing instructions.

To use the guide in the preparation of sailing instructions, first delete all optional instructions that will not be needed. Then, following the instructions in the left margin, fill in the required information and select the alternatives desired. Finally, renumber all instructions in sequential order.

NOTE: The notes in this column contain guidance for preparing sailing instructions. Do not include them in the completed draft.

Insert: The full name of the regatta. The inclusive dates from measurement or the practice race until the final race. The name of the organising authority. The city and the country.

____

____

____

____

Sailing Instructions

*1 Rules

Insert the full names of the national authority when applicable, and the class(es).
Insert the appropriate category in accordance with Appendix A3.

The regatta will be governed by the International Yacht Racing Rules, the prescriptions of the ●, the rules of the ● class(es) (except as any of these are altered by these sailing instructions) and by these sailing instructions. The regatta is designated Category ●.

*2 Entries

Insert the competitor eligibility conditions, if any.

Eligible yachts may be entered by completing registration with the organising authority. Eligible competitors shall be ●.

*3 Notices to Competitors

Insert the specific location(s).

Notices to competitors will be posted on the official notice board(s) located ●.

*4 Changes in Sailing Instructions

Insert the times.

Any change in the sailing instructions will be posted before ● on the day it will take effect, except that any change in the schedule of races will be posted by ● on the day before it will take effect.

5 Signals Made Ashore

Insert the specific location.

5.1 Signals made ashore will be displayed at ●.

Insert the sound signal and time.

5.2 Code flag 'AP' with two ● (one ● when lowered) means 'The race is postponed. The warning signal will be made not less than ● minutes after 'AP' is lowered.'

Insert the sound signal.

5.3 Code flag 'B' fully hoisted with one ● means 'Protest time has begun.' When lowered half way, it means 'There are less than 30 minutes remaining before protest time ends.' When lowered, it means 'Protest time has ended.'

*6 Schedule of Races

Races are scheduled as follows:

Insert the days, dates and times.

Race	Day and Date	Time of Warning Signal

7 Class Flags

Insert the class names and descriptions of flags. Use only for a multi-class regatta.

Class flags will be:

Class	Flag

8 Racing Area

A section of a chart or other suitable map should be copied and marked for this purpose.

The racing area will be as shown in illustration 'A', attached.

9 The Course

Insert the distances. Delete the last sentence when not applicable.

*9.1 The diagram below shows the course, including the approximate angles between legs, the order in which marks are to be rounded or passed, and the side on which each mark is to be left. Mark 1 will be approximately ● nautical miles from Mark 3. The first and last legs will be approximately ● longer than the distance from Mark 3 to Mark 1.

Insert course diagram(s) here. A method of illustrating a course is shown in Addendum A. When there are navigational marks that are to be observed, they should be shown on the course chart.

9.2 The approximate compass bearing from the starting line to Mark 1 will be displayed from the race committee signal boat.

Delete when courses may be shortened.

9.3 Courses will not be shortened.

***10 Marks**

Insert the description of the marks and the instruction number.

Marks 1, 2 and 3 will be •. New marks, when used in accordance with instruction •, Change of Course after the Start, will be •. The starting and finishing marks will be •.

11 The Start

Use the last part of the sentence for a multi-class regatta. Insert the number of minutes. Use instruction 11 in Addendum C when a gate start is to be used.

*11.1 Races will be started in accordance with racing rule 4.3(a) System 1, with classes starting at • minute intervals in the order •.

(OR)

*11.1 Races will be started in accordance with racing rule 4.3(a) System 2, with classes starting at • minute intervals in the order •.

*11.2 The starting line will be between a staff displaying an orange flag or shape on the race committee boat at the starboard end and Mark 3 at the port end.

(OR)

*11.2 The starting line will be between a staff displaying an orange flag or shape on the race committee boat at the starboard end and the port end starting mark.

(OR)

Delete the last sentence when signals will be made from the starboard end race committee boat.

*11.2 The starting line will be between staffs displaying orange flags or shapes on two race committee boats. Signals will be made from a race committee signal boat stationed to windward of the line.

(OR)

*11.2 (a) The starting line will be between staffs displaying orange flags on Starting Marks A and B and between staffs displaying orange flags on Starting Marks B and C as shown below. Mark B may not be on a straight line between Mark A and Mark C.

Mark A •   • Mark B   • Mark C

(b) For the purpose of racing rules 51.1(b) and 51.1(c), the extensions of the starting line are the extensions beyond Mark A and Mark C.

Use only for a multi-class regatta. Insert 'warning' when classes start at ten-minute intervals, 'preparatory' when they start at five-minute intervals.

11.3 Yachts whose ● signal has not been made shall keep clear of the starting area and of all yachts whose ● signal has been made.

Insert the number of minutes.

11.4 A yacht shall not start later than ● minutes after her starting signal.

12 Recalls

Insert 'in accordance with racing rule 7.1' or describe any special procedure.

*12.1 Individual recalls will be signalled ●.

Use only for a multi-class regatta.

12.2 When a general recall has been signalled, the start(s) for the succeeding class(es) will be postponed accordingly.

Use only for a large fleet of a one-design class that has a history of repeated general recalls.

Other penalties, such as a scoring penalty equal to 20% of the number of yachts entered, may be prescribed for infringing this rule. When appropriate it may also be prescribed that yachts that infringed this rule, after proper notification, shall leave the race course immediately. In that case state the procedure for notifying yachts and the rights and obligations of yachts that decide to continue ***racing*** *despite such notification.*

13 Black Flag Rule

When a black flag has been displayed before or with the preparatory signal and lowered, accompanied by one long sound signal, one minute before the starting signal and when any part of a yacht's hull, crew or equipment is identified within the triangle formed by both ends of the starting line and the position of the first mark during the last minute before her starting signal, the yacht shall be disqualified from that race and from any subsequent re-start or re-sail of it. No individual recall signals will be made. Racing rules 7.2(b) and 11 shall not apply to such a yacht.

14 Mark Boats

Insert the description of the flag or shape.

Mark boats will be stationed beyond each mark. At the finish, the mark boat will be stationed beyond the finishing line. When on station only, each mark boat will display a ●. Failure of a mark boat to be on station or to display her signal will not be grounds for redress.

15 Change of Course after the Start

15.1 When changing the course after the start, the race committee will lay a new mark and will lift the original mark as soon as practicable. Any mark to be rounded after rounding the new mark may be relocated to maintain the original course configuration.

Insert the sound signal.

15.2 A change of course will be signalled near the mark beginning the leg being changed by a race committee boat that will display Code flag 'C' and the approximate compass bearing to the new mark and sound a ● periodically. The change will be signalled before the leading yacht has begun the leg, although the new mark may not yet be in position.

15.3 When in a subsequent change of course a new mark is replaced, it will be replaced with an original mark.

*16 The Finish

The finishing line will be between a staff displaying an orange flag or shape on a race committee boat and Mark 1 at the port end.

(OR)

The finishing line will be between a staff displaying an orange flag or shape on a race committee boat and the port end finishing mark.

(OR)

The finishing line will be between staffs displaying orange flags or shapes on two race committee boats.

***17 Time Limit**

Insert the time(s) and class(es). Adjust for a single class regatta or for a single time limit for all classes.

The time limit will be ● for the ● class and ● for the ● class. Yachts failing to finish within ● minutes after the first yacht finishes or after the time limit, whichever is later, will be scored 'Did not finish'.

18 Protests

Insert the location and time.

18.1 Protests shall be written on forms available at ● and lodged there within ● after the time of the last yacht's finish.

(OR)

Insert the location and times.

18.1 Protests shall be written on forms available at ● and lodged there within Protest Time which will begin at ● and end at ●.

Substitute 'race committee' or 'protest comittee' for 'jury' when there is no jury.

18.2 The jury will hear protests in approximately the order of receipt as soon as possible.

(OR)

See above. Insert the time.

18.2 The jury will hear protests in approximately the order of receipt beginning at ●.

18.3 Protest notices will be posted within 30 minutes of the protest time limit to inform competitors where and when there is a hearing in which they are parties to a protest or named as witnesses.

Use only when the requirements of rule 1.5 are met.

18.4 Decisions of the jury will be final in accordance with racing rule 1.5.

***19 Scoring**

The bonus-points scoring system, Appendix B2 of the racing rules, will apply.

(OR)

Use when the bonus-points scoring system is desired but the number of scheduled races is other than seven. Insert the number of races. See Appendix B2 for other possible alterations.

The bonus-points scoring system, Appendix B2 of the racing rules, will apply, except that • races are scheduled, of which • races shall be completed to constitute a series.

(OR)

See Appendix B2 for possible alterations.

The low-point scoring system, Appendix B2 of the racing rules, will apply.

(OR)

State the scoring system to apply by reference to the class rules or other document containing the complete scoring system.

____

____

____

20 Alternative Penalties

The 720° turns penalty, Appendix B1 of the racing rules, will apply.

(OR)

Insert the number of places.

The scoring penalty, Appendix B1 of the racing rules, will apply. The penalty will be • places.

21 Support Boats

Insert the dates or times.

Team leaders, coaches and other support personnel shall not go afloat in the racing area between • inclusive except in boats provided by the organising authority. The penalty for failing to comply with this requirement may be the disqualification of all yachts associated with the infringing support personnel.

22 Haul-out Restrictions

When this applies to some classes only, insert the name(s) of the class(es) between 'all' and 'yachts'. Insert the time. Substitute 'race committee' or 'protest committee' for 'jury' when there is no jury. Use (b) only when there is a scheduled reserve day.

All yachts shall be afloat before ● on the day preceding the first scheduled race and shall not be hauled out during the regatta except:

(a) with and according to the terms of prior written permission of the jury; or

(b) after the race preceding a reserve day. In which case they shall again be afloat before ● on the day preceding the next race.

23 Plastic Pools and Diving Equipment

Insert the class(es) and time.

Underwater breathing apparatus, plastic pools or their equivalent shall not be used around ● class yachts after ● on the day preceding the first scheduled race.

24 Radio Communication

A yacht shall neither make radio transmissions while racing nor receive special radio communications not available to all yachts.

25 Prizes

Alter as required. When perpetual trophies are to be awarded, refer to them by their complete names. State, when appropriate, that cash or cashable prizes and/or appearance payments totalling more than US $10,000 (or its equivalent) may be received by any one yacht.

Prizes will be awarded to each member of the crews placing first, second and third in the regatta.

Addendum A—Illustrating the Course

Shown here is a recommended method for illustrating a course. Any course can be similarly shown, using the same details. When there is more than one course, prepare separate diagrams for each and state how each course will be signalled.

This course is a frequently used course: triangle, windward, leeward, windward, on a 45°-90°-45° triangle. In this example the starting and finishing lines are separate and are between two race committee boats. The third sentence of instruction 9.1 and the third versions of instructions 11.2 and 16 would be used.

Start-1-2-3-1-3-Finish
Marks to be rounded to port

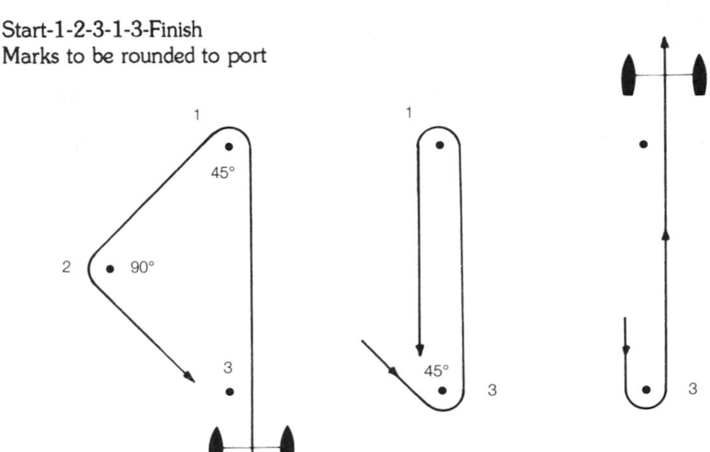

In the next example the course is the same except that the starting and finishing lines are between a race committee boat and Marks 3 and 1 respectively. The third sentence of instruction 9.1 would be deleted and the first versions of instructions 11.2 and 16 would be used.

Start-1-2-3-1-3-Finish
Marks to be rounded to port.

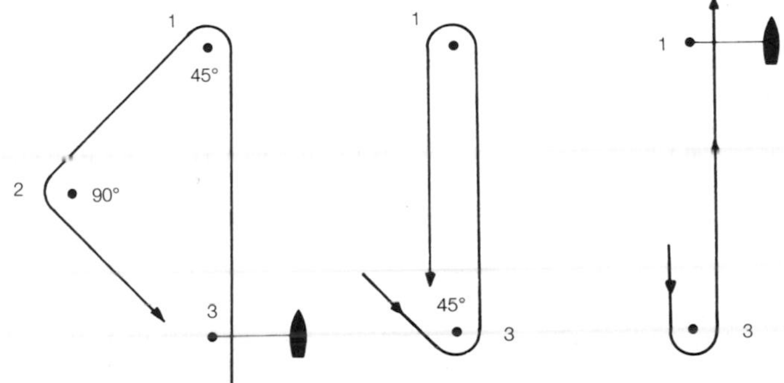

Addendum B—Yachts Provided by the Organising Authority

The following sailing instruction should be used when all yachts will be provided by the organising authority.

The instruction can be added to or altered, or portions deleted to suit the situation. When used, it should be inserted following instruction 5.

X Yachts

X.1 Yachts will be provided for all competitors, who shall not modify them or cause them to be modified in any way except that:

(a) a compass may be tied or taped to the hull or spars;

(b) wind indicators, including yarn or thread, may be tied or taped anywhere on the yacht;

(c) hulls, centreboards and rudders may be cleaned only with water;

(d) adhesive tape may be used anywhere above the water line; and

(e) all fittings or equipment designed to be adjusted may be adjusted, provided that the class rules are observed.

X.2 All equipment provided with the yacht for sailing purposes shall be carried while afloat.

X.3 The penalty for infringement of the above instructions will be disqualification from all races sailed in contravention of the instruction.

Substitute 'race committee' or 'protest committee' for 'jury' when there is no jury.

X.4 Competitors shall report any damage or loss of equipment, however slight, to the organising authority's representative immediately after securing the yacht ashore. The penalty for infringement of this instruction, unless the jury is satisfied that the competitor made a determined effort to comply, will be disqualification from the race most recently sailed.

Use when the regatta is not restricted to class members.

X.5 Class rules requiring competitors to be members of the class association will not apply.